Judge for Yourself

T0383706

Judge for Yourself guides interested and advanced-level readers through the challenge of judging the quality of hyper-contemporary literature. Whether reading the latest bestseller or the book that everyone is recommending, *Judge for Yourself* guides you through the challenge of the text. Reading the long-list of the 2019 International Dylan Thomas Prize through five chapters, *Judge for Yourself* introduces readers to current critical debates that inform engagement and the reading experience of hyper-contemporary writing. Topics covered include feminism, postcolonialism, critical race theory, queer theory, class, and book reviews. Each chapter includes introductory questions for the reader, and *Judge for Yourself* is accompanied by an exploration of book prize culture and the challenge posed by hyper-contemporary literature. *Judge for Yourself* puts judging firmly in the hands of the reader, and not the academic or professional reviewers.

Nicholas Taylor-Collins is a Lecturer in English at Cardiff Metropolitan University, UK. He specialises in both Shakespeare and contemporary writing, especially Irish literature.

Judge for Yourself
Reading Hyper-Contemporary Literature and Book Prize Shortlists

Nicholas Taylor-Collins

Routledge
Taylor & Francis Group
LONDON AND NEW YORK

First published 2021
by Routledge
2 Park Square, Milton Park, Abingdon, Oxon OX14 4RN

and by Routledge
52 Vanderbilt Avenue, New York, NY 10017

Routledge is an imprint of the Taylor & Francis Group, an informa business

© 2021 Nicholas Taylor-Collins

British Library Cataloguing-in-Publication Data
A catalogue record for this book is available from the British Library

Library of Congress Cataloging-in-Publication Data
A catalog record has been requested for this book

ISBN: 978-0-367-37199-9 (hbk)
ISBN: 978-0-367-37197-5 (pbk)
ISBN: 978-0-429-35302-4 (ebk)

Typeset in Bembo
by Newgen Publishing UK

For my parents,
who made our home a library

Contents

Acknowledgements

This book started as a module that I taught at Swansea University in 2018–19. The module went on to win the University's inaugural prize for Best New Module, and I owe many thanks to my students who turned it into the success that it became. Therefore, my primary thanks are to them: John Baddeley, Jacob Butt, Jacob Fleming, Rose Flynn, Georgina Hart, Jay Loader, Molly Holborn, Amy Jones, Jasmine Hunkin, Bronte Leek, Henry Lewis, Chloe McCarthy, Niall McGregor, Daniel Morgan, Nathan Phillips, Danielle Scott, Angharad Stephens, Melissa Tailor, Hannah Trim, Will Turnbull, and Hannah Wadham.

The module would not have happened without the support of my colleagues at Swansea, chief among them Elaine Canning, whose organisation of the International Dylan Thomas Prize was, and continues to be, exceptional. Her assistance and generosity in getting the module up and running proved invaluable. Also, thanks to her team at the Swansea University Cultural Institute for their patience and assistance. Additionally, the module and my thinking for this book were ably helped by the visiting speakers Jacqui Bowen, Tory Lyne-Pirkis, Eddie Matthews, Gary Raymond, and Dai Smith. I also had informative and enlightening discussions with some of the Prize's long-listed authors, including Nana Kwame Adjei-Brenyah, Clare Fisher, Zoe Gilbert, Guy Gunaratne, Louisa Hall, and Novuyo Rosa Tshuma. To you all, thank you.

I'm also indebted to Swansea friends and colleagues. Without your mentorship and confidence, I wouldn't be where I am today, and this book wouldn't have materialised. To Alice Barnaby, Kirsti Bohata, Georgie Lucas, Eóin Price, Richard Robinson, and Daniel Williams, I am extremely grateful.

This book would never have come into being were it not for Polly Dodson at Routledge. To her and to Zoë Meyer, I owe huge thanks.

I have been humbled by all my colleagues at Cardiff Metropolitan University whose hospitality and generosity have helped me to settle in; however, I owe special thanks to Carmen Casaliggi, Elizabeth English, and Meryl Hopwood.

To Ekow Acquah, Kerrie Reading, Alice and Tom Shortland— my guinea pigs—thank you. Additionally, my thanks to Andrew Leach for statistical guidance.

I will always be grateful to my teachers and my thanks in this case go especially to Thomas Docherty and Carol Rutter.

As ever, my undying thanks and love to my family for their support and unending belief in me. I hope you'll be able to find spaces on your shelves for this one.

And finally to Emma Taylor-Collins, to whom I owe it all and for whom words will remain insufficient. I'm sorry the ride sometimes seems a little bumpy, but happily I think we've a clear road ahead of us now. *Céad míle buíochas*.

All infelicities that remain are my own.

Introduction

The judgement of Dr J. Evans Pritchard, PhD; or, in praise of bad literature

For thirty years, students and bibliophiles alike have cited the film *Dead Poets Society* (1989) as the reason they fell in love with reading. The power of poetry—whether via Henry David Thoreau's 'sucking the marrow out of life', or in William Shakespeare's Puck from *A Midsummer Night's Dream*, who dances onstage and pulls the strings of his human marionettes—is affecting and persuasive. Mr Keating's students bond over Romantic poets, they play jazz saxophone, and they loyally defend their teacher's humanist virtues.

It is also a film that resoundingly rejects New Critical assertions of value. In their first lesson with Mr Keating, the students are instructed to rip out the first pages of their textbook by the presumably esteemed, but definitely hyperbolically titled Dr J. Evans Pritchard, PhD. The introduction had urged them to judge what they read by the following criteria:

> To fully understand poetry, we must first be fluent with its meter, rhyme and figures of speech, then ask two questions: 1) How artfully has the objective of the poem been rendered and 2) How important is that objective? Question 1 rates the poem's perfection; question 2 rates its importance. And once these questions have been answered, determining the poem's greatness becomes a relatively simple matter.
>
> If the poem's score for perfection is plotted on the horizontal of a graph and its importance is plotted on the vertical,

then calculating the total area of the poem yields the measure of its greatness.

A sonnet by Byron might score high on the vertical but only average on the horizontal. A Shakespearean sonnet, on the other hand, would score high both horizontally and vertically, yielding a massive total area, thereby revealing the poem to be truly great. As you proceed through the poetry in this book, practice this rating method. As your ability to evaluate poems in this matter grows, so will your enjoyment and understanding of poetry.

Here 'perfection' is brought into conversation with apparently measurable qualities. Not only does Pritchard's argument falsely depict the ability to 'rate' these qualities, but his metric also guarantees a readout of a poem's 'greatness'. Ultimately, this 'evaluation' will help students to 'enjoy' reading poetry all the more.

Pritchard's instructions are rejected because they create a false link between objective 'evaluation' and subjective or affective 'enjoyment'. Keating's teaching, by contrast, invokes what we might nowadays term an affective reader-response theory, in which value is ascribed to literature by individual readers (rather than fusty academics), according to their own emotional response to the poem. In his initial simplified sketch of an affective reader-response theory, Wolfgang Iser wrote that

the literary work has two poles, which we might call the artistic and the aesthetic: the artistic pole is the author's text and the aesthetic is the realization accomplished by the reader. In view of this polarity, it is clear that the work itself cannot be identical with the text or with the concretization, but must be situated somewhere between the two. It must inevitably be virtual in character, as it cannot be reduced to the reality of the text or to the subjectivity of the reader, and it is from this virtuality that it derives its dynamism. As the reader passes through the various perspectives offered by the text and relates the different views and patterns to one another he sets the work in motion, and so sets himself in motion, too.

(1978: 21)

Key words here include those indicating the 'motion' and 'dynamism' generated in the alchemical reaction between 'text' and 'reader'. To read good quality literature is to (re)generate the reading self. This becomes visible in *Dead Poets Society* during the students' Bacchanalian nights spent at the 'old Indian cave'—almost as if the pre-Christian, indigenous gods have a surer mainline to hedonism and art's pleasures—where the students try to woo young women, and declaim their own attempts at poetry. They respond emotively and personally to the poetry they have read, and their own characters change and develop as a result of Keating's favoured approach to reading.

On the surface, it seems that literary judgement is wholeheartedly dismissed from Keating's classroom—at least as far as Pritchard's rigorous methodology is concerned. However, as an academic of literature, this is somewhat problematic for me. After all, a major part of my employment and vocation requires me to make judgements about literary writing, to assess quality, and to cast judgement on that quality through academic discourse. This takes place at conferences, and in written publications through journal articles, book chapters, and whole books. This present book is no exception. I am therefore concerned, much as I deride Pritchard's method, with the same end: to evaluate literature.

The other major part of my vocation is teaching. Across two secondary schools and three universities to date, I have dedicated time to helping students to develop reading and analytical skills—and, yes, to judge and evaluate literature. In fact, if a student should leave my seminars and lectures *without* enhanced abilities to judge literary quality, then by many metrics (perhaps even my own) *I* would be judged as having failed.

Perhaps more worryingly, this teaching and development of analytical skill often takes place through a programmatic method, whereby students can identify features of writing that indicate quality. It's best not to be shocked by this but to reconsider what it is that you learnt by being able to distinguish linguistic features such as metaphors from similes, to identify formal features such as metre, rhythm and rhyme, soliloquies and monologues, epistolary and realist novels, and to recognise 'key themes' such as the representation of women or the class struggle. These all could have been (as some were) on Pritchard's list. Am I, are my students, as bad as that crusty old academic?

In our defence, part of these teaching habits arises from expediency. After all, two to three hours on Samuel Richardson's gargantuan *Clarissa* (1748) is hardly sufficient. Shortcuts must necessarily be taken in order to fulfil the requirements of a degree. On an *x*-axis we could plot 'Number of texts' and on a *y*-axis we could plot 'Time spent on texts'. The resulting graph would show that, in order to read more texts, less time must be spent on them, and *vice versa*. Additionally—and more importantly in what follows over the next five chapters—we are hardly giving students the chance to develop refined analytical and judgemental skills because (and here is the crux of the matter) we have already decided to give them top-quality literature.

Since students are only studying 'the greats', they rarely get the opportunity to judge writing on its own merits. We give students such a refined diet that it is little wonder that they struggle to cook their own meals from scratch. We have only opened half of Pandora's box. The half we have opened we have tended to call the 'canon'. The canon includes Geoffrey Chaucer, Shakespeare, and John Milton, and extends through Alfred Lord Tennyson to T.S. Eliot and W.H. Auden, perhaps most recently including Seamus Heaney. This is a selective group of writers from the canon, but it is not unrepresentative of the canon of Western literature: It is filled with white males. When we introduce these excellent writers to students, we are doing them a good service; after all, students should be familiar with the best that English literature has to offer. 'Originally the Canon meant the choice of books in our teaching institutions,' writes Harold Bloom, 'and despite the recent politics of multiculturalism, the Canon's true question remains: What shall the individual who still desires to read attempt to read, this late in history?' Bloom's canon exists in part as motivation in the race against time 'because we are mortal and also rather belated. There is only so much time, and time must have a stop.' The canon therefore 'exists precisely to impose limits, to set a standard for measurement' (1994: 15, 30, 34). In this argument, the canon is itself a result of the process of literary judgement by academics on behalf of readers.

However, that good service must be reckoned against the bad service we are offering students by primarily asking them to read literature that we, as 'experts', have already qualified and judged as 'good'—and not least because there is a lack of diversity in the canon. From Ngũgĩ wa Thiong'o's *Decolonizing the Mind* (1981) that promoted the end to the use of English in Thiongo's writing, to Karen Lawrence's edited collection *Decolonizing Tradition: New Views of Twentieth-Century 'British' Literary Canons* (1992), and to Achille Joseph Mbembe's 'Decolonizing the university: New Directions' (2016), the decolonising agenda continues apace. For Mbembe, a decolonised 'pluriversity […] embraces' universal knowledge 'via *a horizontal strategy of openness to dialogue among different epistemic traditions*' (37)—that is to say, by moving beyond Western bases of knowledge and undertaking conversations between traditions of knowledge that culminate in a more plural understanding of what knowledge and learning are. That current (lack of) diversity on university syllabuses can be characterised across the intersections of society, including sex, ethnicity, gender, and class. In giving students primarily Chaucer, Shakespeare, and Milton, etc., we are failing to ask them the more practicable questions about literature: We should not just ask, 'Why is this literature good?', but 'Why is *this* literature better than *that other* literature that we are not reading?'

This is all the more problematic because much of what students are reading—and much of what those of us interested in contemporary writing are reading outside class—begs to be evaluated and assessed. The brand-new writing that fills bookshops and their shelves offers the opportunity to learn, practise, and hone the skills of genuine evaluation because these texts have not (yet) gathered a critical consensus as to their quality. However, for the most part this writing does not make it on to undergraduate reading lists. This is in part because many modules treat literature historically ('Mediaeval to Renaissance', 'The Seventeenth Century', 'Literature and Revolution: Modernism' are but three historically-structured courses I have either taught or studied), and so brand-new writing would not suit the lists. But it is also because there is a necessary time-lag between a book's publication, its digestion by the literary world, and its insertion into a discourse or discourses—be they historical, thematic (on or about a specific subject), generic (adhering to conventions of a specific genre), or formal (poetry, prose, drama)—that are already addressed on university syllabuses. In time these texts may make it on to a student's reading list, but by that time, the process of judgement has already been undertaken: The text is now considered of 'good' quality and has gained 'canonical status' (Ross *et al.*, 2006: 190) by being organised 'in a set of evaluative relations' (Docherty, 2018: 142).

At Swansea University in 2019, I was given the opportunity to shift this paradigm. The Swansea University International Dylan Thomas Prize (IDTP) awards a cash prize to the author of any book (regardless of form), as long as they are aged thirty-nine or under. I introduced a module to the Department of English Literature and Creative Writing that used the 2019 longlist as its reading list. The list of twelve was announced on 31 January; the course began exactly a week later on 7 February.[1] The turn-around time limited any possibility of forming opinions about the texts and their selection. All of the texts were published in 2018, and so the students and I came to the texts without prejudice. We had no prior knowledge of the texts, and only our shared reading history to help us interrogate and judge the texts. This approach, I believe, offers a productive way to engage students with the task of separating good literature from bad, and it relies wholly on what I term hyper-contemporary literature.

What is hyper-contemporary literature?

To state the obvious, two words make up 'hyper-contemporary'. Neither is particularly straightforward and both have more than one obvious meaning. 'Contemporary' has long confused students of history, literature, and politics because of its double meaning: It signifies both the temporal now of the reader's world (i.e., 2020), but also the temporal 'now' of the text's world (be it Shakespeare's 1599, Dickens's 1850, or Woolf's 1922). In its Latinate etymology, contemporary is constructed of a prepositional prefix '*con-*', meaning 'together with'. 'Temporary' in this context means 'time', deriving from the Latin '*tempus*'. 'Contemporary' thus means 'together with the time', hence its confusion. Its meaning can only properly be discerned from its context. 'Hyper', which has come to standalone as a word signifying the longer 'hyper-active', is mostly used a prefix. It means excessive or exaggerated. Think of 'hyper-inflation' or 'hypermetropia' (long-sightedness).

And in this new construction, hyper-contemporary, I am designating a particular kind of contemporary: a contemporary moment that is relatively quickly passed through and departed from; a contemporary moment whose effects, consequences, and significances are evident in cultural productions (such as literary texts); and a contemporary moment that, as quickly as it takes shape and emerges, dissolves and disappears. The hyper-contemporary is the 'now, now, very now' (I.i.85) of Iago's insistent present in Shakespeare's *Othello*. It is not surprising that many of the theories I detail in the rest of this book are also concerned with defining the 'now' or the 'present'. For Prudence Chamberlain, her theory of fourth-wave feminism is built on Giorgio Agamben's theory of the present, as she argues that feminist activist 'moments themselves seem to exist slightly outside of a linear understanding of time; they are less specifically defined in terms of time frame and represent a sustained period of feminist activism' (2017: 62). Chamberlain's present is thus conditioned by an 'imperfect coincidence' (62) of events.

For James Penney, the queer contemporary is best reduced to a 'psychoanalytic temporality' that is a 'temporality of discontinuity' and also entails the possibility of future revision: 'At any point in time […] something can happen which, from the perspective of a later moment, will have literally changed the past' (2014: 183). This queer contemporary is inherently unstable, therefore, leading to Penney's move to 'after queer'. Penney's ideas are not unlike Homi K. Bhabha's theory of the postcolonial present that 'comes to be revealed for its discontinuities, its inequalities, its minorities' (2004: 6). Whilst other postcolonial theories exist, Bhabha's is signally influential and therefore worthy of serious consideration. Finally, Paul Mason sees the present opening up to a new kind of revolution of the info-connected human against capitalism. 'By creating millions of networked people, financially exploited but with the whole of human intelligence one thumb-swipe away,' writes Mason, 'info-capitalism has created a new agent of change in history: the educated and connected human being' (2015: loc. 167–8). All of these contemporaries are exciting but also uncertain—much like the hyper-contemporary literature that emerges from these contemporaries.

Consequently, 'hyper-contemporary literature' characterises texts that have *just* been published, that have *just* reached book-shelves, and *just* been devoured by a brand-new readership. Hyper-contemporary literature is exciting, brand-new writing whose merits also lead to problems for the critic—regardless of whether that critic is an academic in a university, a student in the seminar room, or a book-club member who reads the latest bestseller. The merits of hyper-contemporary literature are clear. These texts have not yet been read, pored over, or digested. They are fresh and their stories are new. The ways those stories are told are as yet unknown. The characters are either formed out of an imaginative nothingness or develop previous characters in ways that are unforeseen or long-awaited. Hyper-contemporary litera-ture is unread, untouched, and exciting.

But hyper-contemporary literature also comes with its problems. The frameworks for analysing and examining the texts are either non-existent or insufficiently developed. The subjects are unknown in their specifics and they may offend or (worse yet) bore the reader. The unseen nature of hyper-contemporary literature also means that few people have had eyes on the text and had—let alone taken—the opportunity to amend or improve the writing, either in its subject, characters, style, or form. Worst of all, it is perfectly possible that hyper-contemporary literature, however long-awaited or longed-for from its author's fans, may well be rubbish. In short, many of the problems that may arise from hyper-contemporary lit-erature are to do with the question of judgement.

Hyper-contemporary literature is not the same as 'twenty-first-century literature', such as that expertly surveyed in books like Daniel O'Gorman and Robert Eaglestone's *The Routledge Companion to Twenty-First-Century Literary Fiction* (2019). For one, that text is concerned with a particular type of literature called 'literary fiction' that, as I detailed above, entails thinking about critically as a type of writing that has been co-opted by the academy or other like establishments (the publishing industry, the book prize circuit) into a certain conception of what 'good' writing looks like. As I will discuss, I am as much interested in judging 'bad' literature as I am in judging 'good' literature. Second, *The Routledge Companion* is designed for a particular academic audience who are attempting to survey the literary landscape at the moment and provide a snapshot that may well be redundant in 'eighty years: some of the fictional trends identified in this volume will solidify as others erode' (2019: 1). I am instead undertaking an experiment that is eminently repeatable; moreover, it is an experiment that the majority of readers outside the academy conduct much of the time. By taking the longlist of a book prize as my reading list—though it could equally be the brand-new books that fill the shelves of bookshops, both physical and digital—I am testing how to read these books with available resources (i.e. the five chapters that make up the main body of the book), rather than developing new theories in relation to these texts. I believe that this is a democratising process that makes these twelve primary texts more readily available to public scrutiny. Far from dismissing the work of *The Routledge Companion*, I am instead offering a different kind of book, with different purposes.

Hyper-contemporary literature is therefore literature that has yet to gather a critical consensus. That is to say that no opinion has settled as to whether a particular text is 'good', 'bad', or anything else.[2] This means that the text is risked with the public, and the opinions they form along with reviewers either help or hinder the circulation of the text. There is a duty of care for the first readers of a brand-new text. Hyper-contemporary literature is a risk, for publishers, authors, and readers—and this book hopes to give the first readers of hyper-contemporary literature a series of methods for approaching and analysing it, in order to help form that inaugural critical consensus. This book helps you to judge for yourself.

Book prizes

Some will argue that it is not for the student or book-club member to judge a text; they are reading that text because it has been reviewed well or provocatively, or been long- or shortlisted for a book prize. This is where I want to intercede for two chief reasons. First, as I have already mentioned, I think that the more students of literature are exposed to hyper-contemporary literature, the more likely that literature will not be to the canon's exacting standard, and students will have to develop more acute skills of judgement (this being a good thing). Second, I am firm in the belief that book prizes only occasionally grant their award to the best book or writer, and that prize shortlists include writers who are shoo-ins—in some cases, regardless of the quality of the text—because of the value of their name. Think, for example, of Salman Rushdie who was included on the 1983 Booker Prize shortlist only because of his 'sacred name'; or, even more worryingly, Margaret Atwood's 2019 Booker Prize joint victory for *The Testaments* that, even in the words of Afua Hirsch, one of the jury members, was awarded for her 'titanic career' (2019a: para. 6) rather than the quality of the book.[3] That is what a Nobel Prize is meant to be for, not a book prize. Book prizes are political because they are to do with famous names, and because they award huge sums of money. Euphemistically speaking, book prizes 'have a broad range of motivations and implications' (Squires, 2007: 97). There's no escaping it: There is no way a book prize can be awarded on literary quality alone. And, moreover, literary quality is impossible to describe in absolute terms. The book prize is doomed to fail.

Nevertheless, literary prizes come in a range of formats with a varied assortment of qualifying criteria. At the top of the tree is the Nobel Prize in Literature, which is awarded to a writer in recognition of the continued and growing importance of their complete oeuvre. The Nobel is highly sought in part because it is difficult to win: Winners are drawn from around the world, and they write in any language. Moreover, you cannot enter yourself into the Nobel. Rather, the Nobel Committee takes account of submissions by esteemed individuals (who remain publicly anonymous), wherever the writers are from, and whatever form their writing takes—as Bob Dylan's 2016 award for his songwriting demonstrates—before choosing their annual winner.[4] A writer can only win the prize once, and the prize, which dwarfs every other literary prize in terms of cash award, is worth nearly a million US dollars.

More common literary prizes are book prizes, which award a particular book from the last year of publishing. For example, the IDTP accepts submissions in the autumn from publishers whose books were published at any point that year. Thus the 2019 prize was drawn from over 100 submissions published in 2018—I, myself, read books on behalf of the Prize's organisers, recommending some for the longlist. The Booker Prize similarly draws its entry pool from books published up until September in the year it awards the Prize. Curiously this also means that, when they announce the longlist in late August, there are occasionally books on the list that have not yet been published for the reading public.[5]

On the surface, these two prizes may appear similar in their scope. However, they both place additional restrictions on their qualifying criteria. The IDTP entries must be first published in English and, at the time of publication, the author must be aged thirty-nine or under—Dylan Thomas died at thirty-nine. The book can be a novel, a collection of short stories, a poetry collection, or a play. The Booker Prize criteria are more stringent in some regards—additionally requiring that the book be a novel—but less in others—placing no restriction on the age of the writer. This leads to a hierarchisation of prizes so that the Booker is placed at the top:

> For the Booker is awarded to the best non-genre novel or, in other words, the best 'literary' novel. By not naming the category, though, what the Booker does is to confirm the 'literary' novel at the top of genre hierarchies. The phrase 'best novel' equates with 'best literary novel', and so it is implied that the winner of the Booker is better than the winner of the Arthur C. Clarke [prize].
>
> (Squires, 2007: 98)

We don't have to travel far in our book prize journey to meet the interference of politics yet again. After all, as Thomas Docherty points out, 'the institutionalization of some writing specifically as "literary" is itself an act of criticism', and that 'critical responsibility is the condition of the legitimization of literature' (2018: 16): The book prize needs to endow certain texts as 'literary' in order to sustain its own existence, and the Booker is first among prizes to make its own necessity known.

There are prizes purely for poetry collections—the T.S. Eliot and Forward Prizes—as well as prizes for up-and-coming poets. The Eric Gregory Award annually goes to five early-career poets who can win the Award only once. There are genre fiction awards, such as those awarding crime writing (the Gold Dagger award), Gothic fiction, and dystopian writing. Other awards focus on the age of the intended readers, such as the Blue Peter book prize for children's literature, whilst others restrict their entrants according to the author's sex, notably so in the Women's Prize for Fiction.

There is not an equitable economy of access to these prizes. The Costa Prize, for instance, charges publishers £5000 to enter. For most publishers who aren't mainstream and extremely successful, this is a genuine barrier to submitting their books. Eimear McBride's *A Girl is a Half-formed Thing*, 2014 winner of the Women's Prize for Fiction, was first published by Galley Beggar Press, and only later did publishing monolith Faber and Faber buy the rights and submit it for prizes. The risk/reward calculation is especially important for a publisher in these decisions, not least because making it on to a long- or shortlist does not guarantee success for the publisher. I have heard of smaller presses, for example, who have struggled to buy enough stock to capitalise fully on the successful shortlisting of one of their few submissions. The price to print their own books at short notice in order to supply the booksellers, who were (all of a sudden) clamouring along with their customers to buy the book was a barrier to the cash-poor publisher. When in competition with, say, Penguin Random House—the biggest publishing house in the world—the minnows necessarily lose out via the temptation of the book prize.

Crucially, book prize judges end up conferring a literary value on their winning books or authors. Squires points out that, for example, 'Literary prizes—notably the (Man) Booker, but also a legion of others including the Whitbread (latterly Costa) Awards and the Orange Prize—have promoted writing and also contributed to mid-term canon formation' (2007: 2). In some respects this makes sense: If a text is considered the best of the year by writers aged thirty-nine and under, as judged by esteemed jurors, then why should anyone question the merit of that judgement? James English has problematised this process in his book on prizes, focusing not only on the way in which prizes are engaged in a financial economy, to the extent that 'Prizes obviously are bound up in varying degree with the business end of art […] and no one would question the legitimacy of inquiring into their economic motivations and effects' (2005: 4), but also on the way that a cultural economy is also fostered and disseminated through book prize culture:

> This other economics, which is woven together with, and cannot be understood apart from, the money economy, is not itself based on money. It involves such terms as 'capital,' 'investment,' 'endowment,' 'return,' 'circulation,' 'accumulation,' 'market,' and so forth, and it assumes certain basic continuities between economic behavior […] and the behavior proper to artists, critics, intellectuals, and other important players on the fields of culture.
>
> (2005: 4)

With this framework in mind, the role of the book prize judge seems ever more demanding and also significant: Their role is not only to award a specific prize but also to shore up the cultural structure inherent in contemporary society.

We should remember to recognise the great weight placed upon the jurors. This includes political and economic factors that prize organisers consider when they select their jurors. These selections often lead to an economic burden on the judges that seems especially heinous given the apparently apolitical nature of the judging process. It might seem unusual that many book prize judges are not professionally involved in the book industry, are not writers, or would not qualify for the book prize being judged; their judgements are therefore under increased scrutiny. More famous names necessarily lead to a larger marketing campaign, in turn attracting more interest to a prize: 'The stature of the judges guarantees the stature of the prize' (English, 2005: 123). Those famous names may not necessarily have the required skills or background knowledge, nor the specialist abilities to judge a particular prize. They *should* have those skills and abilities, but there is no guarantee. The difficulties redouble when genre-specific prizes require jurors with an advanced knowledge of, say, Gothic literature, as also when a panel has to read over a hundred books in a matter of months along with compiling a comprehensible and nuanced set of notes and reviews on each text.

The process of judging itself is also not straightforward—Libby Purves, a Booker Prize judge in 1983, has described the experience as 'trauma[tic]' (2019: para. 1). Another Booker Prize judge, Afua Hirsch (2019), has additionally summarised the stresses that result from reading over 100 texts in a short space of time:

> Over the past 10 months I have been sleeping less, answering my phone little, not mentally present in queues or on public transport, and roaming instead the mountains of Kashmir, the villages of the Cotswolds, colonial-era Zambia and superhuman communities in Northern Ireland. I have found myself decrypting Shakespearean time travel and complicated sibling love in Lagos. […] It wasn't all easy. This process also turned out to be an exercise in overcoming my own deep sense of impostor syndrome—a belief that I was not qualified, literary or clever enough to be a judge on this prestigious prize.
>
> (2019b: paras 2–9)

The judges may also feel judged as the culture of capital intraconversion,[6] as English terms it, makes its pressure felt on the judge's shoulders. But there is also the 'literally impossible labor' (English, 2005: 120) of reading all the texts in the given time, which leads to but one reason for thinking of the winner of a book prize as contingent on a number of variables. It would be fair under these circumstances for the judges to make use of Dr J. Evans Pritchard's schema for judgement.

The contingent nature of the book prize leads to healthy disagreements, both on the judging panel and in the reading public. For these reasons, juries are often made up of an odd number of people, or the prize's rules include a provision for the chief judge's veto. There is an anecdote that a Booker Prize jury voted nearly unanimously for one winner from their shortlist, only for the dissenting voter—the jury's chair—to make use of their veto and to vote instead for another text. That text finally won the Prize over and above the jury's democratic favourite.[7] As regards the public, I know the disagreements that arise from first-hand experience of teaching undergraduates about book prizes. In the module I taught at Swansea University, we had a vote narrowing the Prize's longlist of twelve down to our own shortlist of six. The text I ranked twelfth, my students ranked first—much to my dismay.

These disagreements underpin the motivation for writing this book. Whether on the book prize jury, in the university seminar room, or even during a monthly book club in the local pub, judging a book's literary value and quality is difficult—especially so when it's hyper-contemporary writing that lacks the establishment seal of approval. Brand-new writing requires fresh judgement, and in that process, this book is designed to help.

At the heart of that process are two key beliefs. First: that *anyone* is entitled to give their judgement on a book. Second: that being informed about the latest discussions in/around culture, politics, literature, and history can inform *everyone's* judgements. Often those discussions in the pub or the seminar room begin to falter when opinions have reached their limit, and thereafter little further knowledge is brought into the conversations. I am reminded of Jenni Ramone and Helen Cousins's comments about the Richard & Judy Book Club—a television book club that was highly successful in the 2000s—that much of the discussion receded into celebrity descriptions of the book and personal responses that limited developed discussions of the selected text (2011: 6–7). *Judge for Yourself* offers a set of ways of developing those conversations and enhancing those discussions. Armed with those developed and enhanced ideas, my belief is that the reader is better able to judge hyper-contemporary literature for herself.

Crucially, that literature does not need to be pre-determined as 'good' or 'literary'. If this introduction serves one purpose, it is to advocate the reading of *all* literature, embracing the possibility that it might be 'bad' writing or 'poor' quality. It is only by surveying all that there is to read that the best can truly be discerned; to that end, I am in favour of reading bad literature. If it means I can more fully understand how a writer's deftly woven writing is beautiful, how magical landscapes become enchanted, or how characters are endowed with unplumbed depths that bring tears to my eyes, then I am willing to risk a few hours of my life in pursuit of the good.

How this book works

In order to introduce and develop the concepts of judging for yourself, in the substantive chapters, below, I interrogate my questions through a dozen sample texts all published in 2018. These are not selected randomly but are drawn from the IDTP's 2019 longlist—the same longlist that constituted the reading list of the module I taught at Swansea University. They present a cross-section of authors from diverse backgrounds—both in terms of sex, class, ethnicity, and nationality—and writing in a range of forms—short-story collections, poetry collections, and novels are all included. They also happen to provide a near ideal collection of narratives and focuses that allow me to undertake a range of representative literary analyses in the course of this book. In alphabetical order, here is the list of the twelve texts all published in 2018, including a brief summary:

- Nana-Kwame Adjei-Brenyah's *Friday Black* (riverrun) is a short-story collection that depicts a contemporary dystopian USA, overrun by capitalist and racist forces.
- Michael Donkor's *Hold* (4th Estate) is a novel that tells the stories of two Black girls in contemporary Ghana and the UK, exploring the processes of growing up and discovering one's sexuality.
- Clare Fisher's *How the Light Gets In* (Influx Press) is a four-part collection of flash fiction, depicting a young woman's

experiences of the postmodern city and the struggles—in career, in finance, and in mental health—that those experiences forge.

- Zoe Gilbert's *Folk* (Bloomsbury) is a short-story collection-cum-novel that tells fantastic tales of the population of the island Neverness, during the course of a generation.
- Emma Glass's *Peach* (Bloomsbury) is a novel that depicts the rape and the gradual breakdown—both mental and physical—of its eponymous protagonist.
- Guy Gunaratne's *In Our Mad and Furious City* (Tinder Press) is a novel that unites five distinct voices from characters all living in London, but who have other cultural experiences to draw on, during two febrile days of intercultural strife in the city.
- Louisa Hall's *Trinity* (Corsair) is a novel exploring the actions and character of famed nuclear physicist J. Robert Oppenheimer—all through a narrative constructed by voices of seven fictional characters who knew him.
- Sarah Perry's *Melmoth* (Serpent's Tail) is a novel retelling the Gothic tale of the wanderer who presciently predicts the visitant's death.
- Sally Rooney's *Normal People* (Faber and Faber) is a novel that depicts the development of two young people's relationship from secondary school through to university in contemporary Dublin.
- Richard Scott's *Soho* (Faber and Faber) is a poetry collection that puts a queer narrative of becoming at front and centre.
- Novuyo Rosa Tshuma's *House of Stone* (Atlantic Books) is a novel that tells the parallel stories of the transition of Rhodesia into an independent and postcolonial Zimbabwe over the course of the 1980s and 1990s, alongside a contemporary story of a young man in search of another young man who has gone missing.
- Jenny Xie's *Eye Level* (Graywolf Press) is a poetry collection charting the immigrant journey from Southeast Asia into the USA, along with the memories that cannot be forgotten from that journey, or many other journeys taken at another time.

In addition to prioritising the judgement of these texts, this book operates on three key principles. The first principle is that analysing (and judging) literature is best done through what we term 'close reading'. Whilst there are different approaches to close reading, common among them is the focus on the language in the text. This may seem obvious on one level, but I have found myself repeating in many seminars that we need to focus more closely on the words on the page, how they are used, how they surprise us (with specific references), and how the words weave their magic. One of our jobs is to lift the curtain to see and scrutinise the mechanics of the writing. This means focusing on the plainness of the language, or its metaphors and similes, moments of disruption, as well as its moments of silence. I also endeavour to do this below by offering comparative readings about a topic; that is to say, where possible I show how the same ideas are done in various ways in different texts. This comparative approach is improved by a close attention to language. For these reasons, you will find a lot of quotations in my readings of the hyper-contemporary texts.

The second principle is that one of the ways in which to read and judge hyper-contemporary literature is through related writing through, for example, 'intertextuality'. 'Intertextuality' was coined by Julia Kristeva in her essay 'Word, Dialogue, Novel' (1966). In the essay, Kristeva introduces the term as a way of explaining how language and ideas from one text can be taken and transposed into another, showing that all writing is plural, and never singular. Therefore, knowledge of one text may help you to read another text. In the discussions below, for instance, I will have occasion to reference Vladimir Nabokov's *Lolita* (1955) in order to help read the hyper-contemporary novel *House of Stone* (2018) by Novuyo Rosa Tshuma, or Charles Maturin's *Melmoth the Wanderer* (1820) while reflecting on *Melmoth* (2018) by Sarah Perry. Whilst introducing these texts may help me elucidate my readings and ways of judging the hyper-contemporary writing under scrutiny, I appreciate that not everyone will have access to this writing (for instance, I have not read any of Sarah Perry's previous books). Nevertheless, I believe that more knowledge is better than less, and that my audience may have this kind of knowledge to help them read brand-new writing.

My final key principle is that, whilst there are always multiple 'conversations' ongoing in any text—others might call them 'themes' or 'discourses'—a productive way of starting to judge a text is by starting to think about these conversations discretely. As such, the remainder of the book is structured according to different literary conversations and the way they inform the ongoing negotiation of the literary canon.

In the first of these, I explore 'Feminism; or, emasculating the canon' in which I relate contemporary fourth-wave feminism to hyper-contemporary literature. I explain the importance of difference in and to feminism, and the importance of social media to today's fourth-wave feminism and the kinds of feminist discourses that now dominate. I also explain how 'postfeminist' literature is on the rise, rejecting the premise of feminism entirely. I frame these arguments within an idea of utopian and dystopian literature as a way in which feminism gains traction. In the second chapter, 'Postcolonialism and critical race theory; or, decolonising the canon', I explain the crossovers and differences between postcolonial theories and critical race discourses, establishing that much hyper-contemporary literature that is considered 'postcolonial' or addressing the presentation of 'race' itself interrogates colonial and/or racist literature. In my third chapter on 'Queer theory; or, bending the canon', I establish that queerness does not seek acceptance for homosexuality, but it seeks to right/rewrite heterosexuality as the accepted 'norm'. But also, 'queer' is itself contested nowadays with some academics urging us to think about the 'after queer' or 'post-queer'.

In my fourth chapter, I address 'Class; or dividing the canon', probing why there is a continued focus on class antagonism in both culture and literature, and the recurrent Bildungsroman trope of 'escape' from working-class strictures through education and other perceived 'middle-class' opportunities. Underpinning my arguments is the understanding that class is produced by capitalism, that all pervasive controller of social and economic forces. The final chapter considers 'Reviews; or, popularising the canon' and whether we can trust the canon, especially in relation to hyper-contemporary literature. Given the significance of online reviews in shaping purchasing decisions, it is important to see how Amazon reviews compare with, for example, professional reviews in newspapers, as well as on Goodreads, a socially mediated book club that contains millions of book reviews. I recognise that, whilst there is no critical consensus for hyper-contemporary writing, the reviews often provide the reader's first engagement with others' opinions on a text—either the reason for buying the book or to check the reader's opinion in comparison with someone else's. I evaluate these reviews by looking closely at how the twelve primary texts have been rated and reviewed across these fora.

Each chapter is structured into two parts. The first part gives an overview of recent and relevant theory that describes and defines the discourses I am using. Sometimes these theories are densely written in their original context, and I have tried where possible to translate this writing into more accessible English; however, I have also quoted the theories in their original languages in order to share them on their own terms. I think it is important to hide nothing, and present as much as possible. Nevertheless, should a term or idea still be difficult to comprehend, you can turn to the second half of each chapter in which I explore the theories in relation to the primary texts under scrutiny. These explorations are not meant to be exhaustive and are just models of how the theory can be used to read the primary texts. I could easily have written about Sally Rooney's *Normal People* in the feminism chapter or included Clare Fisher's *How the Light Gets In* in my chapter on class. It is perfectly possible—indeed, necessary—to think about the theory in different ways or to read the primary texts with other ideas brought to the fore. However, I hope that I show some ways of making good use of these theories. I believe that, just as students and non-students read more hyper-contemporary literature—and therefore are more likely to read bad writing—so too should they be furnished with the tools to scrutinise that literature. To learn to read is a democratic process of becoming, and it is our duty in the academy to advance the democratic mandate as deeply and broadly as we can.

It is also possible to read this book alongside the twelve primary texts. Some book clubs choose the short- or longlist of a book prize as their yearly reading list. If that is your kind of book club, then feel free to pick up these twelve texts and read this book alongside them. Moreover, each chapter begins with a brief definition of the theories elaborated in the pages that follow, along with a series of questions that may help you to think through whether a particular theory is relevant to the text you are reading. If you are reading a hyper-contemporary text and you would like to add to the conversations and arguments you are already having with your peers, then read those questions to judge whether or not the theory will help you to develop those lines of enquiry.

In the conclusion to the whole book I repeat, at length the following assertion: that hyper-contemporary literature comes to readers as unread, fresh, and new; it brings its own complications with it into the reading experience, as I have sketched above. However, in the process of reading a hyper-contemporary text, and judging it 'good' or 'bad', something happens to that text. It is no longer hyper-contemporary, according to my own definition, but recedes into the (mere) contemporary. It is no longer unknown; it is no longer unread. The reader's opinions cannot be un-thought or de-argued. The judged text now enters the body of intertexts available for authors of new texts, and therefore an instrument of the literary canon. The hyper-contemporary is *temporary*.

This book expedites that process and reading; it will help you to judge hyper-contemporary literature for yourself. I have already written about the importance of judging and the key characteristics of hyper-contemporary writing. However, I need now—in order to finish—to sketch the importance of you, the reader in that judgement. By way of illustration, I want to focus on the possibility of disagreement over agreement. Individual and discrete judgement give rise to the former over the latter, and it is important that everyone's substantiated opinions are heard and considered equally in the process of judging hyper-contemporary literature for which the critical consensus has not yet been established. Above I gave the example of how my students voted for one of the texts as their favourite to win the IDTP, just as I voted it last in my list. This illustrates the diverse opinions that can be formed from reading the same text and engaging with the same discussions.

This shows what happens when a range of dissenting judgements are directly compared and used to judge hyper-contemporary literature. The goal is not agreement (though neither is it merely disagreement). The goal of giving the reader greater opportunities to refine her judgement is to open up discussions to more opinions that are properly informed. From those opportunities, dissenting opinions will emerge more frequently—and also more robustly. *Judge for Yourself* is designed to help you do that.

This book is, ultimately, an invitation to you, my reader. I invite you to read your hyper-contemporary literature in the ways you would ordinarily—and, further, to develop your abilities of literary analysis to enhance your ability to judge good literature from bad. Above all, don't avoid 'bad' literature, and don't only read 'good' literature. After all, on whose opinions are you basing those decisions? It is far better to judge for yourself.

Notes

1 See www.swansea.ac.uk/press-office/news-archive/2019/femaleand debutwritersdominatethe2019longlistfortheswanseauniversityinterna tionaldylanthomasprize.php for the press release.

2 By contrast, texts in *The Routledge Companion* qualify as 'good' by virtue of their inclusion in that text.

3 Former Booker Prize judge and journalist Libby Purves (2019).

4 The Nobel Committee judging the award for literature has had more than its fair share of controversies in recent years, leading to the post-ponement of the 2018 award, with two winners announced in 2019. See Andrew Brown (2018).

5 For instance in 2019, Margaret Atwood's eventual co-winner, *The Testaments*, was long-listed before it had been released to the general public.

6 'Capital intraconversion' is the process by which a purely cultural event—such as the book prize—generates a flow of capital, such as when the winning author's previously out-of-print books suddenly come back to press and generate income (English, 2005: 10–11).

7 In the version of the anecdote I have heard, the eventual winner went on to win the Nobel Prize, so perhaps the chair's final judgement was valid.

Bibliography

Bhabha, Homi K., *The Location of Culture* (London: Routledge, 2004) [1994].

Bloom, Harold, *The Western Canon: The Books and School of the Ages* (New York, NY: Harcourt Brace, 1994).

Brown, Andrew, 'The ugly scandal that cancelled the Nobel prize', *Guardian*, 17 July 2018, www.theguardian.com/news/2018/jul/17/the-ugly-scandal-that-cancelled-the-nobel-prize-in-literature [accessed 20 July 2018].

Chamberlain, Prudence, *The Feminist Fourth Wave: Affective Temporality* (Basingstoke: Palgrave Macmillan, 2017).

Docherty, Thomas, *Literature and Capital* (London: Bloomsbury, 2018).

English, James, *The Economy of Prestige: Prizes, Awards, and the Circulation of Cultural Value* (Cambridge, MA: Harvard University Press, 2005).

Hirsch, Afua, 'Judging the Booker prize: "I'm proud of our decision"', *Guardian*, 16 October 2019a, www.theguardian.com/books/2019/oct/16/booker-prize-winners-margaret-atwood-bernardine-evaristo-judge [accessed 27 November 2019].

———, 'What I learned from my year of reading outside the box', *Guardian*, 10 October 2019b, www.theguardian.com/commentisfree/2019/oct/10/reading-booker-prize-judge [accessed 22 November 2019].

Iser, Wolfgang, *The Act of Reading: A Theory of Aesthetic Response* (London: Routledge & Keegan Paul, 1978).

Kristeva, Julia, *The Kristeva Reader*, ed. by Toril Moi (New York, NY: Columbia University Press, 1986).

Lawrence, Karen R., ed., *Decolonizing Tradition: New Views of Twentieth-Century 'British' Literary Canons* (Urbana: University of Illinois Press, 1992).

Mason, Paul, *Postcapitalism: A Guide to Our Future* (London: Penguin, 2015).

Mbembe, Achille Joseph, 'Decolonizing the university: New directions', *Arts & Humanities in Higher Education*, 15.1 (2016), 29–45. DOI: 10.1177/1474022215618513.

O'Gorman, Daniel, and Robert Eaglestone, 'Introduction', *The Routledge Companion to Twenty-First-Century Literary Fiction*, ed. by Daniel O'Gorman and Robert Eaglestone (London: Routledge, 2019), pp. 1–10.

Penney, James, *After Queer Theory: The Limits of Sexual Politics* (London: Pluto Press, 2014).

Purves, Libby, 'The best novels don't win the Booker prize', *The Times*, 22 July 2019, www.thetimes.co.uk/article/the-best-novels-dont-win-the-booker-prize-6kcnbl086 [accessed 22 November 2019].

Ramone, Jenni, and Helen Cousins, 'On readers and reading', *The Richard & Judy Book Club Reader: Popular Texts and the Practices of Reading*, ed. by Jenni Ramone and Helen Cousins (Farnham: Ashgate, 2011), pp. 1–18.

Ross, Catherine Sheldrick, Lynne McCechnie, and Paulette M. Rothbauer, *Reading Matters: What the Research Reveals about Reading, Libraries, and Community* (Westport, CT: Libraries Unlimited, 2006).

Shakespeare, William, *Othello*, ed. by E.A. Honigmann, Third Series (London: Arden Shakespeare, 2001).

Squires, Claire, *Marketing Literature: The Making of Contemporary Writing in Britain* (London: Palgrave Macmillan, 2007).

1   Feminism; or, emasculating the canon

Theories summary: The current predominant feminist theory comes under the title of **fourth-wave feminism**. In fourth-wave feminism several common threads emerge, focusing on **online activism**, as well as a strategy of **joining the dots** or **spotting the pattern** of seemingly singular sexist incidents in order to create a groundswell of support for new feminist activism. There is hope in the construction of real-time archives of abuse, but worry about the simultaneous backlash against feminist action. We will see an interest in **feminist narratives**—how stories are told—and how women come together in **feminist assemblies**. Finally, fourth-wave feminism comprises a range of texts, but to qualify properly as a fourth-wave text, it must be **activist** itself—merely to describe fourth-wave feminism is not sufficiently contemporary.

Relevant questions

1   Are abusive or exploitative behaviours against women depicted in the text?
2   Is the story about emerging patterns of abusive/exploitative behaviours?

3   Is the text activist or moralistic with regards to feminism, i.e.
    does it try to persuade you of a particular point of view?
4   Are women's bodies the focus of any narrative strand?
5   Does the text depict women coming together in an innova-
    tive or controversial organisation?

Feminism is clearly not a new concept, and it would be easy to
dismiss feminist readings and contemporary feminist arguments
as well-trodden and familiar. However, to do so would pass over
the continued and urgent problems that women encounter in
everyday life and how those problems—however long-lasting
and damaging—have not yet been solved. Hyper-contemporary
writing attests to feminism's continued importance in society,
and the upsurge in writing addressing the so-called 'fourth wave
of feminism' evidences the relevance of these arguments. I will
argue that fourth-wave feminism is important not just because it
has gained significant traction in contemporary debates, but also
because texts—whether literature or criticism—that address or
talk about fourth-wave feminism are examples of fourth-wave
feminism in action.

To understand fourth-wave feminism fully—if that is even
possible—first entails a brief overview of the first, second, and
third waves of feminism. To summarise, first-wave feminism was
defined, after the event, as feminism that was focused on securing
women's suffrage. Second-wave feminism was characterised by
a broader idea of gender equality, taking workplace and familial
equality more firmly into account. The 'personal is political'
mantra is associated with the second wave. Third-wave feminism
thereafter focused on the differences between women, rather
than their essential sameness. This led to a discourse of identity
politics, in which anyone could define their own mode of existence in the world, and the notion of a broad church of feminism
splintered into more individualised, discrete narratives of aspiration and success.[1]

Fourth-wave feminism has, in the last decade, become the
relevant term for current feminist discourses. I stress the plural
because, as with feminist waves before, there is no singular feminism and it has many facets whose successes are championed

to different degrees. Tellingly, as Kira Cochrane (2013) pointed out in *All the Rebel Women*—one of the key texts to introduce the 'fourth wave of feminism' into popular discourse—there are several more prominent strands to these current feminisms. The central chapters of her book outline these:

- Rape culture
- Online feminism
- Humour
- Intersectionality and inclusion

Many of these overlap, with the rise in prominence of contemporary anti-rape culture being propelled on social media such as Facebook and Twitter. Consider also, as Cochrane describes, the overlap between anti-rape culture and the types of jokes told by comedians at the Edinburgh Fringe festival. These overlaps briefly stated also point out the relevance of Cochrane's idea of intersectionality and inclusion 'which seems to be emerging as the defining framework for the fourth wave' (2013: loc. 920). Intersectionality was first defined by Kimberlé Crenshaw in 1989, who later elaborated that

> many of the experiences Black women face are not subsumed within the traditional boundaries of race or gender discrimination as these boundaries are currently understood, and [...] the intersection of racism and sexism factors into Black women's lives in ways that cannot be captured wholly by looking at the race or gender dimensions of those experiences separately.
>
> (Crenshaw, 1991: 1244)

I will focus more on intersectionality in my next chapter on 'Postcolonialism and critical race theory', but for now I want to highlight these ideas of banishing discrete analyses, and considering the unique position of intersectional discourses. It is not, for example, that women who are victims of rape and victims of online trolling undergo two distinct experiences. Rather, to be a victim of rape and online trolling culminates in a unique experience at the intersection of those two violences; it is unique in that it cannot merely be described as an aggregate experience of those of rape and online trolling, but distinct again from that. The activist actions in response to these experiences are similarly unique and cannot be broken down into a simple equation. To this end, the categories that Cochrane uses to structure her book are only separated as part of an argumentative strategy. In reality, there are many permutations of these.

There is a danger that, like the third wave, fourth-wave feminism could descend into the fractious problems of identity politics, or produce an unintended result. For example, third-wave feminism notably gave rise to 'postfeminism' that has continued to prove persuasive. For Rivers, postfeminism 'paradoxically both asserts feminisms' success in claiming that the battle for equality has been won, whilst simultaneously undermining feminist gains in suggesting that feminism has gone too far' (2017: 4). Given feminism's utopian desire to create equality, feminists must necessarily 'dismantle what has already been assembled', including postfeminism gains, and 'we need to ask what it is we are against, what it is we are for, knowing full well that this we is not a foundation but what we are working toward' (Ahmed, 2017: 2). However, where discrete and unique identities were heralded in the third wave, fourth-wave activists have sought to focus on 'working out what we are for' through which 'we are working out that *we*, that hopeful signifier of a feminist collectivity' (Ahmed, 2017: 2). Much of that collective solidarity is catalysed by the openly public and notionally democratising space of the Internet. Online activism and such endeavours as Laura Bates's Everyday Sexism Project prove the possibility of finding solidarity despite diverse experiences and perspectives—a kind of 'unity by volume' (Ohlheiser, 2017: para. 26). The Everyday Sexism Project was first established on Facebook and then Twitter, inviting anyone who had experienced sexism—regardless of sex or gender—to contribute their stories. 'In exactly the same way that raising the subject in a roomful of people led to more and more women chipping in with their own examples,' writes Bates in *Everyday Sexism*, 'the idea spread through social media like wildfire, snowballing and gathering momentum as it travelled' (2014: 16). The stories relayed from the individual to the Twitter account,

@everydaysexism, therefore went from a private, and perhaps silent, space, to the most public and loudest forum. Nicola Rivers consequently notes that 'Laura Bates' Everyday Sexism project could be seen as a return to the kind of collective identity politics that characterized much of the second wave' (2017: 24). This is the kind of online solidarity that can take account of difference and individualism, but use it as a way of consolidating that into a common ground:

> [S]olidarity does not assume that our struggles are the same struggles, or that our pain is the same pain, or that our hope is for the same future [...] even if we do not have the same feelings, or the same lives, or the same bodies, we do live on common ground.
>
> (Ahmed, 2004: 189)

It is clear from some of these ideas that what comes under the label 'fourth-wave feminism' draws on earlier feminisms. This invites the question as to what waves are, and what they are not. Both Prudence Chamberlain and Nicola Rivers have explored this question, coming up with slightly different, though overlapping responses. Chief among the commonalities is that there is no sense that any wave is unique, nor that the different waves should be restrictively considered as purely generational. Whilst there is a chronological order to the waves, it does not imply that there is progress from one wave to the next. Chamberlain prefers the language of chronology over generational linearity that

> denotes a line; a straight connection between historical points that cannot and will not be deviated from. The rigidity of following lines also seems to imply certain methodologies. Moving from one point to another narrows the scope of feminism and creates paths through history that negate anything other than what is clearly and easily accessible.
>
> (2017: 55)

Chronology, by contrast, 'recognises how events have unfolded. As opposed to being linear, it recognises how waves have fallen at specific, different points throughout time' evidencing how, Chamberlain continues, 'waves' existences are determined through responsiveness to their contemporary moment, which has heralded significant social change' (2017: 55, 57). Waves, then, are much more concerned with the contemporary than with improving on the past. Rivers thinks of a 'solution' to the problem of defining waves when she 'envisage[s] a wave as allowing for a movement that is constantly in flux, rolling back as often as it rolls forward, gaining strength from what it brings with it rather than losing momentum due to what it leaves behind' (2017: 21–2). This contemporary focus leads to Chamberlain's convincing argument that waves in general, and the fourth wave in particular, come about because of an upsurge of common feeling at a particular moment that spills over into action and activism. In Chamberlain's (2017: *passim*) terminology, this is 'affective temporality', and relies on a flexible sense of what a 'contemporary moment' is, not unlike my own understanding of hyper-contemporary literature. Chamberlain draws on Agamben's theory of the contemporary (62) to help make the case. Fourth-wave feminism, then, is hyper-contemporary, much like the literature under scrutiny here.

The idea of activism that is central to feminism takes on a new hue in fourth-wave feminism. That is because, I argue, the texts describing and categorising fourth-wave feminism are also examples of fourth-wave feminism at work. For example, in *Living a Feminist Life*, Sara Ahmed declares early and explicitly that 'I consider this book primarily as a contribution to feminist of color scholarship and activism' (2017: 16). In this statement, Ahmed is tacitly following Crenshaw's footnote that framed her own intersectional arguments as more than descriptive, arguing that 'I hope to suggest a methodology that will ultimately disrupt the tendencies to see race and gender as exclusive or separable' (Crenshaw, 1991: 1244, n. 9). Chamberlain looks to Bates's Everyday Sexism archive as 'a form of online activism, using its social media forum to document and disseminate thousands of women's experience of sexism in the hope that wider society will no longer overlook these incidents' (2017: 15). Bates ends her book on a note of activist urgency, commanding her readers to 'Be the aunt or uncle who buys their niece a chemistry set and their nephew a toy stove. Be the teenager who […] Be the colleague who' (2014: 381–2), etc. while Cochrane contrasts the second wave of the 1970s that 'was awash with theory' with the fourth wave that 'feels quite different, generally more active than academic' (2013: loc. 917).

That activism takes place largely online. With the advent of the hashtag as a way of curating microblogs around a single or several ideas, feminist activists have (along with others) made the most of the online meeting space. Few can forget the #metoo explosion for much of 2018, after actor Alyssa Milano tweeted simply enough on 15 October 2017: 'If you've been sexually harassed or assaulted write "me too" as a reply to this tweet.' As of 21 December 2019, it has been retweeted 22,779 times and received 51,267 likes. That viral success only tells the beginning of the story: 'Capturing both public and media attention, the hashtag was used 12 million times in the first 24 hours alone' (Mendes *et al.*, 2018: 236). As an activist urge, it was hugely successful and led to the downing of famous powerful men, particularly in the film and television industry, where a permissive culture of sexual harassment had gone long unchecked. #metoo prominently led to the shameful downfalls of Oscar-winning producer Harvey Weinstein (who was later imprisoned) and Oscar-winning actor Kevin Spacey. Online activism is fast acting and can be effective if it catches the right wind.

What often goes unmentioned, however, is how Milano was not the first to use the 'Me too' phrase as an activist rallying cry— and she did not even use the hashtag #metoo at all, preferring the simple phrasal variant. 'Me too' was first used by Tarana Burke in 2006, a Black activist working with girls and young women who had experienced sexual harassment (Ohlheiser, 2017). Milano's tweet's detachment from the prior history of #metoo is significant because it illustrates a larger trend in fourth-wave feminism to emphasise the novelty of this feminist activism, even at the cost of a genuine engagement with past activism. In this case, the apparent novelty of Milano's tweet serves to erase the Black women's experiences that gave initial rise to the phrase 'me too'. Rivers is critical of this element of fourth-wave feminism, first thinking about Caitlin Moran's *How to be a Woman* (2011), in which Moran's '"new" brand of feminism can be seen as an extension of postfeminism that, whilst bringing "feminist" ideas to the fore in popular culture and consciousness, simultaneously functions by reinforcing notions of established feminist theory as stuffy and outdated' (Rivers, 2017: 67). Rivers proceeds to make the same point about Bates ('Bates is positioned in media accounts and interviews as having somehow discovered sexism, and by extension, feminism, anew' [67]) and Emma Watson, who presents her 'He for She' campaign 'without historical and social context' (68). For Rivers, this strategy has two chief effects. First, it connects fourth-wave feminism uneasily with postfeminism, a branch of discourse that threatens the necessity and virtue of feminism. Second, 'the current popularizing of feminism also relies on it appearing to be non-threatening' (67), thereby neutering its power.

The idea that feminism should no longer threaten is particularly acute in the fourth wave because of the online activist space. Not only is that space fast-paced, but so is the response to online activism. Chamberlain points out how the idealised and democratised Internet space and 'the possibility of genderless spaces of freedom' (2017: 136) have failed to materialise, mainly 'On account of the backlash happening with greater rapidity, [and] to the point that it in fact overlaps with the wave's temporality, the wave itself is feeding on that negativity' (137). In turn, this allows activists to engage dialogically with their trolls, 'consolidating the fact that the wave and its counter are occurring within the same temporality' (137). In light of this, it is easy to see why a neutered, non-offensive feminism appeals if it can attract little attention and provoke little argument. It could be argued, therefore, that some fourth-wave activists seek to pass by unnoticed, adopting a strategy that women of colour have long been forced to practise: '[I]n order to pass through (a street a neighborhood, an organization), you have to pass as something you are assumed not to be' (Ahmed, 2017: 115). To this end, 'Feminists are diversity workers' because 'we are trying to transform institutions by challenging who they are for' (110), and both diversity work and feminism 'could thus be described as willful work. You have to persist because they resist' (113). There is thus a tension encoded into fourth-wave feminism that both wants to appear unthreatening, but must also push through the simultaneous backlash that is unleashed against its online activism, proving as ever its necessity because it always threatens structures of power.

Given the varied examples of fourth-wave feminism, it would be simple to dismiss the existence of any coherence. However, there appears to be one idea that recurs across many of the activists' work: the process of connecting disparate ideas into a larger story of sexism and sexual harassment in a bid to galvanise activism. Rebecca Solnit writes that

> I think we would understand misogyny and violence against women even better if we looked at the abuse of power as a whole rather than treating domestic violence separately from rape and murder and harassment and intimidation, online and at home and in the workplace and in the streets; seen together, the pattern is clear.
>
> (2014: 16)

Indeed, more than 'clear', the 'pattern is plain as day' (Solnit, 2014: 25). For Bates in *Misogynation*, 'Until we join the dots, we haven't any hope at all of stopping misogyny. We can't tackle any one of these incidents in isolation' (2018: x), which is similar to Ahmed's argument that also invokes activism. Ahmed writes that 'Apparently unrelated phenomena, things that seem "just to happen," to fall this way or that, become part of a system, a system that works. It is a system that works because of how it smooths progression. We need to throw a wrench in the works', but 'Before we can do that, before we can be that, we have to recognize that there is a system' (2017: 157–8). However, this tendency to narrativise must be set against the feminist 'need to delineate and differentiate' (Chamberlain, 2017: 6). Narratives, therefore, must also be suspected and not believed wholesale, such as in the constructions of celebrity feminists, as Rivers pointed out.

These are but the outlines of fourth-wave feminism, including a brief allusion to postfeminism that opposes feminism by suggesting its utopian goals have already been realised. In my discussions below, these ideas will recur and shape my reading of the texts. In particular I will focus on three constellations of ideas in order to question the quality of the texts and to judge them in their evocation and use of feminism:

- Feminist narratives
- Online feminism
- Embodied feminism

Feminist narratives

A narrative is a way of stringing single events together into a story. One way of analogising the idea of narrative—and how it can be problematic—is by thinking through the relation between the 'past' and 'history'. Chamberlain explains that 'History […] is understood in two ways; it is not purely the events of the past, but the way in which we record, document and account for what has happened in the past' (2017: 54). In this mode, narrative is problematic because there are 'past' events omitted from 'history' that are therefore not considered. The past is forgotten in and through historical narrative. This is the battle facing feminists, especially those of the fourth wave for whom the single event can catalyse an entire movement, as with Milano's tweet in October 2017, or the Slut Walk movement originating in Canada.

One way of responding to the pressure to narrativise and to tell a story that can be used to galvanise feminists and persuade non-believers is through a new method of archiving and curating events. If the narrative is the problem, that is, then the process of how you select what is included in the narrative is under greater scrutiny. Chamberlain thus praises Bates's work in the Everyday Sexism Project because her 'kind of archival practice […] prioritises a multiplicity of voices […] without creating hierarchies of experience' (2017: 119). This new archival practice 'unfolds within the present moment' (119) and leads to a process of 'curation [that] is less selective. The curator is working almost as a mediator for the information' (120). These archival ideas and their praise provide a way of judging the 'narrative' structure and content of Claire Fisher's *How the Light Gets In*.

How the Light Gets In is a collection of flash fiction 'stories' structured in four parts: 'learning to live with cracks', 'how the light gets between you and me', 'how the light gets out', and 'learning to live with cracks again'. The names of the first and last of the sections point toward an inescapable circularity to experience, therefore corroborating the idea that new feminist waves do not necessarily build on or progress past previous waves, but interlink across generations. This idea is intensified in the course of the book given the narratives of women's experiences in twenty-first-century London. The book's form, making use of flash fiction, creates a sense of fracture with sixty-one chapters populating only 145 pages of text. The shortest chapter, 'insomniac', is just five lines long, and the longest, 'no further than a selfie stick', stretches to nearly seven pages.

Between and among these chapters, however, Fisher is able to create a disparate sense of narrative for the women who populate the voices in this modern city. This is partly achieved through the explicit nods and returns to specific topics. For example, 'dark places to watch out for [1]' introduces the darknesses that assail people in the modern world, including 'The days when you hate everyone, everyone—including all the ones who are not yet born. In fact, *especially* those ones' (Fisher, 2018: 35), which morphs in 'dark places to watch out for [3]' into 'The days when you love everyone, everyone, even the ones you have never met. Especially the ones you have never met' (97). The transformation from hate to love illustrates an overt concern for women's mental health. Its greater prominence in recent cultural discourses—from Princes William and Harry speaking openly about their own struggles with mental health following their mother's death, to model-cum-actor Cara Delevingne confessing openly to her own feelings of depression—shows how conversations about mental health are on the rise. Moreover, Young Women's Trust CEO, Sophie Walker (2019), has written about how women suffer in specific ways from mental health, and therefore need particular, and not generalised, provision and treatment. As such, it is instructive to read Fisher's fifth and final iteration of 'dark places to watch out for [5]', in which

> No matter the tongue-in-cheek and cheek-in-tongue self-help books […] when that phone rings, when you trip, fall or slowly, slowly slide back into that dark place, it will not feel like any darkness you've known before. It will suck. And digging your way out will not be any easier than it was the last time, or the time before[.]
>
> (2018: 143)

The stress on 'digging your way out' as a repeated action reminds us, yet again, of the circularity of experience in the text, and therefore also the circularity of *women's* experience in the world.

In 'dark places to watch out for [1]', the narrator tells of a sexual assault in a bar:

> Revs on a Friday night when already you won't want to be there, and some idiot spills raspberry vodka shots down your top and shouts as if this is your fault, and them some other idiot gropes your arse and the friends of the other idiot tell everyone you love it, and so, when—finally!—you fight your way back to the people who, if not exactly your friends, are not as idiotic as the other people in there, you think the fluttering in your chest means you're happy.
>
> (2018: 34)

This paragraph reads like a number of the entries to Laura Bates's Everyday Sexism Project (e.g. Bates, 2014: 167, 175), and the way in which Fisher has curated and constructed these examples of 'dark places to watch out for' allows the reader to connect these discrete episodes—the sexual harassment, the 'slid[ing] back' into depression and anxiety—and proposes a causal link between the two, even if there is no explicit narrative connection.

'[R]epeat' (Fisher, 2018: 113–15) also tells of a sexual assault in a nightclub. The first-person narrator explains, in the first of the fictions from the 'how the light gets out' section, how she got the scar on her face. The story begins with the narrator accusing the reader of 'star[ing] at me', thereby positioning the reader as one of the passive passers-by who is also implicated in the stories of the Everyday Sexism Project. The story is known by now as 'His hands slide into my pockets, my pants, my bra' before she spots a knife in his hands. The narrator's subjectivity drops out of the grammar of the experience when she explains how she lost any sensation: 'Didn't really feel anything when he did it.' The missing 'I' from the sentence points to the fractured state of the narrator's selfhood. This fracture is compounded by her 'mates [who] are sick of this story, jammed on repeat, hoping that each telling will nudge me closer and closer to the end—to when I feel the cut of the blade'. It is not just the repetitious experience of assault that comes under scrutiny, but also the narrator's friends and their own desensitisation to the story, such that it will feel real once the narrator can tell the story more properly and more fully.

Fractures and fractured experiences are at the heart of this text—and here is a way of seeing the fracture and its repetition as the prominent fourth-wave element of the story. Above I wrote that it is between and among the stories that Fisher's text forges a narrative of sorts. This sense of between-ness is central to Chamberlain's argument about affect—that force of feeling that encourages political action and activism—and she writes that

> Affect, then, becomes important in that it seems to mediate the thinking and feeling emotional side, and then the embodied experiences of such feeling. It situates itself somewhere between the physical experience, and then the more internalised emotional responses inevitable in the face of a patriarchal society.
>
> (Chamberlain, 2017: 9)

This affective experience is visible in 'repeat' through the self's fracture, as in elsewhere in *How the Light Gets In*. After all, the text's overall focus is the cracks that either permit or refuse the entrance of light. The text's opening salvo is 'in praise of cracks' and cites a fridge magnet that reads '*blessed are the cracked for they let the light in*' (Fisher, 2018: 15). This in-between-ness helps to construct the sense of narrative in the text, and is nearly as common as the number of stories themselves.[2] Given the seemingly super-ficial connection between many of the stories, it is perhaps easier to argue that the running thread in the collection *is* the series of cracks themselves.

This is, therefore, a fourth-wave archive of stories that are held together by what separates them. In a certain slant of light, to paraphrase Emily Dickinson, the stories join together in a loose narrative of tales about woman's experience in the modern city—in spite of their more apparent dissonances and separations. To that end, they seem to reflect the practice of fourth-wave feminist activism that enlarges a single incident synecdochic-ally to represent a whole movement, and that joins to create a 'common ground' (Ahmed, 2004: 189). It is worth comparing this use of difference and fracture to Sarah Perry's *Melmoth*, which retells a Gothic story of Melmoth the Wanderer, a monster who is dedicated to tempting mortals to damnation.

Charles Robert Maturin's *Melmoth the Wanderer* (1820) provides the blueprint for Perry's 2018 variation, including the framework of nested and parallel stories-within-stories. For Maturin, there is the overarching story of John Melmoth, who encounters the story of the ancestor-Wanderer through three other stories: Stanton's manuscript, The Tale of the Spaniard, The Tale of the Indian, The Tale of Guzman's Family, and The Lovers' Tale. In terms of narrative, therefore, the novel offers a smooth narrative of stories told from realistic perspectives. The overarching story that joins the re-told stories together remains permanently in view. This is the same pattern that Perry reproduces. However, she adapts this structure in one chief way: by allowing more women to tell their own stories and confess to their own guilty feelings. The monster is, too, transformed into a woman. Melmoth the Witness—as she is in Perry's adaptation—visits those who feel guilt from which they would like to be absolved, and who possess stories they would like to confess. Instead of John Melmoth, Perry introduces Helen Franklin. Here, then, is an explicitly feminist twist on an otherwise masculinist story.

There are intimations that Helen is characterised as postfeminist—someone whose success has come in spite of being a woman in a man's world. Her friend Karel says to her that "You are so ordinary your very existence makes the extraordinary seem impossible." This, he claims, is meant "as a compliment" (Perry, 2018: 9). Moreover, when Helen was admitted to a grammar school as a child, her 'mother wept, because she could not reconcile maternal pride with her feeling that she was now marked out among the neighbours—had transgressed, somehow, and would in due course be punished for it' (58). This hints at a postfeminist attitude from Helen's mother that 'asserts feminisms' success in claiming that the battle for equality has been won, whilst simultaneously undermining feminist gains in suggesting that feminism has gone too far' (Rivers, 2017: 3). The strength of this postfeminist sensibility is encouraged by the lack of overt feminist discourse in the text, with the characters neither individually focusing on how their life as a woman is particularly difficult nor undertaking specific conversations about womanhood. However, Helen is ultimately inscrutable, as the narrator explores later in the text:

> Where is the evidence of who she is, this Helen Franklin: small, insignificant, having about her an air of sadness whose source you cannot guess at; of self-punishment, self-hatred, carried out quietly and diligently and with a minimum of fuss?
>
> (Perry, 2018: 57)

The successes she has had appear to have come in spite of herself, with a box beneath her bed encasing her past successes: 'Everything before it was prologue: everything after, a footnote' (60).

The novel begins to reach its climax when Helen organises an evening birthday celebration for her landlady, Albína. Sat around the table near the Prague opera house where they will go after dinner are four women: Helen, Albína, Thea—a former Barrister from Britain—and Adaya, who turns out to be the contemporary manifestation of Melmoth the Witness. This is the scene for Helen's confession to her friends. The confessional act reflects the story she tells of sorority when, as a visitor to a Manila hospital when she was younger, she visited a very sick patient, Rosa, who 'has no one' (Perry, 2018: 194). After a few days of visiting Rosa, the latter invites 'Helen into a contract which she had never sought but could not break'. Rosa achieves this by asking of Helen one thing: '"My friend, my friend. Let me die"' (199). By interpellating Helen as her 'friend', Helen is bound by a kinship that she cannot shrug off, and eventually takes it on herself, calling Rose '"my older sister"' (203) and resolving to do as Rosa requests: helping her to die with an overdose of painkillers.

When Helen tells her companions this story, she worries that either 'disgust' or 'contempt' 'silences the women'. It is neither, for all of the women console Helen and, to an extent, invite her to absolve herself of her sins. The sisterhood that Helen had forged between herself and Rosa extends beyond the frame of her story to reach out to Albína, Thea, and even Adaya the Melmoth who speaks gently to her (Perry, 2018: 208). Given the age differences between the women, there appears another way of considering this sorority of stories, underpinned as it is by a series of confessions and witnessings. In *Men Explain Things to Me*, Solnit considers how to reintegrate lost stories of previous generations of women. 'Everyone is influenced by those things that precede formal education,' writes Solnit, and she calls those 'excluded influences […] grandmothers' (2014: 73). The community of women who gather around Helen, including the ninety-one-year-old Albína, testifies to the reintegration of grandmothers in Perry's *Melmoth*. The exchange of stories between the women gives voice to the 'excluded influences'. After all, 'The ability to tell your own story […] is already a victory' in Solnit's fourth-wave feminism, wherein 'to be able to sing and not be silenced' (2014: 78, 82) is celebrated. It is pertinent, therefore, that at the end of *Melmoth* 'there is music' (Perry, 2018: 268).

Here, then, is *Melmoth*'s version of contemporary feminism: giving voice to women's stories and bringing a grandmotherly sorority to the fore. Set against the fractured and dissonant narrative content and style of Fisher's *How the Light Gets In*, there is a clear opportunity for readers to judge how feminist narrative styles play a role in determining the quality and success of hyper-contemporary writing.

Online and digital

It is clear that instant communication has made an immeasurable change to how we interact with others in the world and, as has been pointed out above, this is especially significant for activist communities. The important characteristic of media such as Twitter is the instantaneous method of communicating, and of sharing in public what would otherwise have remained private. As Chamberlain points out, this link between technology and the public sphere is central to feminist activism:

> Current technologies cultivate an environment of public intimacy and its affective results. This suggests that the privacy traditionally associated with the body and personal experience have been necessarily transferred into the public sphere, such that the affect these feelings produce can galvanise feminist collectives.
>
> (2017: 82)

Replacing the importance of intimacy is another term: extimacy. The ideas of instantaneity and extimacy help us to judge how important hyper-contemporary literature can be in relation to, and in advancing, fourth-wave feminism.

Fisher devotes an entire story to parodying this topic. In 'things smartphones make you less likely to do when alone, in a public place', the text playfully explores the way that digital extimacy actually constrains activity in the so-called 'real' world of material, and not virtual, objects. The text does this through eight single-sentence paragraphs, each detailing a different 'thing' that smartphones limit in public. For example, smartphones help us to 'find' ourselves on a map through geolocation. However, smartphone geolocation neuters our ability to discover where we are located in our physical surroundings, either through looking around us or by looking at a traditional map. Thus, the text suggests trying to 'Work out where you are by looking up, down, around and around, trying left, trying right, trying straight ahead, even though you can only hope this is the direction in which you are meant to be headed' (Fisher, 2018: 51). Moreover, being awake to your location also allows you to 'Ask strangers for the time or directions […] to the nearest coffee shop […], oh, and cake—cake is always good' (50). This hints at the possibility of a real, lived intimacy, rather than the digitally-forged extimacy.

   The first two items in this list of 'things smartphones make you less likely to do when alone, in a public place' are about erotic love. The text suggests, in turn, two similar strategies: 'Stare at every passing stranger who is a similar size/shape/sex/style to the one you are waiting for in case they are indeed the one you are waiting for.' and 'Stare at strangers who are a completely different size/shape/sex/style to the one you are waiting for because you do not want to admit to yourself that the one you are waiting for is still not here' (Fisher, 2018: 50). In both, Fisher's text mocks several aspects of fourth-wave practice. First, that with smartphones we are less likely to make eye contact with strangers. Second, that on a phone dating app we are more likely to stick to the limits of what 'size/shape/sex/style' we think we like—we take fewer risks. Third, that the instantaneity of smartphone technology makes us less likely to wait. Since all of this is written in a tongue-in-cheek tone, it suggests that Fisher's text is not *rejecting* the possibilities afforded by digital and online feminism, but simply poking fun at those who are too locked into digital extimacy to see that physical intimacy is still possible. Fisher's narrator doubles down on these ideas in 'things smartphones make you less likely to do when in a private place, with or without other people', when asserting that 'being lost with a crappy map in your pocket is better than being lost with no map at all' (91)—neither of which is likely to happen in a world teeming with smartphones.

   In 'blip blip blip' the narrator shows how the immediacy of online communication might not provide a panacea. The 'blip blip blip' of the title is 'the sound submarines would make if they ever tried to communicate underwater [and] of Skype trying to reconnect' (Fisher, 2018: 82). The pause in the supposedly instantaneous conversation between the two speakers separated by '1.67 thousand miles and two time zones' begins to grow in feeling, becoming 'Six minutes, ten years, three lifetimes and twelve box sets later' (82–3) as the sensibility of the distant connection alters the passage of ordinary time: Something that should be instantaneous leads to mere minutes feeling like days. This is a problem consequent to the possibility of extimacy in an online setting that forestalls proper intimacy. This is a particularly feminist issue because historically women have had less access to public spaces and to long-distance travel. In the collapse of time and space in online environments—you could be talking to a friend on the other side of the world with speed-of-light efficiency—the Internet purports to offer a more equal space in which women can engage even from their own home. The success of Mumsnet, for example, demonstrates the viability for forging online communities of women where a real-world community might be more difficult (if not impossible) to create. Fisher's text challenges the possibilities of online feminism by pointing out flaws in the virtual world, and by mocking the asocial behaviours that follow too great a focus on smartphone technology.

Embodied

The idea that bodies are central to feminism is not new. Suffragette Emily Davison's death under the trampling hooves of the king's horse in 1913 testifies to the importance of the body in feminist activism: The body suffers under the patriarchy, and so the body can help to liberate women's oppression. In *Bodies that Matter* (1993), Judith Butler argues that all genders and sexualities are performed and are neither 'essential' nor 'natural', ideas that have become a mainstay of third-wave feminism. The fact of the body should not be overlooked as merely a discursive subject or object, but as a material object that either enabled or obstructed discourse, depending on how it was used. Butler's theories urged a consideration of difference and identity politics that underpinned third-wave feminism.

Questions of the body have changed in the twenty-five years since Butler's *Bodies that Matter*. Chamberlain argues that the development of a wave is itself an embodied phenomenon and ties it into her theory of the 'force' (2017: 35) of affective temporality. She writes that

> Affect, then, becomes important in that it seems to mediate the thinking and feeling emotional side, and then the embodied experiences of such feeling. It situates itself somewhere between the physical experience, and then the more internalised emotional responses inevitable in the face of a patriarchal society.
>
> (9)

Without the body to feel the physical side of affect, feminism cannot rise to become a wave phenomenon. Chamberlain later develops these ideas, suggesting that the body must become an agent of feminism, not just its barometer, since 'Feminism […] embodies a kind of difficulty' and it is therefore necessary for feminism to 'avoid a sense of comfort' (2017: 103). The discomfiting essence of feminism, as Chamberlain reads it, responds directly to the bodily discomfort many women feel in public spaces when—in an inversion of online fourth-wave activism—women's private bodies are made objects of public inquiry, ridicule, and become subject to physical and sexual abuse. Laura Bates's *Everyday Sexism* devotes an entire chapter to the phenomenon ('Women in Public Spaces'). Chamberlain notes, in line with other ethics of fourth-wave feminism, that whilst the 'embodied experience [of abuse] is one that unfolds quite individually', it is nonetheless an 'endemic social problem' (2017: 109): Contemporary feminists are beginning to join the dots of women's embodied experience.

In *Peach*, Emma Glass explores the mental degradation of a school-aged teenage girl, Peach, who has suffered sexual abuse. The mental degradation is accompanied by a physical degradation that is depicted in surrealist terms: Peach emaciates and becomes the stone at the heart of the fruit at the end of the novel (Glass, 2018: 98), while her boyfriend Green is a tree who 'shakes little leaves as he laughs' (98), and her abuser Lincoln (another shade of green) is figured as greasy, phallic sausages (12 and *passim*). Other characters include Mr Custard, Peach's biology teacher, and Sandy, Peach's friend. Colours and non-geometric shapes abound, as Mr Custard's 'blobby body [...] slips directly on to the floor' (24) because he is made of liquid. There is no translation provided in the text to make sense of these surrealist depictions, and instead the reader is invited to read it as they might a Dalí painting in which realist representation is forgone without explanation.

To say this book is surrealist would suggest that it is modernist—an artistic period across all media that encompassed much of the first half of the twentieth century—rather than contemporary. This raises questions when judging *Peach* as to whether it can be considered a valuable fourth-wave feminist text. But it is important to assess whether this is pure surrealism, which took the symbolic images of dreams to depict the malaise of the post-First World War, or whether some other meaning or interpretation is available in Glass's text. I think an answer is found in Peach's embodied experience of abuse at the hands of Lincoln, and her embodied response to that abuse.

Her body comes to stand in as her mediator in the world, similar to the way that Chamberlain described, above. After she is first raped by Lincoln, Peach looks at her wounds through a mirror and decides she must sew them up (Glass, 2018: 7). The attempt to fix the body in this literal way shows that the mental apparatus that we might expect to read at the forefront of a post-rape narrative is supplanted by a literalisation of the body: Peach's body is used as a tool to respond to the abuse the body has suffered. A few pages later, her boyfriend Green 'touches my tummy. [...] His hand donates a damp peat print to my stomach. I put my hand in its place and press. Firm. Fat. I frown. I look down. Can't see my shoes' (19). Later, 'My thighs don't feel like they can balance the weight of my swelling belly any more' (22). Following the abuse, Peach has entered into a body-hating discourse, the likes of which prompted celebrity feminists such as Caitlin Moran, Lena Dunham, and Jameela Jamil to start what has been called the 'love your body' discourses of fourth-wave feminism. These are not necessarily positive discourses and, following Gill and Elias (2014), Rivers summarises that

> within such apparently 'empowering' discourses the burden of change is still placed upon women who are encouraged to look internally for a solution to prevailing currents of sexism, rather than externally to challenge a system that supports and promotes such sexist values.
>
> (2017: 63)

For Gill and Elias, the 'love your body' discourses *look* like they are fourth-wave feminism in action, but actually constitute postfeminism that serves to undo the successes of feminism. In another context, the *Observer*'s Eva Wiseman has recently lamented the same phenomenon, suggesting that these discourses lead to a woman feeling a 'doubling of guilt': 'Guilt both for living in a body that doesn't fit and for wanting to change it' (2020: para. 8). It follows that if Peach were to engage with this discourse, she might be letting Lincoln totally conquer her body, both as a mediator for her feelings, and as a way of becoming a fourth-wave activist. Indeed, at the end of the book when Peach sheds her skin and becomes the hard stone at the heart of her fruit-like body, she has only just finished trying symbolically to cut herself off from her experience of rape by 'tug[ging] the thread' with which she sewed herself back together. Trying to love her body, therefore, leads to Peach's knowing failure as she 'rip[s] [...] The slit the split that hasn't healed' (Glass, 2018: 96).

Peach did temporarily seem to succeed in the face of this traumatic experience. The solution that Peach reaches is as radical as the text itself: She decides to kill Lincoln and cook his sausage-body over a barbecue for all her friends to eat and enjoy. Thus, while 'My eyes meet his chest, where his sternum should be, [...] instead thick chunks of gristle and flesh' appear, and Peach attacks: 'Fight. Knife. Fight. Knife. Find. Find the hateful face. The knife moves fast, flashing silver chrome. [...] I am calm' (Glass, 2018: 78–9). Green soon asks where Peach got the meat from—'Did you rob a sausage factory?' (89)—before Peach's friends 'gather[] round the barbecue' with 'Plates [...] stacked with sausages' (92), including Peach's, who has previously been a vegetarian. 'It didn't taste as bad as I thought I would', Peach tells the reader, just before declaring that 'I am contented in [Green's] arms. I feel the trauma and tension of the last few days fall away like an old dry scab' (93). The surrealist body here seems to give way to representative language through Peach's use of a simile ('*like* an old dry scab'), perhaps indicating that Peach has responded in her own way. Ahmed, writing about her own tactics against a violent father, noted that when she screamed while she was attacking him, he would stop. 'Why did this work?', Ahmed asks, continuing, 'By screaming, I announced my father's violence. I made it audible' (2017: 73). In a way, Peach's embodied response to embodied violence, like Ahmed's scream, makes Lincoln's violence known to him at the moment of his death. His actions are not innocent. Peach thus becomes 'wilful', a key term for Ahmed's feminism, because wilfulness is 'the acquisition of a voice as a refusal to be beaten' (Ahmed, 2017: 73). Peach thus can be read as a fourth-wave feminist paragon by becoming wilful and responding bodily. Glass's *Peach* thus updates modernist surrealist ethics and aesthetics for the contemporary moment.

Zoe Gilbert's *Folk* offers a radically different version of the feminist body, one that is also radically positive. It is therefore useful to read it under the guidance of fourth-wave feminism's utopian ideal that, as Ahmed described, involves a 'we' that is not yet 'a foundation but what we are working toward' (2017: 2). This utopian vision has long had a history in relation to fantasy writing, the genre to which *Folk* most readily belongs. Fantasy envisages a secondary world that may be either similar or extremely different to 'our' world, but by constructing that secondary world, fantasy plays with the question of *u*-topia: the *no*-place, the non-existent, as well as the *eu*-topia, the happy place. *Folk*'s island Neverness is just such a place.

In 'Long Have I Lain Beside the Water' May, daughter of Galushen and Vina, is about to undergo an important coming-of-age ritual as she turns sixteen. She intends to become a professional fiddle player, but to do so requires that she find her 'spirit'. Finding her spirit in turn will lead to her making her own professional fiddle, better than the 'mock up' she has already made:

> 'All Quayle's apprentices have to make one. It took me a month, at his workshop.' She raises it to her chin, and mimes a bow across the strings. 'Quayle says it's good enough. It proves I'm ready.'
>
> 'And what does this mean?' asks Galushen.
>
> 'It means I'm to go out and find my fiddle-playing spirit. All the true fiddlers do it. Nine days is long enough, Quayle says. I'll just stay out, and when I find it, I'll make my own fiddle like he did. I'll be able to play like him.'
>
> (Gilbert, 2018: 79)

May thus undertakes her task, disappearing into the woods and swimming in the stream before returning after nine days with her fiddle in hand. This is thus a story of feminine becoming with a sense of Chamerblain's 'affective temporality' indelibly inked into the story. For May, discovering her spirit '"will be a new feeling. Not like any other"' (Gilbert, 2018: 83), with this radically new present (the temporality) defined by its sentiment (its affect). To reiterate, for Chamberlain this affective temporality 'situates itself somewhere between the physical experience, and then the more internalised emotional responses' (2017: 9), and this seems a useful description of May's expectation.

A story of lovelorn grief shadows May's narrative. It is the story of Oline, Vina's late sister and Galushen's first love. Oline drowned when she was sixteen, the same age as May. May, however, has never been told of her aunt's death, thereby keeping Oline's history literally beneath the surface. There are tantalising allusions to the tragedy when, while May is on her search for her spirit, Galushen catches sight of her at the stream:

> There on the rippling, ridging surface of the water he sees a dark mass, long black hair flowing. As he stares, it vanishes, and he looks up, to be sure it was not a bird shadow. After

a few moments he sees it again, further downstream. He stumbles along the bank, his eyes on the rag of black, and is certain he sees a head rise from the water, as if to breathe, before diving down again. 'Oline,' he calls, as it vanishes, but the rough thrum of his own voice makes him stop in shame. He must look like a man losing his mind. As he watches, the head rises again, and turns. He sees the pale face beneath the black hair. So like Oline, his daughter.

(Gilbert, 2018: 89)

The uncanny similarities between May and Oline are central to this story, suggesting that the women's body cannot just be excised from memory (Vina refuses to tell May the truth), and that it can provide a link to the past that will also help to create this utopian 'we' into the future.

The uncanny link between May's and Oline's bodies is confirmed in the fiddle May has made. It is made entirely from 'bone[, found b]uried in the bank': 'The neck is white, a long, polished bone. The pegs that wind the strings are the same: thin, white spindles' (Gilbert, 2018: 92). These are Oline's long-lost bones, her body thus being resurfaced by her niece who is her uncanny double. I read this as a positive affirmation that women's bodies persist in spite of their suppression and oppression, their omission from narrative history, and from memory. This is a utopian fourth-wave feminism in which 'we' now includes the written-out voice of Oline.

Furthermore, this fourth-wave feminism is broadly inclusive as we read that Galushen himself experiences what could be thought of as a moment of affective temporality. As he listens to May playing her new fiddle, the music

is rich as raven black, as glowing black hair, but with a ghostly light, high notes like glimpses of white. He feels cold. […] Struggle pulses through him. He cannot open his eyes but only feels himself flailing against the hands that catch about his head and push him down.

(Gilbert, 2018: 91)

Galushen, who had wanted to tell May about her aunt's death, is now affectively joined with Oline's tragic experience, but in a way that connects him utopically with his daughter in a broad fourth-wave feminist unity. This feminism is not restricted to women, but is born out of woman's becoming, i.e. May's coming-of-age as fiddle-master, and reconnection with woman's body, i.e. Oline's bones.

In this chapter I surveyed fourth-wave feminist texts and argued that fourth-wave feminism can be defined as such in part because the texts that *describe* it also become its activist texts. Across these texts and others, I have shown the importance of discourses of the use of narrative, online feminism, and embodied feminism. I also highlighted the importance of 'joining the dots' in fourth-wave feminism, as well as the centrality of intersectionality (more on which in the next chapter).

These discussions allowed me to consider four hyper-contemporary literary texts—Clare Fisher's *How the Light Gets In*, Sarah Perry's *Melmoth,* Emma Glass's *Peach*, and Zoe Gilbert's *Folk*—and to explore how they engage with fourth-wave feminist discourses. *How the Light Gets In* uses a fractured narrative, whereas *Melmoth* favours the long-form narrative in which a confessional story allows a woman's voice to be heard. *How the Light Gets In* also engages with online and digital feminism, while *Peach* and *Folk* help us to explore embodied feminism with different outcomes. You may now have judged which of these texts is your favourite based on the style, the story, or even its success at engaging with these discourses. I have explored these texts with only a few strands of analysis in mind, which has helped me to isolate certain aspects of these stories, but by no means all of them. It is therefore possible that you may, for example, judge *How the Light Gets In* as a better text than *Melmoth* because it engages more radically with the question of narrative in fourth-wave feminism. Alternatively, you may judge *Peach* as the best text under consideration because its engagement with sexual abuse, trauma, and the body is not only significant, but also more important than the other discourses of feminist narrative or online feminism.

Notes

1 Intersectionality, an idea examined at length in this and the next chapter on 'Postcolonialism and critical race theory', emerged during third-wave feminism, but has become much more readily used in fourth-wave feminism.
2 There are sixty-one stories and sixty 'cracks' between the stories.

Bibliography

Ahmed, Sara, *The Cultural Politics of Emotion* (Edinburgh: Edinburgh University Press, 2004).

———, *Living a Feminist Life* (Durham, NC: Duke University Press, 2017).

Bates, Laura, *Everyday Sexism* (London: Simon & Schuster, 2014).

———, *Misogynation: The True Scale of Sexism* (London: Simon & Schuster, 2018).

Butler, Judith, *Bodies That Matter: On the Discursive Limits of 'Sex'* (London: Routledge, 2011) [1993].

Chamberlain, Prudence, *The Feminist Fourth Wave: Affective Temporality* (Basingstoke: Palgrave Macmillan, 2017).

Cochrane, Kira, *All the Rebel Women: The Rise of the Fourth Wave of Feminism* (London: Guardian Books, 2013).

Crenshaw, Kimberlé, 'Mapping the margins: Intersectionality, identity politics and violence against women of color', *Stanford Law Review*, 43.6 (1991), 1241–99.

Fisher, Clare, *How the Light Gets In* (London: Influx Press, 2018).

Gilbert, Zoe, *Folk* (London: Bloomsbury, 2018).

Gill, Rosalind, and Ann Sofia Elias, '"Awaken your incredible": Love your body discourses and postfeminist contradictions', *International Journal of Media & Cultural Politics*, 10.2 (2014), 179–88. DOI: 10.1386/macp.10.2.179_1.

Glass, Emma, *Peach* (London: Bloomsbury, 2018).

Mendes, Kaitlynn, Jessica Ringrose, and Jessalynn Keller, '#MeToo and the promise and pitfalls of challenging rape culture through digital feminist activism', *European Journal of Women's Studies*, 25.2 (2018), 236–46. DOI: 10.1177/1350506818765318.

Ohlheiser, Abby, 'The woman behind "Me Too" knew the power of the phrase when she created it—10 years ago', *Washington Post*, 19 October 2017, www.washingtonpost.com/news/the-intersect/wp/2017/10/19/the-woman-behind-me-too-knew-the-power-of-the-phrase-when-she-created-it-10-years-ago/ [accessed 21 December 2019].

Perry, Sarah, *Melmoth* (London: Serpent's Tail, 2018).

Rivers, Nicola, *Postfeminism(s) and the Fourth Wave: Turning Tides* (Basingstoke: Palgrave Macmillan, 2017).

Solnit, Rebecca, *Men Explain Things to Me* (Chicago, IL: Haymarket, 2014).

Walker, Sophie, 'Women's Mental Illness is a Reaction to Oppression', *Huffington Post*, 27 November 2019, www.huffingtonpost.co.uk/entry/women-sexism-mental-health-illness_uk_5ddd55ace4b0913e6f74b4b9? [accessed 24 December 2019].

Wiseman, Eva, '"Body positivity" has had its day. Let's find peace with ourselves', *Observer*, 12 January 2020, www.theguardian.com/lifeandstyle/2020/jan/12/body-positivity-has-had-its-day-lets-find-peace-with-ourselves#maincontent [accessed 12 January 2020].

2 Postcolonialism and critical race theory; or, decolonising the canon

Theories summary: I explore two theories in this chapter. **Postcolonialism** describes a range of theories that take places and peoples who have suffered, or who continue to suffer, from colonial and imperial rule, and think through how they experience the world after colonialism is over or as it is finishing. There is no singular postcolonial theory, but **migrants** are a privileged demographic. The postcolonial citizen's **hybridity**—being between times, between places, between communities—is also a recurring topic. For one postcolonial theorist, attention must be paid to **literary disconsolation**: the ability of literature to be shocking, surprising, and ironical, and to exceed or deny what we have come to expect from postcolonial writing. **Critical race theory** shares some of the same critical ground as postcolonialism but offers a renewed focus on the idea that 'race' is a sociohistorical construct. This means that what 'race' comes to mean changes according to time and place. Central to both of these theories is **intersectionality**, which describes how identity is more complex than we thought. For example, instead of experiencing your gender (and any sexism) separately from your race (and any racism), intersectionality describes how these identities intersect and produce a third experience of identity for which the first two categories cannot account. The identity permutations are near endless.

Relevant questions

1 Are racism and/or colonialism depicted in the text?
2 Is there difficulty in representing historical events?
3 Are narratives of migration depicted in the text?
4 Is identity depicted as complex, and is that complexity problematic?

In this chapter I summarise and explore two complementary theories: postcolonialism and critical race theory. They are separate, though related, and I will take them in turn. As Neil Lazarus summarises regarding the former, 'Emerging at the end of the 1970s and consolidating itself over the course of the following decade and a half, postcolonial studies was very much a creature of its time—or, better, it was a creature *of* and *against* its time' (Lazarus, 2011: 1–2), while critical race theory can be understood as addressing the idea of race as a critical, discursive construct:

> I refer to 'race' here as one of those major or master concepts (the masculine form is deliberate) that organize the great classificatory systems of difference that operate in human societies. Race, in this sense, is the centerpiece of a hierarchical system that produces differences.
>
> (Hall, 2017: 32–3)

Though closely entwined, in terms of both subject matter and historical development, I suggest it is helpful to explore postcolonialism first before moving on to critical race theory.

Postcolonialism

Postcolonialism is more than a single theory, rather being a set of theories that compete to describe the ways in which individuals, communities, and nations who have been colonised—or who *remain* colonised—can respond to the acts of colonisation. These theories pertain not only to literature, which is our concern here, but also to history, sociology, psychology, economics, and in many other subject fields. Postcolonialism, dealing with politics above all, is also a politicised field, which is why in the sentence that started this paragraph I was careful to avoid certain phrases, such as: 'how nations emerge from colonization', 'how nations develop after colonization', 'how nations become autonomous/ independent'. This politicised field is also why I offered 'individuals, communities, and nations' as the subject of postcolonialism, rather than 'nations' purely, because there is a justified belief that colonial forces have imposed the idea of 'nation' on to colonised communities, and that there is an alarming trend to homogenise—to flatten out the unevenness of—postcolonial groups. In postcolonial theory, even the term 'nation' is contested.

To simplify the field, it is fair to triangulate postcolonial discourses around three key figures: Edward Said, Homi K. Bhabha, and Gayatri Chakravorty Spivak. Behind each of them is the 'master' postcolonialist, Frantz Fanon, who wrote emphatically about how nations can overthrow colonial forces, in his *Black Skin, White Masks* (1951), and *The Wretched of the Earth* (1962). As Lazarus explains:

> The work of Frantz Fanon served as a central node of focus, discussion, and dispute in the institutionalisation and consolidation of postcolonial studies during the 1980s and 1990s […] and if the best-known surveys, primers, and introductions to the field tended to devote pride of place to individual chapters on Edward W. Said, Gayatri Chakravorty Spivak, and Homi K. Bhabha—the three critics whose publications they typically presented as field-defining—rather than to Fanon, they nevertheless all took time to acknowledge and explore the centrality of Fanon 'beyond' or 'behind' the emergent critical discussion.
>
> (2011: 161)

Fanon prominently voiced the idea that post-colonial[1] attitudes were also bound up with *anti*-colonialism, and that

'Third-Worldism'—the belief that decolonised nations can become a homogenised force in global politics to compete with the Western capitalist 'First World' and Soviet socialist/ communist 'Second World'—provided a viable alternative to thriving on a global scale. Part of that 'Third-Worldism' was an antagonism against nationalism, a force that Fanon viewed as coming from the colonisers into the colonised nations. Fanon argued in *The Wretched of the Earth* that 'nationalism, that magnificent song that made the people rise against their oppressors, stops short, falters and dies away on the day that independence is proclaimed' (1970: 163). Instead, of that poison, Fanon advocated 'a rapid step [… to be] taken from national consciousness to political and social consciousness', which included theorising a pan-African unity because 'The people of Africa have only recently come to know themselves' and so they desire a '"Utopia"' (132). Whilst this thought could see Fanon accused of flattening out differences between individuals and nations in Africa, this sentiment also reveals the importance of identity in postcolonial thinking.

Homi K. Bhabha focuses on the urgency of identity when defining 'vernacular cosmopolitanism' that is opposed to a global cosmopolitanism, the latter merely a proxy for worldwide capitalism. Instead 'vernacular cosmopolitanism' prioritises a 'right to difference' that

> does not require the restoration of an original [or essentialist] cultural or group identity; nor does it consider equality to be a neutralization of differences in the name of the 'universality' of rights where implementation is often subject to ideological and institutional definitions of what counts as 'human' in any specific cultural or political context. […] The vernacular cosmopolitan takes the view that the commitment to a 'right to difference in equality' as a process of constituting emergent groups and affiliations has less to do with the affirmation or authentication of origins and 'identities,' and more to do with political practices and ethical choices.
>
> (Bhabha, 2004: xvi–xvii)

There is a lot to unpack in this passage. First is the idea that there is no original (or essential) identity, and that vernacular cosmopolitanism celebrates that fact. Second, that difference— as opposed to 'diversity'—ought to be celebrated, meaning that the individual as opposed to the group is privileged. And third, that anything approximating identity develops out of 'political practices and ethical choices'. This means that to identify as anything or anyone is a political and moral decision. In *The Location of Culture*, Bhabha proceeds to celebrate hybridity, ambiguity, liminality, and interstitiality—but not as qualities. Rather, these entail a *process* through 'passage[s] between fixed identifications [that] open[] up the possibility of a cultural hybridity that entertains difference without an assumed or imposed hierarchy' (2004: 5). For Bhabha, to be postcolonial—and to explore post-colonial writing, for example—requires exploring this passage through hybrid identity and travelling down it. For this reason, migrants are a privileged demographic, substituting the 'transmission of national traditions'—that is, inherited traditions—with migrant 'transnational histories' (17). Rosi Braidotti, a philosopher in another branch of cultural theory, describes this passage as 'becoming minotarian' (2011: 20 and *passim*). In practice, for Bhabha this involves avoiding the simplistic binaries and dialectics of the 'oppressor and oppressed, centre and periphery, negative image and positive image' (Bhabha, 2004: 28).

Typically for Bhabha, this leads to a sophisticated kind of analysis. For example, Bhabha focuses on '"fixity" in the ideological construction of otherness' because 'Fixity, as the sign of cultural/historical/racial difference in the discourse of colonialism, is a paradoxical mode of representation: it connotes rigidity and an unchanging order as well as disorder, degeneracy and daemonic repetition' (2004: 94). 'Fixity' is visible in the idea of an ethnic stereotype, Bhabha proceeds, arguing that the stereotype is fixity's 'major discursive strategy'; yet there is a 'force of ambivalence' in the stereotype's fixed nature—read 'characterless object'—'that gives the colonial stereotype its currency' of resistance.

According to Bhabha, part of this ambivalence is the fear that the colonial, stereotyped Other—a key word in postcolonial discourses—will revolt against the colonial 'master'. He analogises

this revolt through the idea of the Other gazing back at the col-
oniser. This returned gaze only troubles the idea of the stereotype
and, 'To put it succinctly, [first,] the recognition and [second, the]
disavowal of "difference" is always disturbed by the question of
its re-presentation or construction'. For Bhabha this means 'The
stereotype is in that sense an "impossible" object' (2004: 116) that
destabilises colonisers' narratives about the colonial—even as it is
necessary for colonisers to justify their civilising mission and 'dis-
criminatory and authoritarian forms of political control' (119). In
other words, if the stereotyped Other gazes back, then the fixed
nature of the stereotype becomes essentially questionable because
it defies its 'fixed' and characterless being, and therefore cannot be
restricted to its fixity. It earns another value on top of the stereo-
typical fixity, becoming an uncontrollable, characterful object,
thus becoming 'ambivalent' (the etymology of which means
'doubly valued'). Via this potential ambivalence through resistance, Bhabha's postcolonialism thrives and becomes 'a fighting
term, a theoretical weapon that "intervenes" in existing debates
and "resists" certain political and philosophical constructions'
(Lazarus, 2011: 12).

Edward Said is also aware of this colonial gaze, registering it
under the term 'Orientalism'. In Said's far more transparent prose,

> The Orient is not only adjacent to Europe; it is also the
> place of Europe's greatest and richest and oldest colonies,
> the source of its civilizations and languages, its cultural con-
> testant, and one of its deepest and most recurring images
> of the Other. In addition, the Orient has helped to define
> Europe (or the West) as its contrasting image, idea, person-
> ality, experience.
>
> (1979: 1–2)

Orientalism is 'a way of coming to terms with the Orient that is
based on the Orient's special place in European Western experience' (Said, 1979: 1). In a way, this is Said's version of Bhabha's
debate about the stereotype: The stereotype of the Orient shapes
the Westerner as much as it shapes they who suffer under the
weight of the stereotype.

Said distils his idea further into what is, usefully for us in a book about literature, called a 'textual attitude' (1979: 83–95). He describes 'Two situations [that] favor a textual attitude'. First,

> when a human being confronts […] something relatively unknown and threatening and previously distant. In such a case one has recourse not only to what in one's previous experience the novelty resembles but also to what one has read about it. Travel books or guidebooks are about as 'natural' a kind of text[.]
>
> (93)

The guidebook then 'explains' the threatening situation to the reader.

Second:

> [T]he appearance of success. If one reads a book claiming that lions are fierce and then encounters a fierce lion (I simplify, of course), the chances are that one will be encouraged to read more books by that same author […]. But if […] the lion book instructs one how to deal with a fierce lion, and the instructions work perfectly, then not only will the author be greatly believed, he will also be impelled to try his hand at other kinds of written performance[.]
>
> (93–4)

In both cases, the text appears more materially viable *as* the Orient than the Orient itself. Said's warning about the textual attitude includes the tethering of this Orientalist narrative to Western desires for power and a violence that succeeds those desires. Indeed, in a 1985 interview with Jonathan Crary and Phil Mariani, Said noted that representation 'almost always involves violence of some sort to the *subject* of the representation' (2004: 40). For Said, the textual attitude is bound up with violent representation because of its effects in the material, lived world of action.

Lazarus notes that, as the 1980s developed, Said moved away from this position of the dangerousness of representing the colonial Other. Nonetheless, Lazarus adds, that 'this repudiation' of the ability to represent the colonial Other—that which some have called the unrepresentable—'remain[s] a central plank in the postcolonial discussion' (2011: 140). This 'plank' is no more vociferous than in the subject area known as Subaltern Studies, which also has its roots in the 1980s. After a 1985 lecture by Gayatri Chakravorty Spivak, 'Can the subaltern speak?', Subaltern Studies continues to this day to interpret and reinterpret Spivak's arguments. In addition to citations the original publication of the essay lecture has received,[2] in the last decade there have been at least two essay collections of essays dedicated to continuing Spivak's conversation.[3] Spivak's argument was originally based on a story of a Hindu widow in India who sought to commit ritual suicide after the death of her husband, thereby becoming a *sati*; this ritual suicide was made illegal by the British colonial forces. In relation to this story, Spivak's argument, which she herself revised, is that

> An imperial tradition that rendered widow sacrifice as the sign of a cultural failure subsequently outlawed it and misidentified it as *sati* […]. This imperial tradition legitimated itself as a rule of law and resignified a ritual—a performatively compulsive discourse—as a crime (and not merely as superstition), while discerning in it the evidence of a retrograde patriarchy. Even contemporary commentators realized, however, that the prevalence of *sati* was historically recent and theologically illegitimate.
>
> (Morris, 2010: 5)

Even in this dense description, it is noticeable how the woman who committed the (perceived) ritual suicide—the *sati* herself—is marginalised and voiceless. She is irredeemably the *object* of these discourses, and never their *subject*. This leads Spivak to exclaim that 'The subaltern cannot speak' (1988: 308). This is a failure of two kinds for Spivak: metaphorical–artistic re-presentation and metonymical–political representation.[4] In neither art nor politics can the subaltern women speak. Spivak admonishes contemporary French philosophers (Michel Foucault and Gilles Deleuze, especially) for asserting that their politics and their approach to philosophy allow the unrepresentable to be represented, with Spivak instead arguing that this 'leads to an essentialist utopian politics' (1999: 259) that just repeats the silencing of the subaltern woman.

It is then beholden to the reader of literary texts to look for the silences and the characters and communities whose voiced self-representation is denied—not to un-silence them or to *speak for*, but to pay attention to these silences in order that they might be heard. Lazarus laments the gravitational pull of Spivak's essay, yet highlights the need to pay attention to how

> the writer's desire to speak *for* others—to endow 'them' with consciousness and voice—shades over into ventriloquisation, into speaking *instead* of 'them': what starts out as an attempt to speak on behalf of others, or at least about others (in the interests of 'putting them on the map') ends up, paradoxically, as a silencing of 'them' through the writer's own speech.
> (2011: 145)

There is no handy schema to detect whether a writer is speaking *for* or *instead* of the subaltern; it nonetheless requires deep readerly attention.

Critical race theory

Perhaps quite expectedly, discussions surrounding Spivak's essay have begun to 'engage the deepening intersectionalities of oppression in the world today' (Darder and Griffiths, 2018: 83). In 1991—though drawing on an earlier paper—Kimberlé Crenshaw described intersectionality as a way of 'account[ing] for multiple grounds of identity when considering how the social world is constructed' (1991: 1245). In the political landscape, for example, Crenshaw highlighted the problem of discounting one of the identities constituting the subject, since these groups 'frequently pursue conflicting political agendas' (1251). Making use of this intersectional approach in a cultural analysis, such as when reading literature, is possible by the end of Crenshaw's article when she argues that 'A beginning response to these questions requires that we first recognize that the organized identity groups in which we find ourselves in are in fact coalitions, or at least potential coalitions waiting to be formed' (1299). If we are able to spot the formation and/or operation of coalitions of identity within narratives of oppression, then we know we are in the realm of literature responding to the demands of intersectional analysis.

Intersectionality, as with other theories of representation, relies on categorical definitions of myriad identities. In the mid 1990s—and, indeed, throughout his work—Stuart Hall addressed this question in relation particularly to 'race'. That these lectures were eventually published in *The Fateful Triangle* in 2017 testifies to their continued relevance. The development in Hall's thought of a critical race theory is continued in Michael Omi and Howard Winant's *Racial Formation in the United States*, the completely revised third edition of which was published in 2015. Whilst Hall is rarely mentioned in Omi and Winant's text, I believe his ideas are relevant to the latter text, even if the critics approach the question of defining race from different angles.

Hall asserts, as I showed at the beginning of this chapter, that 'race' is a discursive category rather than a definitive scientific phenomenon. In Hall's terms, this means that

> socially, historically, and politically, race is a discourse; that it operates like a language [...]; that its signifiers reference not genetically established facts but the systems of meaning that have come to be fixed in the classifications of culture; and that those meanings have real effects not because of some truth that inheres in their scientific classification but because of the will to power and the regime of truth that are instituted in the shifting relations of discourse[.]
>
> (2017: 45)

Race is therefore a second-level description of certain human qualities—only some of which are real. In an explicitly deconstructivist argument, following in the footsteps of French theorist and philosopher Jacques Derrida, Hall calls 'race' a 'sliding signifier' (2017: *passim*) in order to explain that 'race' changes its meaning according to its context, be that a social, historical, or geographical one.

Hall develops this argument more widely, arguing that 'race', when discussed and used to signify a material object, is linked to a 'chain of equivalences in culture, which is to say that these signifiers of epidermilization'—the significance of someone's skin colour—'work precisely by metaphor and metonymy'. The latter terms point us, again, back to Spivak's metaphoric–artistic re-presentation and metonymic–political representation. Put simply, 'race' is also a representative for another signifier ('skin colour') that also represents another signifier ('genetics') that also represents another signifier ('phenome'), on which is built a *social* categorisation that is used to produce oppression. A racist says: I am of a different race, because I have a different skin colour, because I am genetically different, because I have distinct phenomes, and for these reasons I believe that I am better socially/better culturally/more intelligent/more important than the person of the other race.

'Race' thus produces difference, and yet the discursive concept 'race' is so distant from a phenomic code that it makes no sense to produce a political belief on its foundations. Hall adds that 'Nothing I am saying should be construed as arguing that there are no physiological, morphological, or genetic differences among groups of people in the world. But my question is this: what do these differences mean?' (2017: 55). Hall argues that these differences change according to time and space and, for that reason, 'race' should be analysed in its 'transcoded' meaning in history and geography.[5] As with contemporary postcolonial theories, the migrant demographic is privileged in this transcoding, in part because migrants, like discourse, traverse history and geography. Hall writes that 'The crisis of identity among the post-Enlightenment, postimperial Western nation-states and their national identities' is catalysed by the 'joker in the pack, the element that really unfixes a certain conception of homogeneous national cultural identity' that is 'mass migration' (147–8).

Hall's *The Fateful Triangle* connects race with ethnicity and nation, arguing in each case that these terms need to be explored in their proper contexts. Omi and Winant, in a similar construction (with interesting differences), suggest that 'race' as a concept is underpinned by three paradigms: ethnicity, class, and nation. The chief overlap between the two arguments, however, is in the idea that 'race', to reiterate, is 'one of those major or master concepts […] that organize the great classificatory systems of difference that operate in human societies' (Hall, 2017: 32–3). Or, in Omi and Winant's terms, with their acknowledged focus on the USA: 'race is a master category—a fundamental concept that has profoundly shaped, and continues to shape, the history, polity, economic structure, and culture of the United States' (2015: 106). As a master category, for Omi and Winant the process of '"Making up people" racially'—what other theorists term 'Othering'—'has been "portable" across US history. It has spread from one oppressed group to another and proved transferable to other marginalized identities, social cleavages, and political struggles' (108). Again, since 'migration recasts concepts of race, racial meaning and racial identity' (126), migrant narratives are privileged in Omi and Winant's critical race theory. It follows that the multiple oppressions of gender, sexuality, class, etc. can be understood in the USA as following the trend set by racialised narratives; nevertheless the critics assert that 'We hold these truths of intersectional analysis to be self-evident' (106). Thus, whilst race has an 'unsettled' 'meaning' (106)—much as in Hall's analysis—it continues to dominate as a constant in intersectional analyses.

As in fourth-wave feminism,[6] online activism is a prominent feature of contemporary critical race activism. This is notably so in the #BlackLivesMatter and #SayHerName movements. Nikita Carney summarises how the #BlackLivesMatter 'movement began in 2012 when George Zimmerman was acquitted after shooting and killing 17-year-old Trayvon Martin in Florida. Three Black women activists, Alicia Garza, Patrisse Cullors, and Opal Tometi, started the movement that subsequently engaged many, including many youth of color, in social justice activism across the country' and 'The hashtag #BlackLivesMatter gained prominence once again and became the rallying call for protesters after the killing of Michael Brown in Ferguson, MO, in August 2014' (2016: 181). The latter sought to counter 'Stereotypes of young Black men, especially those who come from low-income neighborhoods', especially as those stereotypes have led to police brutality. By linking race to class and wealth, Carney notes the intensely intersectional nature of the movement that, as Crenshaw hoped and predicted in 1991, 'came to represent the identities of groups of people' (Carney, 2016: 185). These are Crenshaw's 'potential coalitions' as they are being formed online.

Crenshaw, along with others, herself advanced the #SayHerName project because of a perceived lack of intersectionality in the #BlackLivesMatter movement. Whilst Carney noted that 'a focus on Black men as victims of police violence led to an emphasis on the role of racism in police brutality at the expense of other issues, such as class, gender, and sexuality' (2016: 195), Crenshaw *et al.* argued that

> The failure to highlight and demand accountability for the countless Black women killed by police over the past two decades, including Eleanor Bumpurs, Tyisha Miller, LaTanya Haggerty, Margaret Mitchell, Kayla Moore and Tarika Wilson, to name just a few among scores, leaves Black women unnamed and thus under-protected in the face of their continued vulnerability to racialized police violence.
>
> (2015: n.p)

#SayHerName seeks to correct that erasure and pays attention to Black women killed in a range of incidents involving societal and, in some cases, state forces. In an analysis of the use of hashtags in social media activism, Melissa Brown pointed out that 'the users of #SayHerName indicate an awareness of the multiple jeopardies facing Black women. Twitter helps users amplify their consciousness raising in the digital sphere through the network ties people form as they follow and interact with other users' (2017: 1842).

It leads me to the conclusion that hyper-contemporary literature that pays attention to critical race discourses may also engage with the erasure of women in a nonintersectional way—and therefore 'limit the opportunities for meaningful intervention on [...] behalf' of 'minority women who suffer from the effects of multiple subordination' (Crenshaw, 1991: 1251)—but also may catalyse the formation of Crenshaw's coalitions.

This brief tour of postcolonial thinking and critical race theory gives us a few topics for analysis in hyper-contemporary literature. The latter should have a lot to say on the matter, as Omi and Winant claim that 'The racial present always needs to be studied and explained anew' (2015: 1), which in a way accords with Bhabha's idea that our immediate present 'comes to be revealed for its discontinuities, its inequalities, its minorities' (2004: 6). The topics under which I will investigate the literature in the following sections are:

• History and (the problem of) representation
• Migration
• Online racial discourse

History and (the problem of) representation

Novuyo Rosa Tshuma's *House of Stone* retells the history of Zimbabwe's painful emergence from British colonial rule in the 1970s, the ensuing civil war, and continued frustrations with the quasi-dictatorship led by Robert Mugabe. Those are at most half of the important details about *House of Stone*, because the novel is also concerned with 'hi-stories'—fabricated or fictionalised narrativisation—family, and identity. In *House of Stone*, Zamani records the story of the family of Abednego, Agnes, and their son Bukhosi, with whom he lodges in his late uncle's former home. He details their stories in a journal of sorts, after having interviewed them. Bukhosi has gone missing, and Zamani sees an answer to his disappearance through his parents' stories about Zimbabwe's birth pangs. Tonally, *House of Stone* is reminiscent of Nabokov's *Lolita* (1958), John Banville's *The Book of Evidence* (1989), and even Joseph Heller's *Catch-22* (1961).

The book ties these European texts to a postcolonial narrative. Zacchaeus is Abednego's brother, and is never given the opportunity to speak for himself in the text. Instead, his story is filtered through Abednego's narrative and, after that, Zamani's own experience of Abednego. Zacchaeus was there when Mugabe took his oath of office in 1980, performing at the Independence Day celebrations. However, for an unknown reason, Zacchaeus is later 'disappeared from the official records' and exiled to the USA. From there, he pens an essay 'praising [his fellow Zimbabweans] for reclaiming their dignity from undignifying white slavery'. However, Zacchaeus 'was dismayed to discover that home […] was still tinged with the sinister tones of the past, and his illusions about the Great Emancipation of The Niggers of Africa gave way to disillusions of our government' (Tshuma, 2018: 131, 133). Zacchaeus becomes an amalgam of the 'native intellectual' and 'native poet' that Fanon (1970: 175 ff.) describes, and Zacchaeus comes up against Mugabe's and Zanu PF's 'authentic ethnical' and 'tribal dictatorship' (Fanon, 1970: 147). This nod to postcolonial scholarship—and the parodic tone that dominates *House of Stone*[7]—assures the reader that there is an ongoing conversation between Zamani's narrative and the way Zimbabwe's history has been described (and on occasion *predicted*) in postcolonial discourses.

Significant in *House of Stone*'s narrative is the intense focus on the past as a constructed—and *constructable*—narrative. Zamani's strategy is one of collage and fabrication, both by piecing others' narratives together and by inventing himself in the process. This invention takes place in the present tense—'I am a man on a mission' begins the Prologue (Tshuma, 2018: 1)—and the narrative keeps returning to the now. This collage therefore allows the reader to see Zamani *as* a hyperbolic discontinuity, to use Bhabha's term, and yet a discontinuity who is authoritative over the story he tells. In a microscopic way, Zamani can be read as metonymically standing in for the modern Zimbabwe nation itself. The question then follows: Is this a just representation?

One of the most compelling episodes that Zamani relates is the murder of Abednego's first love, Thandi, by the character called Black Jesus during the Gukuruhandi massacre in Matabeleland;

readers should be warned before they read this next quotation. In a killing that invokes pre-industrial incivility as well as popular symbolic depictions of the Grim Reaper, Zamani describes the killing in terms that are designed to provoke a visceral reaction:

> In his hand was a scythe. The scythe sliced through the air. It sliced into her belly. Sliced her belly open. She staggered. Clutched her belly. Her belly was spilling. Spilling her intestines, her colon, her stomach. Spilling her spleen, her pancreas, her liver. Spilling her foetus.
>
> (Tshuma, 2018: 148–9)

Beyond the shock of Thandi's barbaric murder, this incident becomes a metonymical representation for the nation as a whole. Thandi had been a force in the liberation movement before Zimbabwe threw off the colonial shackles, and she is now invoked as Zamani's surrogate mother and therefore mother to the modern Zimbabwe nation. Her unborn foetus comes to symbolise the lost hopeful future of Zimbabwe.

This kind of narrative is not unique in its evocation of politics as a family. However, where I think *House of Stone* adds another distinctive voice to postcolonial narratives is through Zamani's immediate turn to a European cultural framework to respond to Thandi's death. First there is the crowing cock (Tshuma, 2018: 151), subtly alluding to the Christian belief that the devil appears when the cock crows three times. Then, at the beginning of the next chapter, Zamani laments the death of his 'Inamorata' Thandi, calling her 'My Laodamia', invoking the lovelorn Greek prophet who killed herself at Troy.[8] Zamani proceeds to rewrite Laodamia's part in the Trojan myth in order to make space for Thandi's story. Zamani then apostrophises (in a one-sentence section and paragraph) to the gods in the manner of the great epicists: 'Celestial pity, I again implore;—Restore her to my sight—great Jove, restore!' However, at the beginning of the next section, bathos interrupts with Zamani confirming that 'Celestial pity refuses to restore you to my sight' (2018: 151–3). These appeals to and from a European *mythos* further complicate our reading of Zamani and the presentist narrative of himself and Zimbabwe he is piecing together.

Before drawing full conclusions from the points I have made, I will turn to Guy Gunaratne's *In Our Mad and Furious City* by way of comparison. *In Our Mad* tells the story of five Londoners from different cultural and ethnic heritages and their experience of two febrile days in the city. The stories are told from the characters' first-person perspectives, with each voice restricted to one chapter at a time. Three narratives are from young people who are all friends—Selvon, Ardan, and Yusuf—one from Ardan's Northern Irish mother (Caroline), and the final narrative from the internal monologue of Nelson, a Windrush-generation immigrant from Montserrat, and father to Selvon. Nelson's narrative is completely interior because, following a stroke, Nelson is unable to speak.

Nelson's name already points us to a heterogeneous heritage, with it directly calling on Britain's greatest admiral, Horatio Nelson, whose exploits in the Napoleonic Wars secured Britain's sovereign autonomy at the beginning of the nineteenth century: The Battle of Trafalgar stopped Napoleon's invasion of Britain. Meanwhile, Montserrat's colonial history began in 1632 with Irish colonists settling on the island. It was then colonised by the French until its colonial sovereignty was allocated to Britain in 1783 as part of the Treaty of Paris. In a dual sense, therefore, Nelson's personal history is a marker of the history of Britain's global exploits and its pattern of repeated and insistent colonisation.

And yet, with the advent of the Commonwealth citizenship agreements and the Windrush generation of immigrants from the late 1940s until 1970, Nelson is one of those who feels the blackmailed call from the United Kingdom to assist her economy:

> And after everything Britain call me, I explain, the Mother Country call we come. That great and grand old Britain, the poster and film reel call all the young gully fools to hop on the boat-train to London. I buy the story hook and sinker.
>
> (Gunaratne, 2018: 72)

The effective use of vernacular English to signal Nelson's strangeness from the 'Mother Country' compounds the irony of his willingness to answer the call from overseas. The postcolonial irony is further highlighted by the bathetic reaction Nelson experiences when he arrives in Britain and is able to 'see Britain for what it was. Nothing like the postcard image, never. Not like the wonder we think up on the boat over […] Everybody poor, everybody ailing' (Gunaratne, 2018: 73). This comment inverts the Oriental strategy that Said outlines, in which visitors to the Orient rely on a 'textual attitude'. Whilst Nelson shows up the folly in that strategy by refusing the authenticity of the postcard image—instead agreeing with the image of destitution before him—he nonetheless refuses to 'feel' the 'hardness. Instead I have a sorta rush. Was like the noise possess me' (73). This ambivalent response to the real situation in Britain might be characterised as Bhabha's 'vernacular cosmopolitanism which measures global progress from the minoritarian perspective' (2004: xvi), and it is interesting to track Nelson's vernacular cosmopolitanism elsewhere in the text.

The first instance worth noting is when Nelson sees a 'KBW' sign graffitied on to a wall and is told what it means: '*Keep Britain White*'. In response, Nelson realises that 'the same yellow light I had mistook for a gentle haze look like a portent, like some damnations what fill my chest with a heavy weight'. Now Nelson sees 'an ugliness in this Britain' that means this becomes the moment 'when I realise that this Britain here did not love me back, no matter how much I feel for it' (Gunaratne, 2018: 78–9). Nelson's experience of post-war cosmopolitanism is emphatically negative. Nevertheless, when the Notting Hill Race Riots start, Nelson is faced with a choice: either to take part in throwing petrol bombs at supporters of the British fascist Oswald Mosley, or to flee. He chooses the latter. His monologue while fleeing is instructive, and I quote it at length:

> Home never feel so far away as I ran. […] How we go from talking about we rights and decent living to being march out like foot-soldiers bent and unthinking and hollow? We dusty group of angered lacks, my brothers and sisters them. How quickly honest talk is exchange for speeching […]

How we plunge and grapple and seize all them loose ideas
of unbelonging and offence. Leave all them, I thought. Leave
all them behind me. […] For the cruel world is too close in
this city. Them madmen like Mosley, the violent stories, them
images of torn faces in the tabloid paper. It suffocate we own
sense and have it replace with some lower code. For see all
them who I called my blood, see them lost to it, lost to a city
what hate them.

(Gunaratne, 2018: 212)

In this passage 'Home'—which, for a cosmopolitan, is technic-
ally everywhere and, for a migrant, is in constant flux—becomes
fluid. The 'home' that it designates is both Montserrat and west
London where Nelson now lives and spends his time. And yet,
it becomes more distant as Nelson travels, suggesting that he
is not travelling towards either home, and instead constantly
departing his homes. This vernacular cosmopolitanism from the
minoritarian position is one of perpetual flight. The reason for
this exponentially-distancing flight is given later in the paragraph when Nelson laments the effectiveness of Mosley's and the
tabloids' textual attitude, through which images of immigrants
represent them as dangerous and inhuman. But the lament is
less about the artistic representations in the paper, and more
about how they exert pressure on the migrants to change their
own behaviours. Returning to the idea of 'home', the passage's
final sentence suggests that Nelson's friends are in fact home-
less and unmoored in London. In this particular narrative of *In
Our Mad and Furious City*, vernacular cosmopolitanism leads to
destabilised identity.

Here, then, is the comparison of the representation of history
through this postcolonial exploration. On the one hand, Zamani's
turn in *House of Stone* towards European civility in the lament over
the death of his pseudo-love—a turn that is mocked and queried
in the text's tone; on the other hand, Nelson's rejection in *In Our
Mad* of European practices of colonial representation because of
the way they debase the behaviours of his fellow immigrants,
those subject to the violent representations. The colonial question
is levelled, in both texts, against European civility. In *House of*

Stone, Zamani's zealous turn to Jove and high European culture
as antidote to Black Jesus's behaviour—even though Zimbabwe's
'authentic' 'ethnic dictatorship' is modelled on British colonial
practices—undermines the notional civility that European art
can confer on the colonised. In *In Our Mad*, European (here,
British) hospitality is shown for its true colours of *in*hospitality
and of generating violent behaviours. (I return to the question of
hospitality in my next section on migrant narratives.) Both texts
attempt to situate the colonised individual *outside* the European
framework, but do so from different perspectives. At this point
of the narrative, Zamani is the 'native intellectual' who becomes
a 'vigilant sentinel ready to defend the Graeco-Latin pedestal',
whilst Nelson's actions reveal 'Mediterranean values—the tri-
umph of the human individual, or clarity and of beauty—[to be]
lifeless, colourless knick-knacks' (Fanon, 1970: 36). In *House of
Stone* the reader recognises the text's mockery of Zamani, while
in Gunaratne's novel, Nelson does the work on the reader's behalf
and, in both cases, the issue of historical representation permits an
interesting debate around postcolonialism.

Migration

As both postcolonial and critical race theorists have pointed out,
migrants can become a privileged demographic for theories that
have emerged. It is interesting that, in quite another literary landscape, Declan Kiberd (2017) has made similar claims about the
topics *du jour* in Irish literature: Migration and hybridity have
come to dominate, but not just migration *away* from Ireland (a
historic phenomenon going back centuries), but also migration
into Ireland. In their own ways, Jenny Xie's *Eye Level* and Michael
Donkor's *Hold* also query what it means to be a migrant and
how that experience shapes identity. In both these texts, we are
emboldened in our intersectional analysis because Xie's poetic
persona and Donkor's protagonists are all women. We are therefore reading about what it is like to immigrate, both as an outsider
of a so-called 'Other' ethnicity and as a woman. Zoe Gilbert's
Folk provides an alternative, potentially opposing perspective on

migrancy, as she records what happens to a community when an uninvited visitor comes to stay.

Whilst Bhabha wants to explore migrant characters' identities to see how they 'deploy the cultural hybridity of their border-line conditions to "translate" [...] the social imaginary of both metropolis and modernity' (2004: 9)—which is to say, how they make their new home-city their own space—Lazarus warns against this contemporary turn to hybridity in case the literature that includes migrant identities *as* hybrid might be doing so *in response to* postcolonial theories that privilege migrant hybridity (2011: 23). Lazarus wants to prioritise a literary 'disconsolation' (31) in criticism: the idea that postcolonial texts *exceed* or *deny* the reader's expectations because they question received critical and scholarly frameworks—such as Bhabha's hybridity—both in terms of narrative and of expected responses. Furthermore, Eli Park Sorensen has defined Lazarus's 'disconsolation' as 'a mode of writing that involves all the trademarks of high modernism, a style of fragmentation, parataxis,[9] irony, alienation, discontinuity, and disruption' (2010: 37). In my comparative discussion of migration in *Eye Level* and *Hold*, and in my further exploration of *Folk*, I shall try to identify those places where theories of migrant hybridity raise the quality of my reading, as well as those moments of disconsolation.

Eye Level charts the migrant journeys of its persona[10] through forty-one poems. The persona journeys from China to the USA with further stops along the way. There are explicit invocations of the idea of migrant hybridity throughout the collection. The first poem, 'Rootless' (Xie, 2018: 1), asks whether 'this solitude [can] be rootless, unhooked from the ground?' in a question that explicitly desires the rootlessness of nomadism. The poem ends with a half-rhyming couplet, signalling a unified, complete thought and a sense of certainty:

> At present, on this sleeper train, there's nowhere to arrive.
> Me? I'm just here in my traveler's clothes, trying on each passing town for size.

(1)

The reference to the 'present' tells the reader that this is a current state of rootlessness, linking to Bhabha's sense of discontinuity. The ability to 'arrive' 'nowhere' cements the thrill for the persona who, moving from the literal to metaphorical clothes, enjoys continuously moving on. Restless rootlessness is a mode of being the speaker enjoys; or, as the persona explains in 'Phnom Penh Diptych: Dry Season', 'I developed an appetite for elsewhere' (Xie, 2018: 16). Accordingly, this poem could be read as 'having been produced precisely with an eye to their postcolonialist reception' (Lazarus, 2011: 23).

Xie's persona continues the clothing metaphor in 'Naturalization', a poem that describes the father's struggle to become a naturalised US citizen. In this poem the USA is described as a 'new country' that is 'ill fitting, lined / with cheap polyester, soiled at the sleeves' (Xie, 2018: 35). Far from celebrating migrant indeterminacy in this poem, the persona is noting the way that the father cannot speak English fluently, 'confus[ing] / *snacks* for *snakes*, *kitchen* for *chicken*'. This experience and its record seem to speak to Bhabha's idea that 'The migrant culture of the "in-between", the minority position, dramatizes the activity of culture's untranslatability' (2004: 321). The dramatisation is also visible in the persona's reference to the 'ill fitting' country, which I read as an allusion to Shakespeare's *Macbeth* (1606), in which Macbeth's ill-fitting clothes are used on several occasions to characterise his 'unmerited accession' (Fowler, 2004: 74) to the Scottish throne. In the reference to *Macbeth*, Xie's persona 'dramatizes the activity' of Anglo-American culture's untranslatability. It is not that the poem fails to translate *Macbeth*—if the allusion registers at all, it can only register as successful—but that the poem is *about* the father's failure to translate English, and the US failure to translate the father through the process of 'naturalization'. The poem's drama is in the steady revelation that 'naturalization' is ironised, and, unlike in 'Rootless', this poem constitutes literary disconsolation because it surprises through the ironic presentation of a failed naturalisation.

Where *Eye Level* rarely offers insight into intersectional migration, Michael Donkor's novel *Hold* offers quite a different sense of migration, this time from the perspective of Belinda, a young Ghanaian woman who is hired to travel to London from Kamasi, an inland city in the southern half of Ghana. Husband and wife, 'Nana' and Doctor Otuo, would like Belinda to keep their daughter, Amma, company in London and to try to keep her from getting in trouble. Belinda is therefore seconded from her post as a housegirl—where she has already been sent by her mother in order to help pay her own way in the world— to travel to south London. From 'inner émigré' (to use Seamus Heaney's term [2001: 68]), Belinda becomes a female trans-national migrant worker.

The text 'dramatizes the activity of culture's untranslatability' by printing Twi language phrases and their translations in the book's opening pages. These are supposed to be used by the reader to make sense of, or to translate, the many uses of Twi in the text, and their very presence makes it known to the reader that this is an in-between, migratory text, much as its story is of a woman who migrates from the former colony to the old imperial centre. The Twi phrase list also turns the text into an attempted riposte to the Oriental textual attitude that Said described. *Hold* tries to re-centre the migrant story in the Other language as it infuses into English—the dialogue from the Ghanaian characters is a syncretic mix of English and Twi—rather than substituting an English text for what is a hybrid dialect. This Oriental textual attitude is visibly critiqued when Belinda, still in Kamasi, watches 'Two old men […] engrossed in *Oware*'. As she watches, 'A group of white tourists pointed at the game. […] She heard them talking about how friendly the "locals" were' (Donkor, 2018: 18–19). No explanation is given about the game, nor any note of judgement from Belinda. This scene lives up to the Orient that Said describes as '*watched*' and 'the European, whose sensibility tours the Orient, is a watcher, never involved, always detached, always ready for new examples […]. The Orient becomes a living tableau of queerness' (1979: 103). Instead the text offers up this scene—doubly transcribed as Belinda *watches* the tourists *watching* the men playing *Oware*—as a disruptive way of refusing the assumption that this text could be considered an Orientalist text perfect for creating a textual attitude. *Hold*, even at this early stage, thus seems to offer a postcolonial text of disconsolation.

Hold contributes to an intersectional discourse about race. Towards the end of the novel, Amma wonders about a racist experience she and Belinda experienced on a London bus, realising that 'A line connected them all—[the aggressor] Monique, Belinda, Belinda's mum, her—all these black women mired in different kinds of shit' (Donkor, 2018: 174). But the experience of racism and of Othering is not the only way that intersectionality is discursively presented. Belinda's identification as working class migrates with her to London where, on her first afternoon in her new home, she begins cleaning, tidying, and serving her hosts. 'Beneath the sink,' we are told, 'sprays that smelled safe and familiar were carefully arranged. The man on Mr Muscle was good. Belinda lunged for it. [… S]he wanted to clap as the foam's bubbles cracked over the splodges on the table and the coiling in the small of her back stopped' (41). The ease of bodily tension in Belinda's back signals the comfort she feels in cleaning; not because she necessarily enjoys cleaning in itself, but because she feels she can pay back the Otuos for looking after her. Later, Nana Otuo reminds Belinda of her duties:

> This my house been seeming remarkably cleaner and more neat since you arrive. […] You understanding we not expecting this from you? Eh? My, my husband he worries that you thinking we want you to do this cleaning scrubbing on your hands and knees? No way, girl! No, absolute no.
>
> (Donkor, 2018: 134)

This scene merits a close analysis. Here, Nana—a Londoner who migrated from Ghana—asks her migrant guest to stop living out her classed existence as a worker and servant to others. Nana pays for Belinda to study and to look after their daughter (Donkor, 2018: 134). Nana, however, is not the authority behind this sentiment, but rather her husband, Dr Otuo ('my husband he worries'), who earns the family's money as a medic. The whole conversation acknowledges Belinda's (feeling of) debt to the Otuos, and her seeking to pay off that debt through cleaning and cooking— typically traditional tasks for women. However, the conversation elides Nana's own middle-classed existence as a 'homemaker' and 'housewife'. Lazarus's comment that '"Postcolonial" writing is centrally and vitally concerned with the representation of class [...] as a primary source, and site, of social division and violence' (2011: 40) helps us to identify this passage as one *about* class, but does not necessarily help us to *interrogate* how these nodes of identity—race, migrant, class, women—intersect and produce 'effects of multiple subordination' (Crenshaw, 1991: 1251).

In a *New York Times* article, the academic Henry Louis Gates, Jr argued that 'The class divide is [...] one of the most important and overlooked factors in the rise of Black Lives Matter' (2016: para. 11). Whilst the context in *Hold* is different for a number of reasons, Gates's argument is nonetheless helpful here because he highlights the burden on financially successful African-Americans to help those who continue to be beset by class inequality. This burden has lighted on the Otuos who, though unintentionally, have helped Belinda to climb the social ladder, to use an ill-equipped idiom, in a way that can help her to exit working-class poverty that forced her into work to support her household finances at the age of seventeen—even though, as she says, she had a one hundred per cent attendance record at her school in Adurubaa (Donkor, 2018: 150). Her social class forced her *out of* education, and migrant middle-class compatriots enabled her re-entry *into* education. Nonetheless, Belinda's sense of debt burden—an idea that comes from her own sense of class inequality—leads her to attempt to clear debt by means of trad-itional women's working-class practice.[11] This situation helps us to triangulate the intersection of several elements of Belinda's identity that condition her behaviour: her migrancy (as proxy for her race), her social class, and her gender.

It is interesting to compare Belinda's behaviour to Amma, her hosts' daughter, who is also ethnically marked as Other but who has grown up in London throughout her life. Where British culture is strange to Belinda, Amma is at home with it, for example noticing Belinda's '"allusion to [Lady Macbeth's] damned spot"' (Donkor, 2018: 150). Amma is also firmly middle class and feels a sense of guilt about her own social status, rem-onstrating with Belinda that, '"Look, just because I've got, like, I'm lucky and privileged and all that [...] it doesn't mean I can't

wish what I had was better"', and hates "'being called spoiled"',
tacitly acknowledging Sara Ahmed's point that 'class might seem
to be immaterial or less material if you benefit from class privilege' (2017: 148). Interestingly, as Belinda reminds her, "'I never
mention 'spoiled'. That's something you put in there all by yourself"' (Donkor, 2018: 120–1): This confirms Amma's guilt about
her class status. Finally, Amma is more astute in detecting the evil
of racism when on the bus, asking Belinda to stop talking to the
girls of Jamaican heritage who mock Belinda for being 'African'
(162–4). Whilst this scene merits further scrutiny to unpick the
reasons for this intra-racial racism—confirming at the least Hall's,
and Omi and Winant's theories that 'race' is purely discursive
and fails in its attempt to smoothen a heterogeneous group of
people—it also corroborates the idea that Amma is different to
Belinda in her multiple identities, in spite of their shared heritage in Ghana. In the triad of race, class, and gender that shape
Belinda's experiences of London, it is notionally only class that
distinguishes Amma from Belinda; and yet, their aggregated identities and experiences are much further apart than that difference
alone can account for. They share a social status-related guilt, but
it manifests in distinct ways.

   Zoe Gilbert's *Folk* gives us an opportunity to scrutinise migrant
narratives from a different perspective: from the viewpoint of
the community into which the migrant arrives. *Folk* is either a
collection of short stories, or a novel—or both. Over eleven tales
the island of Neverness is depicted in fantastical and fairytale-like
terms. Characters recur across the stories, and those who are children in the first story 'Prick Song' have their own children in the
final story 'Tether'. In 'A Winter Guest', a visitor called Redwing
comes to Neverness who, later in the text, is described as the
'Only one who ever leaves' (2018: 125). Paying attention to his
story allows us to see how his migrancy becomes more about the
community of Neverness, and less about Redwing.

   Folk is not written with race as a part of its fabric; nevertheless,
the close community can sometimes act as a 'race' unto itself in
the way that it can appear closed off and aware of strangers. At
the beginning of 'A Winter Guest', we are told that 'By night-
fall, everyone knew the man's name was Redwing' (2018: 110),

signalling the close knit of the community and the speed of the gossip across the island. However, the biggest impression Redwing makes in the community is a sexual one. Bhabha noted this element of colonial attitudes in response to reading Fanon and describes how 'the deep cultural fear of the black [is often] figured in the psychic trembling of Western sexuality' (2004: 59). I argue that Redwing can be configured as a version of a colonial subject visiting the 'West' that is configured as Neverness; his 'fiery' (Gilbert, 2018: 110) red hair signifies his racial otherness. In this vein, it is interesting to note that soon after his name is known across the island, Gad confirms what the real talk of the island is: '"Gossip is, he's a fine one," said Gad, when she came knocking on Clotha's window. "And a head taller than any of them. Hair like a bonfire. I want a look"' (110). The intellectual curiosity of the dominant community therefore quickly transforms into a sexual one.

When Redwing returns to Clotha's house, the ethics of hospitality are fully adhered to as 'She did not ask him where he had come from' (Gilbert, 2018: 111), but instead offers her home to him for the night. That one night stretches to two, and those nights stretch to months until Redwing stays for the whole winter. The ethics of hospitality dictate that a guest is welcomed without question and without reserve into the host's home; however, these ethics have a potentially negative consequence because the guest could (legitimately) overthrow the host in their home and rewrite the rules of that home.[12] This threat is manifested in 'A Winter Guest'. First when they have run out of food in the house and Clotha says she will go to buy some more, Redwing replies that '"I'll stay"' (112) that later turns into more aggressively pressurising behaviour. For example, Redwing compels Clotha to ignore the customs in Neverness, instead promising to '"keep the bed warm for you"' (114). But, more worryingly, in response to the invitation to attend the 'year-turning fair'—Neverness's new year's party— Redwing eventually refuses to go: 'Redwing could not let her alone even long enough to get dressed. "I'm more hungry for you than ever," he said, and pulled her skirt from her hips' (114). The inversion of the sexual interest in the Other—that Clotha fancies Redwing—into the Other's sexual predation of the host—that

Redwing sexually pressurises Clotha—seems to confirm all of the fears of the immigrant Other coming into a community. This kind of behaviour gives legitimacy to the closed-off nature of Neverness and bolsters the so-called 'island mentality'.

Clotha and Redwing's relationship also breeds envy in other parts of the community. First, 'March and Iska stopped their work so they could nudge each other' before Iska asks whether Clotha is '"Keeping him all to yourself?"' (Gilbert, 2018: 112). Clearly the sexual interest in the Other maintains, perhaps because the story of claustrophobic control is not yet public. This is confirmed when Redwing, who has travelled away from Neverness for the spring and summer months, returns for the following winter. As Clotha hides away and does not open the door to Redwing's 'scratch[es]', she then 'heard footsteps, a woman's voice and, answering, unmistakable, Redwing's deep tones' (116). The woman is Iska and she takes Redwing home for the winter, repeating the attempt at sexual domination at which Clotha failed.

I read 'A Winter Guest' as a parable, though its moral can be read in two ways. One is the way in which, as Sarah Gibson has pointed out, 'Hospitality is invoked precisely as a way of curtailing […] hospitableness' (2007: 169). In 'A Winter Guest', the sexual threat that Redwing becomes after taking advantage of Clotha's sexual interest suggests that Redwing is an unwelcome guest whose behaviour should lead to greater limits on Neverness's borders. In this moral, the lesson is that 'open borders' are a bad thing, especially when the guest is a racial or cultural Other. Conversely, when thinking through the full logic of *Folk*'s allegorical reference to Britain—in his review of *Folk*, Benjamin Myers noted Neverness offers 'a dark historical mirror held up to the harried face of modern Britain' (2018: para. 1)—the moral is to beware the fear of the Other that follows a perceived infraction of the law of hospitality. That is, 'A Winter Guest' warns against closing down borders because of the kind of society it produces. This society is described by Gibson: 'The narcissistic pride in Britain's hospitality and tolerance is strengthened through the distinction between those genuine, deserving, and grateful refugees, and those bogus, undeserving abusive asylum seekers and economic migrants' (2007: 163). I am not suggesting that we ignore

Redwing's controlling sexual behaviours—these are heinous and should not escape our critical ire—but that we should also pay attention to the kind of society to which Redwing immigrates. In the case of Neverness, this is a community that is generally shuttered off from the rest of the world (whatever that 'world' is in *Folk*'s fantastic landscape), and in which on their arrival the Other is immediately sexualised as a proxy for control.

Eye Level and *Hold* are comparable because they share narratives of migration. In theory, they also share a focus on female characters who come to new countries as Others, but the way in which this migrancy is signified in the texts differs greatly, and one way of conceiving these differences is through the stress laid on intersectional elements of characters' identities. In *Eye Level*, the question of migration is at the forefront of the persona's characterisation and her 'coarse immigrant blood', as it is labelled in 'Chinatown Diptych' (Xie, 2018: 38), whereas the codeterminacy of race/ migration, gender, and class in *Hold* provides a more productive interrogation. Meanwhile *Folk* represents a society that welcomes migrant guests to its shores, but not without its own hypocrisy. By offering a reading of postcolonialism from the perspective of the centre of socio-cultural laws and ethics, *Folk* offers another way of critiquing how migrant narratives are represented. Whether these make any of these texts 'ready-made' for postcolonial analysis—and therefore weaker texts, according to Lazarus—or deeper and more interesting explorations of migration is ultimately up to the reader.

Online racial discourse

By its very nature, literature remains primarily a print medium. As such, the use of representation of digital or online discourses needs to be translated in some way. In *Friday Black*, Nana-Kwame Adjei-Brenyah's collection of bitingly satirical short stories, the first story 'The Finkelstein 5' translates an online campaign into a different medium. Given the satirical nature of the stories, it is clear that 'The Finkelstein 5' does not cite the #SayHerName campaign in a purely realist fashion, but uses it as a model to discuss race and to literalise the discursive practice of race. In doing so, Adjei-Brenyah's text calls on critical race theories from critics like Hall, and Omi and Winant, and pierces the apparently opaque idea of 'race' as essential and unchangeable. In 'The Finkelstein 5', race is knowingly performed and used as a springboard to respond to systemically endorsed racism.

'The Finkelstein 5' tells the story of Emmanuel, a Black US citizen who feels himself constantly surveilled by fellow citizens who judge him according to how 'Black' he looks. Emmanuel thus literalises the discourse of race by quantifying it as he performs it, taking his clothes, accent, and gait (among other things) into account. In addition to Emmanuel's narrative, there is the overarching background story of the injustice surrounding the murder of five Black children killed with horrific violence by a white man, George Wilson Dunn. With Dunn cleared of murder, protests against systemic racism arise everywhere, and there also emerges a revenge movement called 'Naming' in which protesters say one of the names of the Finkelstein 5 before assaulting white passers-by. One Namer, Boogie, is an old acquaintance of Emmanuel's:

> Boogie walked to the bus's rear door. He turned, smiled at Emmanuel, then at the top of his lungs screamed, 'J.D. HEROY!' The name was still echoing off the windows when Boogie his fist and crashed it against a white woman's jaw. She didn't make a sound. She slumped in her seat.
>
> (Adjei-Brenyah, 2018: 10)

The Namers are an offline version of the #SayHerName project. As Crenshaw *et al.* make clear, the #SayHerName campaign wants to 'honor the intention of the #BlackLivesMatter movement to lift up the intrinsic value of all Black lives by serving as a resource to answer the increasingly persistent call for attention to the Black women killed by police' (2015: n.p.). As such, #SayHerName, as the title suggests, is focused purely on women's intersectional experiences of racism, but builds on #BlackLivesMatter's catch-all ideas of celebrating Black lives and highlighting the nature of systemic racism. As part of the generic transformation in 'The Finkelstein 5'—from tragedy to satire—the story also translates an extra-literary medium—that is, Twitter—into a literary one. Emmanuel confirms this when, on the brink of beating a white man and woman with a baseball bat, he urges them to '"Say her name"' (Adjei-Brenyah, 2018: 23).

A concomitant part of the translation of an online campaign into an active protest strategy is Emmanuel's literalisation of race. As a reminder, both Hall and Omi and Winant make solid claims for the discursivity of race and its social construction. Hall asserts that 'hateful as racism may be as a historical fact'—a hatred evident in 'The Finkelstein 5'—'it is nevertheless also a system of meaning, a way of organizing and meaningfully classifying the world' (2017: 33). Hall proceeds to argue that, in the wake of US W.E.B. Du Bois's revolutionary arguments in the first half of the twentieth century, the idea of race as a '"mark" and "badge" are all-important because they signify, because they carry a certain meaning, because they are, in other words, *signifiers of difference*' (39). Emmanuel's behaviour shows clear signs of wearing race as if a badge, and he is keenly aware that he wears that badge not to smooth over differences between him and others, but to accentuate them. Hall's theory develops Fanon's ideas in *Black Skin, White Masks* in which he argues that 'not only must the black man be black; he must be black in relation to the white man' (2008: 82–3). Difference constructs meaning.

Emmanuel's literalisation of race takes place through a rating system in which 10 equates to superlative Blackness and 0 equals an empty or non-existent Blackness. Emmanuel daily and consciously tries to reduce his Blackness, but 'it was impossible to get his Blackness down to anywhere near a 1.5. If he wore a tie [...] he could get his Blackness as low as 4.0'. Later, Emmanuel deliberately wears a cap with which the Finkelstein Five have been associated, and consequently 'his Blackness [is] at a solid 7.6'. By the end of the text, when Emmanuel has joined his friend Boogie and others to kill as part of a Namers group, and he is about to be shot by police officers, 'Emmanuel felt his Blackness slide and plummet to an absolute nothing point nothing' (Adjei-Brenyah, 2018: 1, 3, 26). Importantly, it is impossible for Emmanuel's Blackness rating to reach zero, perhaps because zero is an irrational number on the representation of race: Race always has a positive value. Through this literalisation, the text is able to critique the social construction of race.

Part of the evaluation of Emmanuel's Blackness comes from the unavoidable fact of the colour of his skin that 'was a deep, constant brown' (Adjei-Brenyah, 2018: 1). In the 1950s, Fanon called this 'a racial, epidermal schema' (2008: 84) that forced its way on to him against his will. Fanon's ideas have since been superseded by poststructuralist theory. For Hall, this means that whatever it is that 'epidermalizes' the bodily qualities that signify 'Black'

> is something *that cannot be seen*: the genetic codes. So what precisely tends to fix race in its obviousness and visibility— in physical characteristics of 'color, hair and bone'—are themselves nothing but the signifiers of an invisible code that writes difference upon the black body.
>
> (2017: 63)

However, Judith Butler tacks in a different direction, arguing instead for a concept of performativity. As I explain in more detail in my next chapter, performativity is a cyclical act in which a 'discursive practice […] enacts or produces that which it names' (Butler, 2011: xxi). In connecting Butler's performativity with critical race theory, Charlotte Chadderton has argued that 'race […] function[s] as a performative: race is produced and reproduced through actions, practices and utterances' (2018: 110). Performativity is *not* identical with performance—the former belongs to the category of philosophy, the latter to drama[13]— but they share a vocabulary. '[E]ach society requires that an individual displays a raced subjectivity,' Chadderton continues, 'which matches the conventions of that particular society and what is expected of a given (perceived) racial, ethnic or cultural group' (2018: 110). With this connection between performativity and the expectations and institutions of contemporary culture, Chadderton points out how we each 'perform' our racial iden- tities. Emmanuel's quantifiable evaluation of his Blackness is the literalised version of this performativity, especially as he is able to choose his 'level of Blackness' according to the clothes he wears and the accent with which he speaks on the phone (Adjei-Brenyah, 2018: 1, 13).

Chadderton reminds us that performativity cannot be considered solely a conscious act or confirmation of subjective agency—the individual's ability to will or desire something—even if performative acts can be consciously performed. To this end, Emmanuel's change in tone of voice and change of clothes would seem, again, to literalise a philosophical category. However, Chadderton also notes that 'Butler's notion of performativity opens up the possibility for resistance' (2018: 112). In this vein, it is easier to see 'The Finkelstein 5' as a satire that is also able to voice and construct a mode of textual resistance against systemic racism—in this case the legal system—through the literalisation of a philosophical idea to which we are all subject and to which we all contribute.

Thus on the one hand 'The Finkelstein 5' *translates* an online campaign into the short story literary form, and on the other hand 'The Finkelstein 5' *literalises* the performance of race and racial difference. In attempting to establish these ideas effectively, the story is written in a satirical tone sets a mirror to face reality. The text is therefore *about* race as a social construct and turns its face *towards* society in order to land its criticism.

In this chapter I have offered a brief tour of how postcolonial theory and criticism emerges into certain critical race theories. This included the problem of representation, whether of the colonial 'Other' in general or the female subaltern in particular. Representation, too, was troubled, split between the metonymical–political and the metaphorical–artistic. This tour also included a focus on theories of hybridity and migrant narratives, as also the problem with literature that seems to be written with those theories in mind. Critical race theory established race as a discursive practice that is in fact detached from reality, but which nonetheless has material and artistic purchase in the so-called real world. These theories helped me to raise certain questions regarding historical representation in hyper-contemporary literature, of migrancy, and of the representation of race as a social discourse in this writing. Whether one or other of these texts is more important because of the topic(s) it addresses, or whether one deft artistic technique is better than another when a text engages with postcolonialism or responds to critical race theory: Those questions are now up to you to judge for yourself.

Notes

1 I use 'post-colonial' when referring to the period of time after colonialism has ended; I use 'postcolonial' when referring to the body of theory that thinks through how colonialism and postcolonialism operate and are represented in society.
2 The original publication is Spivak (1988).
3 There are other engagements beyond these two collections, but I am referring to Antonia Darder and Tom Griffith's 2018 special issue of the *Qualitative Research Journal*, and Rosalind Morris's 2010 edited book.
4 A metonym is either a representative part that stands in for, or represents, the whole; or, an associated idea that represents its associate.
5 'History' and 'geography' are politicised versions of 'time' and 'space'.
6 See above, pp. 41–3.
7 After Zacchaeus is disillusioned 'about our government', he became 'reckless in his disquisitions on the nation's leaders. Anyone could have foreseen that mysterious car accident in 2003 in which he met with Death' (Tshuma, 2018: 133).
8 Earlier, Zacchaeus had called Thandi 'Laodamia' in his diary, for which Zamani criticised him (Tshuma, 2018: 103–4).
9 The *OED* defines parataxis as: 'The placing of propositions or clauses one after another, without indicating by connecting words the relation (of coordination or subordination) between them, as in *Tell me, how are you?*' It is therefore a way of structuring sentences without hierarchy and, to that end in modernist writing, it destabilises and questions authority.
10 I prefer the word 'persona'—the Latin word for 'mask'—instead of 'protagonist' or 'poet' for two key reasons. First, a narrative protagonist is considered a unitary character, whereas a poetic persona can change from poem to poem. Second—on which my first reason is

premised—I am convinced that all poetry is fictional and as such the poetic voice ('persona') cannot be reduced to the poet's, even if the two often share a name, origin, history, identity, etc.

11 In the first part of the book it is clear that it is women who work as cooks and cleaners in Uncle and Aunty's household.

12 For more details on this 'Law' of hospitality, see Taylor-Collins (2020: esp. 25–8).

13 Judith Butler writes that

> performance as bounded 'act' is distinguished from performativity insofar as the latter consists in a reiteration of norms which precede, constrain, and exceed the performer and in that sense cannot be taken as the fabrication of the performer's 'will' or 'choice'; further, what is 'performed' works to conceal, if not to disavow, what remains opaque, unconscious, unperformable. The reduction of performativity to performance would be a mistake.
>
> (2011: 178)

Bibliography

Adjei-Brenyah, Nana-Kwame, *Friday Black* (London: riverrun, 2018).

Ahmed, Sara, *Living a Feminist Life* (Durham, NC: Duke University Press, 2017).

Bhabha, Homi K., *The Location of Culture* (London: Routledge, 2004) [1994].

Braidotti, Rosi, *Nomadic Theory: The Portable Rosi Braidotti* (New York, NY: Columbia University Press, 2011).

Brown, Melissa, Rashawn Ray, Ed Summers, and Neil Fraistat, '#SayHerName: a case study of intersectional social media activism', *Ethnic and Racial Studies*, 40.11 (2017), 1831–46. DOI: 10.1080/01419870.2017.1334934.

Butler, Judith, *Bodies That Matter: On the Discursive Limits of 'Sex'* (London: Routledge, 2011) [1993].

Carney, Nikita, 'All lives matter, but so does race: Black lives matter and the evolving role of social media', *Humanity & Society*, 40.2 (2016), 180–99. DOI: 10.1177/0160597616643868.

Chadderton, Charlotte, *Judith Butler, Race and Education* (Basingstoke: Palgrave Macmillan, 2018). DOI: 10.1007/978-3-319-73365-4.

Crenshaw, Kimberlé, 'Mapping the margins: Intersectionality, identity politics and violence against women of color', *Stanford Law Review*, 43.6 (1991), 1241–99.

Crenshaw, Kimberlé, Andrea J. Ritchie, Rachel Anspach, Rachel Gilmer, and Luke Harris, 'Say her name: Resisting police brutality against black women', *African American Policy Forum* (New York, NY), 2015, http://static1.squarespace.com/static/53f20d90e4b0b80451158d8c/t/555cced8e4b03d4fad3b7ea3/1432145624102/merged_document_2+%281%29.pdf [accessed 1 February 2020].

Darder, Antonia, and Tom G. Griffiths, 'Revisiting "Can the subaltern speak?": introduction', *Qualitative Research Journal*, 18.2 (2018), 82–8.

Donkor, Michael, *Hold* (London: 4th Estate, 2018).

Fanon, Frantz, *The Wretched of the Earth*, trans. by Constance Farrington (London: Penguin, 1970) [1961].

———, *Black Skin, White Masks*, trans. by Charles Lam Markmann (London: Pluto Books, 2008) [1952].

Fowler, Elizabeth, '*Macbeth* and the rhetoric of political forms', *Shakespeare and Scotland*, ed. by Willy Maley and Andrew Murphy (Manchester: Manchester University Press, 2004), pp. 67–86.

Gates, Jr, Henry Louis, 'Black America and the class divide', *New York Times*, 1 February 2016, www.nytimes.com/2016/02/07/education/edlife/black-america-and-the-class-divide.html [accessed 1 February 2020].

Gibson, Sarah, '"Abusing our hospitality": Inhospitableness and the politics of deterrence', *Mobilizing Hospitality*, ed. by Jennie Germann Molz and Sarah Gibson (Farnham: Ashgate, 2007), pp. 159–74.

Gilbert, Zoe, *Folk* (London: Bloomsbury, 2018).

Gunaratne, Guy, *In Our Mad and Furious City* (London: Tinder Press, 2018).

Hall, Stuart, *The Fateful Triangle: Race, Ethnicity, Nation*, ed. by Kobena Mercer (Cambridge, MA: Harvard University Press, 2017).

Heaney, Seamus, *North* (London: Faber and Faber, 2001) [1975].

Kiberd, Declan, *After Ireland: Writing the Nation from Beckett to the Present* (London: Head of Zeus, 2017).

Lazarus, Neil, *The Postcolonial Unconscious* (Cambridge: Cambridge University Press, 2011).

Morris, Rosalind C., 'Introduction', *Can the Subaltern Speak? Reflections on the History of an Idea* (New York, NY: Columbia University Press, 2010), pp. 1–18.

Myers, Benjamin, '*Folk* by Zoe Gilbert review—a dreamlike tapestry of island fables', *Guardian*, 8 March 2018, www.theguardian.com/books/2018/mar/08/folk-zoe-gilbert-review-island-fables [accessed 28 March 2020].

Omi, Michael, and Howard Winant, *Racial Formation in the United States*, 3rd edn (New York, NY: Routledge, 2015).

Said, Edward W., *Orientalism* (New York, NY: Vintage, 1979) [1978].

———, 'In the shadow of the West', *Power, Politics and Culture: Interviews with Edward W. Said*, ed. by Gauri Viswanathan (London: Bloomsbury, 2004), pp. 39–52.

Sorensen, Eli Park, *Postcolonial Studies and the Literary: Theory, Interpretation and the Novel* (Basingstoke: Palgrave Macmillan, 2010).

Spivak, Gayatri Chakravorty, 'Can the subaltern speak?', *Marxism and the Interpretation of Culture*, ed. by Lawrence Grossberg and Cary Nelson (Urbana: University of Illinois Press, 1988), pp. 271–313.

———, *A Critique of Postcolonial Reason: Toward a History of the Vanishing Present* (Cambridge, MA: Harvard University Press, 1999).

Swift, Jonathan, *Battle of the Books: And Other Works, Including 'A Modest Proposal'* (Auckland: Floating Press, 2010) [1886].

Taylor-Collins, Nicholas, 'The city's hostile bodies: Coriolanus's Rome and Carson's Belfast', *Modern Language Review*, 115.1 (2020), 17–45. DOI: 10.5699/modelangrevi.115.1.0017.

Tshuma, Novuyo Rosa, *House of Stone* (London: Atlantic Books, 2018).

Xie, Jenny, *Eye Level* (Minneapolis, MA: Graywolf Press, 2018).

3   Queer theory; or, bending the canon

Theories summary: Queer is not a singular theory, but an ever-expanding set of theories. They start with the premise that homophobia needs stamping out in society. In order to do so, it is important to recognise that **heteronormativity**—the ideology that being heterosexual is 'normal' and that all social rules and expectations should be based on female–male relationships—is problematic. Instead of prioritising homonormativity, queer theorists prefer to show how the opposition between heterosexuality and homosexuality is false, and that therefore society has been living a lie. This lie is **compulsory heterosexuality**, the idea that everyone is primarily straight. The answers to this problem lie in recasting the word 'queer' as a banner around which to rally, rather than a paralysing slur. There are therefore both philosophical and activist strands of queer theory. Contemporary queer theories want to make use of the **queer archive** to rewrite history to include stories of **queer identity** that have been wilfully or negligently omitted. Other queer theorists show how that everyone is sexually perverse—some are sadists, some like bondage, some like polyamory, while only some like single-partnered heterosexuality—and therefore **everyone is queer**.

However, others find this dilution unhelpful politically, and these theorists offer 'post-queer' or 'after queer' theories. As such, there is now an attempt to create a theory of **queer universality** that brings people together, rather than suggesting that queer identity is increasingly atomised.

Relevant questions

1 Are queer characters or relationships depicted in the text?
2 Is there an attempt to look back to, or to research, what might be termed a queer archive?
3 Are there any unexplained silences or secrets in the text?

'*Queer* is a slippery term', says Alexandra Parsons (2019: 136), which creates a problem for me in this chapter as I attempt to define it simply. Of the discourses addressed in this book, 'queer' is the youngest. After Michel Foucault's *The History of Sexuality*, volume 1 (1976), the field was more fully fleshed out in Judith Butler's *Gender Trouble* and Eve Kosofsky Sedgwick's *The Epistemology of the Closet*, both from 1990. These latter texts provide a theoretical outline that has been developed in the thirty subsequent years. Butler and Sedgwick base their theories on Foucault's ideas about discourse and biopolitics. Foucault's discourses are perceived unities of thought—such as feminism, postcolonialsm, race, etc.—that are socially constructed and reconstructed in time and place. Biopolitics is the idea that the human is reduced to the sum total power of its body, and that body is remotely controlled by the authorities, often unknowingly or against the human's will. These concepts of discourses and biopolitics allowed Butler and Sedgwick to think through ways of challenging established ideas about homosexuality and queerness, ultimately using 'queer' to define an undertaking that is both theoretical and political, and that highlights the inequalities in society that arise from the idea that being heterosexual is normal. Furthermore, 'queer' does not just *describe* these inequalities, but also seeks to *correct* those inequalities by envisioning a world in which no sexuality type is privileged. This also entails proving that even heterosexuality itself is a myth, and that many— if not most—people have more varied sexual preferences than they like to disclose.

Moreover, both Butler and Sedgwick rely on a theory of performativity of gender that is defined as, first,

> revolv[ing] around […] the way in which the anticipation of a gendered essence produces that which it posits as outside itself. Secondly, performativity is not a singular act, but a repetition and a ritual, which achieves its effects through its naturalization in the context of a body.
>
> (Butler, 2006: xv)

In other words, performativity means that we behave the way we think we should as 'female' or 'male', and we repeat these behaviours. This seems to suggest an individual's *lack* of agency if they take part in the 'naturalization'—the making normal—of a gendered essence 'in the context of a body'. And yet, for Butler, this enforced genderisation also makes available the possibility of resistance against the heterosexual norm through the term 'queer' (2011: 172). 'Queer' thus becomes the banner for resisting, and thinking through resistance of, the invisible power of authorities, be they state authorities who license heterosexual marriage, for example, or ideological authorities who speak against homosexuality, such as religious bodies. In doing so 'queer' can be reclaimed as a term of positive description, rather than a 'paralyzing slur' (169).

At the same time that 'queer' becomes reclaimed as a form of protest, 'queer' also becomes the focal point for an activist politics. In 'Queers Read This', an anonymous pamphlet distributed at a rally in New York in 1990, the authors resent 'Straight people' who 'have a privilege that allows them do whatever they please and fuck without fear' (1990: 1). The pamphlet is knowingly underpinned by anger and rage, and also questions whether 'we really have to use' the word 'queer' because 'It's trouble' (9). However, the authors resolve to do so because, 'Yeah, QUEER can be a rough word but it is also a sly and ironic weapon we can steal from the homophobe's hands and use against him' (9). For Butler and Sedgwick, after Foucault, it is the 'heteronormative'[1] establishment that wields that power; for the pamphlet's authors, it is the homophobes who maliciously use their power against homosexuals. The activist foundation for queer politics therefore also avows to use the term as a way of reclaiming agency and turning the power back against those who wield it. This is similar, though distinct, from the way in which the word 'nigger' has been reclaimed by the Black community, as Robin Jeshion recently explains: 'Two [slur reclamations] predominate. One I call *pride reclamation*, exemplified by the reclamation of "queer". The other, I call *insular reclamation*, exemplified by the reclamation of "nigger"/"nigga"' (2020: 106). In either reclamation, the net result is that the term is rekeyed for use in another, less harmful manner.

Both sets of activists—the philosophical and the political— were animated by the AIDS crisis in the 1980s. It was not just the rapid and uncontrolled spread of HIV that provoked these movements, but the establishment's homophobic response to the spread of the disease. As Sedgwick explains, 'The intense dread of that period included a political fear that AIDS phobia and the attendant sex panic would offer a pretext on which the entire society would be stripped of its liberties' (2008: xv). The agitation around the spread of HIV has greatly lessened in the thirty years since, but the energy of queer theory and queer politics has not diminished. In what follows, I want to point out some of the ways that queer theory has segmented in the last decade or so, and, whilst in the previous chapters I have been able to use individual topics or themes to summarise the theories' arguments, when it comes to queer theory it is easier to point out tensions between positions. The overarching tension remains between the theoretical–philosophical and the political, as writers often question the validity of a queer theory that *thinks through* rather than *activates* queer resistance.

The first tension I highlight is that between the forward-looking and backward-looking focuses of current queer theory. This is not a simple binary between those who are future oriented and those interested solely in the past, but also includes those who use queer theory to undermine the very idea of futurity at all. For example, in Lee Edelman's influential *No Future: Queer Theory and the Death Drive* (2004), the theorist argues that the future as a utopian ideal is only constructed so through heteronormativity and its focus on 'the Child'—capitalised because Edelman is referring to an idealised concept. For Edelman, society is problematically structured around the family and the future as it is manifested in the Child, in a framework Edelman calls 'reproductive futurism'. The consequence of such a limiting focus on the idealised heteronormative families is that it 'render[s] unthinkable […] the possibility of a queer resistance' (2004: 2).

This normative understanding of a family—comically sent up in 1990s British sitcom *2point4 Children*—is of a mother, father, and their biologically conceived children. Edelman's position is that this 'fantasy' limits discussion of relationships that do not fit this mould. Furthermore, the Child is intimately linked to the ideals of tomorrow that imply that queer relationships and queer families are, conversely, excluded from the future. Edelman's argument is not to deny the facts as they are, but rather to adopt the privilege of the heteronormative family positively as a base to establish meaningful opposition, claiming that 'queerness attains its ethical value' by accepting that it has no future, and therefore accepting its 'status as resistance to the viability' (2004: 3) of the future. Similar to the way in which 'queer' as a term of abuse has been accepted and resignified as a term forging a community, Edelman's proposal is to make a virtue out of necessary social constraints.

This is not the only way that queer theorists engage with the future. Jennifer L. Miller has recently considered the growing presence of utopian queer theories that consider tomorrow's world better than today's. Writing about Madison Moore's *Fabulous: The Rise of the Beautiful Eccentric* (2018), Miller describes how Moore 'connect[s] fabulousness to utopia, specifically claiming it as producing a utopian space in the present' (2019: 96). This signals a move towards 'critical optimism' (*passim*) for Miller, in contrast to Edelman's negative acceptance. This critical optimism is visible in Kathryn Stockton's review of queer theory, in which she argues that 'Imagining a queerer coalitional politics requires counter-DREAMING and counter-concocting a utopian space as yet unseen, the no-space, the u-topia, the non-nation entity of a resistance trying to grasp worlds-coming-to-be' (2016: 89). Stockton's counter-concoction includes the idea that the imagined alternative is precisely that: imagined, a no-space, a dream. The implication is that, whilst Moore's 'fabulousness' radically changes the now by virtue of a better tomorrow, an alternative queer landscape thrives on hope rather than pragmatic, effective politics.

In tension with this future orientation is the backward look. Sara Ahmed advocates a re-examination and recuperation of the queer archive. This is an important task, argues Ahmed, because 'When a lesbian feminist past is reassembled as a heterosexual present, the future, her future, is lost' (2017: 220). This means that if the queer archive is inexpertly accessed and used, therefore, it could suffer from the same heteronormative ideological control—i.e. heterosexuality is normal and desired—that exists in the lived present. Prudence Chamberlain, explaining what is meant by the queer archive, declares that it is about 'The ways in which queer figures are remembered and re-told' (2017: 47). This is important for Chamberlain because, much like Edelman's argument, 'In spite of legislative process'—such as the Marriage (Same Sex Couples) Act (2013) and the Adoption and Children Act (2002)—'it is still not possible for the LGBT movement to settle comfortably into the logical and linear progression of time'—that is, the 'natural' order of events that T.S. Eliot once coarsely and comically summarised: 'We're born. We fuck. We die.' Chamberlain continues that, by 'purely focusing on the present and future, the past is negated' (47), and therefore a return to the past is necessary.

Ahmed's conception of the queer archive differs only slightly from Chamberlain's. Whilst Ahmed similarly wants to 'return[] to the archives of lesbian feminism' (2017: 213), it is not just to uncover stories, but to uncover those stories so that they can help us navigate a world outside 'the requirements of compulsory heterosexuality'[2] (216). As with conceptions of utopia that rely on an imagined future or no-space, Ahmed advances the argument that to be a 'lesbian feminis[t]' is imaginatively and paradoxically to 'remember a scene that has yet to happen, a scene of the ordinary' (217), because 'Sometimes you have to battle for an ordinary'. The 'ordinary' might be how two cohabiting lovers go about their daily lives, as Ahmed suggests—a scene that is rarely represented with lesbians as the lovers. This is a battle over queer representation, in other words. The lesbian archive that supports the ordinary battle helps to 'chip[] at the blocks of heteropatriarchy', therefore turning lesbians into a 'we' who 'have to become willful. I want to think of lesbian feminism as a will-fulness archive, a living and a lively archive made up and made out of our own experiences of struggling against what we come up against' (222). The present political battles are thus shaped by an archive that both acknowledges the difficulty of the past, but also reveals the emergence of a lesbian community who have shared in ordinary battles.

Ahmed warns against rehearsing only the negative aspects of the archive. The wilfulness archive 'is thus not only an unhappy archive, even though it includes unhappiness' (2017: 228). There may be experiences recorded in this nebulous archive that have been overlooked by conventional categorisations of 'resistance', 'defiance', or 'acceptance' that can nonetheless be considered positive and pleasurable. It is therefore enjoined on the wilful lesbian to become 'intimate' with the archive's stories in order to 'write ourselves into existence'. Moreover, for Ahmed the archive is also created from the literal experience of writing, such that 'This intimacy of standing against [the heteropatriarchy] and creativity can take the form of a book', with the implica-tion that Ahmed's *Living a Feminist Life* is an example of such a wilful book. 'Books are themselves material, paper, pen, ink, even blood', writes Ahmed. As such, 'Words can pulse with life; words as flesh, leaking; words as heart, beating' (230). In these archives— the archive full of stories that need retelling, and the archive full of models of resistance, both happy and sad—the past can also provide an avenue to form queer theoretical resistance.

A second tension is that between the poststructural underpinnings of much queer theory and reactions against those underpinnings. Poststructuralism is a type of theory and phil-osophy that explains how necessary structures that underpin society are actually fundamentally unstable. These structures include, for example, those that divide genders only into two and structures that divide sexuality into a heterosexual and homosexual binary. Moreover, poststructuralists consider language as the primary mode of creating (and destabilising) social 'meaning'. A sub-practice of poststructuralism is deconstruction, defined by Sedgwick as follows. Deconstruction

> demonstrate[s] that categories presented in a culture as symmetrical binary oppositions—heterosexual/homosexual, in this case—actually exist in a more unsettled and dynamic tacit relation according to which, first, term B is not symmetrical with but subordinated to term A; but, second, the [...] valorized term A actually depends on its meaning on the simultaneous subsumption and exclusion of term B; hence, third, the question of priority between the supposed central and supposed marginal category of each dyad is irresolvably unstable, an instability caused by the fact that term B is constituted as at once internal and external to term A.
>
> (2008: 10)

The result is that the A/B binary is dissolved into a more authentic understanding of how the structures that give meaning to the world actually operate. In practice, it is easier to take an example. For Sedgwick, the heterosexual/homosexual binary that is often considered symmetrical—the former describes opposite-sex relationships, the latter describes same-sex relationships— is actually asymmetrical. This is because heterosexuality is considered more 'powerful' or 'normal' than homosexuality, and therefore a hierarchy is formed in this binary: Heterosexuality is considered superior to homosexuality. Furthermore, Sedgwick's deconstructive framework reveals that, whilst it may look like heterosexuality is opposed to homosexuality, the former instead relies on the latter to give it meaning. Heterosexuals are therefore heterosexuals because they are *not* homosexuals. By using the inferior part of the 'dyad' as an element against which the superior is constructed, we are able to see how the asymmetrical heterosexual/homosexual binary is unstable. If homosexuality were eradicated, then heterosexuals would no longer have any-thing against which to define themselves. Heterosexuality would therefore cease to exist, because heterosexuality needs homo-sexuality. The political argument therefore runs that homosexu-ality should be 'valorized' in society on its own terms, because it is a necessary part of the normalising and making-superior of heterosexuality.

This deconstructive understanding allows Sedgwick to argue that 'the appropriate place for [the] critical analysis [of society] to begin is from the relatively decentered perspective of modern gay and antihomophobic theory' (2008: 1). In doing so, Sedgwick is using queer theory to offer an alternative perspective in which homosexuality is the central referent for meaning. A crucial aspect of this poststructural manoeuvre is the destabilisation of the sex/gender binary. Queer theory has spent enormous energy questioning the supposedly natural division between 'sex' based on chromosomes and 'gender'. For poststructuralists, gender does not equate to sex because it is a social construct that is 'far more elaborated, more fully and rigidly dichotomized […] in a cultural system for which "male"/"female" functions as a primary and perhaps model binarism' (Sedgwick, 2008: 27). Gender divided into 'male' and 'female' thus needs deconstructing along the lines cited above.

Butler develops this argument in *Gender Trouble* in two ways. First, by signalling that gender is an artificial social category, it

> does not follow that the construction of 'man' will accrue exclusively to the bodies of males or that 'women' will inter-pret only female bodies. […] [M]*an* and *masculine* might just easily signify a female body as a male one, and *woman* and *feminine* a male body as easily as a female one.

Second, by querying even the notion of a stable idea of 'chromosomal sex':

> And what is 'sex' anyway? […] Does sex have a history? Does each sex have a different history, or histories? […] If the

immutable character of sex is contested, perhaps this construct called 'sex' is as culturally constructed as gender.

(2006: 9)

Not only has Butler deconstructed the man/male and woman/
female binaries, but she has also deconstructed the sex/gender
binary. She goes further by suggesting that it is also only a social
assertion that sex and/or gender is split into two—male/female,
man/woman—and that, therefore, there are more than two sexes,
and more than two genders. From this queer-theoretical manoeuvre, trans★ theories begin to develop.

The theoretical consequences for poststructural queer theory
are dramatic: Everyone is queer. For Sedgwick, this is because it
seems ridiculous that 'of the very many dimensions along which
the genital activity of one person can be differentiated from […]
another […] precisely one […] has remained, as *the* dimension
denoted by the now ubiquitous category of "sexual orientation"'
(2008: 8). Sedgwick therefore implies that, since none of us is
truly singly oriented, and since sex/gender are unstable categories
and much more plural than just the two we think we know,
'queer' is the best way we can find to define our sexual orientation. This 'queer' is not synonymous with 'homosexual', but
with 'unusual', and 'out of the ordinary'. However, by situating
everyone as queer, Sedgwick subtly reiterates the idea that 'queer'
is normal. This is typical of poststructural queer theories, such as
when Stockton argues that 'if we're for the queer', 'It's the strange
we like', and queer is a 'plea for pleasure, however ephemeral'
(2016: 85). In this mode, to be queer is to be Bacchanalian—and
that is available to everyone. Robert McRuer takes the argument
sideways in his formulation of 'crip' theory that focuses on the
social construction of 'able-bodiedness' and its binary companion
'disable-bodiedness'. For McRuer, 'crip' 'connotes "outness",
"pride" and a location of "the problem" not as disabled bodies
but instead inaccessible environments' (2019: 89). 'To be crip' is
therefore to experience the world *as* inaccessible, much as 'to be
queer' means to 'get at processes that unsettle, or processes that
make strange or twisted' (McRuer, qtd in Miller, 2019: 89). This

crip–queer theory has gained added traction in recent months because of the way the global lockdowns owing to the spread of the Covid-19 virus have made much more of the world inaccessible to people who are able-bodied, therefore turning many more of us criply queer. Through these queer poststructural theories, queer is loosely detached from the activism of antihomophobia and attached to many other theories that highlight or lift off from the idea that identity is socially constructed, and therefore that any fixed identity is a fallacy that can and should be avoided. To queer or to be queer is therefore to render unstable or to thrive in continuous instability.

However, several theorists have begun to question the usefulness of poststructural queer theories. The main point of contention is the poststructural idea that no identity is fixed. The next step in this argument is that myriad identities are possible, which therefore leads to a splitting of society and the subject into increasingly smaller units of identification. Instead of identities such as 'male' or 'female', 'gay' or 'straight', poststructural queer theories lead to minoritarian identities that combine identity categories ('homosexual *and* Black *and* Jewish') or intersect them ('homosexual Black Jew'). Whilst many argue that these newly-forged identity categories are a positive phenomenon, others such as James Penney and David Ruffolo perceive them as problematic.

Ruffolo argues that 'the current politics of queer, as seen through its relations to subjectivity, are limiting for the future of queer studies because of its unequivocal commitment to the queer/heteronormative binary'. In this way, Ruffolo targets precisely the deconstructive tactic that Sedgwick placed at the heart of her queer theory. Where Sedgwick argued that the focus on a binary defused its power and reoriented its logic, Ruffolo considers that this leads to 'restricted' arguments because it results in an 'endless cycle of significations that reposition subjects on fixed planes' (2009: 4). In other words, the problem is the terminology that opposes 'queer' and 'heteronormative' because these terms, in themselves, are too static to reflect accurately human identity. Ruffolo thus rejects the idea of a fixed 'being' at any single point in time ('*I am* homosexual (and) Black (and) Jewish') on which he sees poststructural queer theories relying, even as they appear to reject stasis.

Ruffolo gives the example of the diversity questionnaire that job applicants are required to fill in. Whether you select 'M', 'F', or 'Other', 'these procedures allow subjects to believe in the possibility that the self can be fully knowable' (2009: 15). These forms, which include options beyond the heteronormative 'male', 'female', and now include questions like, 'Are you the same gender you were at birth?', nonetheless require a subject to take note of their identity *now*. The queer theories that have made gains by adding boxes to the questionnaire nonetheless abide by the logic that 'identity politics are in many respects inapplicable beyond the study of fixed identity categories': Orthodox, poststructural queer theory leads to the entrenchment of fixed identity, argues Ruffolo.[3]

Penney's argument is not dissimilar in his focus on the development of minoritarian and particular identity categories. Penney's major problem with this process is the subsequent impossibility

> to ground a notion of community on queer, if queer is what stops you from identifying any quality its members might share. If everyone is potentially queer, then there are no definite exclusions by means of which that community might be defined against society, or the people, at large. And yet, it's impossible to deny that wide swathes of queer theory manage to do just that, even when it explicitly endorses the position that sex subverts any and all identity claims.

> (2014: 10)

Penney's problem is thus (a) that queer community is impossible if no one shares an identity with anyone else, and (b) that poststructural queer theories nonetheless try to establish this logically impossible community. Whilst Ruffolo is not interested in undermining poststructuralism, Penney is offended by it, even going so far as to polemicise that 'queer theory discourse is so entrenched in the presuppositions of poststructuralism that it should simply be abandoned' (2014: 48).

Penney proposes two arguments against poststructuralism throughout his book *After Queer Theory*. For the first, he suggests that poststructuralism is flawed in itself. Targeting Foucault's

> premise that sexuality discourse is essentially an elaborate ruse designed to have us chatter endlessly about sex, [...] while further tethering ourselves to the omnipotent forces of power, then clearly the conclusion is warranted that the very existence of queer theory can be read as a demonstration of this ruse's spectacular success.
>
> (2014: 74)

His argument is therefore that Foucault's ideas on discourse have reinforced the problems that poststructural queer theory sought to alleviate. For this ineptitude, queer theory should be abandoned. For the second, Penney proceeds to lament other theorists' incompetence, such as when he admonishes Edelman for his misuse of Freud's death drive when Edelman tries to use the queer position as powerful, even without a future. Penney complains that 'Edelman's position at the most fundamental level relates to its undialectical notion of a radically pure brand of negativity. Arguably, this version of the negative sees Edelman shirk responsibility for the content of his own argument' (181). This complaint is typical of Penney's vitriol, targeting as he does the notion of stasis at the heart of Edelman's argument, much like Ruffolo pointed out the inadequacies of poststructuralism's assumption of static identity categories even as it refuses them. Therefore, whilst the tone and vocabulary used to dismiss post-structural queer theory differs, the tenor of the arguments does not.

Needless to say, the fact that these poststructural queer theories come under such scrutiny testifies to their success. Any theorist that wants to supersede the poststructural strain of queer theory must take account of it before offering their own—and this is what both Ruffolo and Penney do in *Post-Queer Politics* and *After Queer Theory*, respectively. This question of afterwards-ness or post-ness is my final tension as it sets up a question surrounding the continued validity of queer theory at all. In the titles of these two books are the twin thrusts of queer that I noted in my opening paragraphs to this chapter: on the one hand 'politics', and on the other hand 'theory'. Counterintuitively, Ruffolo's *Post-Queer Politics* is more concerned with establishing a new queer theory,[4] whereas in *After Queer Theory*, Penney is interested in establishing a universal queer politics.

Ruffolo's *Post-Queer Politics* offers a parallel version of queer theory that takes account of, and yet moves beyond, poststructural theorisations of the queer. Noting that 'Queer has reached a political peak' and 'Its theoretical movements have become limited by its incessant investment in identity politics' (2009: 1), Ruffolo argues that 'post-queer attends to the *becomings* of life that do not reiterate the past but move forward as continuous productions' (7). This process is not oppositional to poststructural queer theories, but a recasting of what Foucault, Sedgwick, and Butler can offer:

> I do not intend to establish an opposition to Foucault (as this would create another unnecessary binary) but to reconsider Foucault's role in relation to queer and politics. this inevitably entails a rereading of Butler and the monumental role that performativity has played and continues to play in contemporary queer studies and politics. The purpose of reimagining queer's relationship to Foucault and Butler is to create the spaces to engage a post-queer politics of dialogical-becomings rather than subjugated subjectivities.
>
> (Ruffolo, 2009: 9)

This word 'becomings' is, however, opposed to what Ruffolo perceives as the static focus on 'beings' in poststructural theory. In order to do this, Ruffolo moves his theoretical hinterland from Foucault, Butler, and Sedgwick to Mikahil Bakhtin, Gilles Deleuze, and Félix Guattari.[5] As an example of what Ruffolo means, he contrasts Butler's idea of performativity that, to reiterate, repeatedly creates and enshrines normal structures of society. Butler's performativity is thus 'citational' (2011: *passim*).

However, Ruffolo 'differentiate[s] performative bodies as *copies* from dialogical bodies as *quotes* where the body is not something exclusively given—it does not strictly reiterate existing norms—but is instead always something given and something created' (2009: 35). This is a subtle theoretical difference that can be analogised through Julia Kristeva's theory of 'intertextuality'[6] through which she argues that 'any text is constructed as a mosaic of quotations [of other texts]; any text is the *absorption* and *transformation* of another' (1986: 37; my emphasis). Where Butler would agree that performativity is about 'absorption' and copying (to use Ruffolo's term), Ruffolo would focus on the notion of 'transformation' in his theory of queer 'becomings'.

James Penney's *After Queer Theory* tacks in a different direction, taking his theoretical lead from the father of psychoanalysis, Sigmund Freud, his disciple Jacques Lacan, and chief critic of capitalism, Karl Marx. The twin poles of Penney's theoretical ideas—the psychoanalytic and the Marxist—contribute to his construction of a new 'after queer' theory that is fundamentally historical in nature. This contrasts with Ruffolo's future-oriented 'post-queer' (2009: 30). Penney is adamant that 'queer discourse has run its course', which allows him 'to rethink the relation between sexuality and politics': 'I argue that the way to implant sexuality in the field of political antagonism is paradoxically to abandon the exhausted project of sexuality's politicisation' (2014: 1). Penney's position is straightforward enough: A universal queer politics should replace the particularised, post-structural queer theory that relies on identity politics; and the universal queer politics should be premised on Freud's insights into the individual's and the group's psyche—with their traumatic and repressed sexualities, etc.—and Marx's insights into the fundamentally unequal spread of modernity and modern wealth throughout the world.

Penney's argument, after debunking many other queer theories and explaining their shortfalls, always turns to these two poles—either singly or in combination—in order to offer a corrective. Ultimately, as a summary of what kind of universal queer theory Penney envisages, he thinks through Lacan's idea of the universal–particular, based on 'the concept of the subject with

the premise that all particular subjects share the same estrangement from themselves' (2014: 186). He also writes that 'It's time
to substitute the left-deconstructionist motif of subversion with
the contrasting, properly neutral, attitude of indifference' (178).
Whilst seemingly abstract, it is easy to think of Penney's queer
'indifference' as diametrically opposed to Ahmed's 'wilful lesbian'
who, to reiterate, helps to 'chip[] at the blocks of heteropatriarchy'
in her 'battle for an ordinary' (2017: 217). Penney's indifference
to identity politics encourages less of a focus on what separates
people from one another, and instead a focus on what unites.

Indifference also relies on waiting for and paying attention to
the 'political event' as described by Alain Badiou: '[A] disruptive
event, a "truth procedure" which has the potential literally to
transform what it's possible to think in a given political situation'
(Penney, 2014: 177). An example of an event of this kind is the
9/11 terrorist attacks on New York City. In this context, it might
seem strange to argue for an indifferent response to such a devas-
tating attack, but Penney's argument helps to make sense of how
to unite disparate communities, arguing that,

> Subjectivated by the political event, we subtract ourselves
> from the field of substantive markers of identity—hetero-
> sexual or homosexual; Jew, Muslim, Hindu, Christian; black,
> white, yellow, brown—to 'refind' ourselves 'outside', as it
> were, in a movement of generic subjectivity. Transported by
> this modality of indifference, what distinguishes me from
> others, including in particular my sexuality, ceases to bear
> significant consequences for thought.
>
> (2014: 178)

In this vein, Penney's queer theory is not dedicated solely to
queer citizens and is truly 'after' queer theory in that it suggests
that anything under that rubric is meaningless and therefore
should not be pursued. Where Ruffolo's 'post-queer' runs alongside prior queer theories, Penney's 'after queer' signals the end of
queer, such as it currently is.

For others looking beyond queer—however that 'beyond'
is figured—it is not always as dramatic. Dana Luciano and Mel

Y. Chen, asking whether the queer has ever been human, argue that 'the figure of the queer/trans body does not merely unsettle the human as norm; it generates other possibilities—multiple, cyborgian, spectral, transcorpo-real, transmaterial—for living' (2015: 187). Furthermore, they answer their own question 'equivocally but deliberately, yes and no. *Yes*, because this sustained interrogation of the unjust dehumanization of queers insistently, if implicitly, posits the human as standard form', but also '*no* because queer theory has long been suspicious of the politics of rehabilitation and inclusion to which liberal-humanist values lead'. Luciano and Chen's theory sits comfortably within current transhumanist theories, showing how queer theories intersect with others. For instance, Ahmed made the race–queer intersection a central part of her thesis, arguing that 'I am not a lesbian one moment and a person of color the next and a feminist at another. I am all of these at every moment' (2017: 230). It is possible to see Luciano and Chen's theories in dialogue with Ahmed's.

Moreover, Miller has stated that 'collective survival is echoed throughout queer theory published in 2018, which seeks to theorize and organize beyond single axes of identity in order to imagine ways to be together with our differences' (2019: 88): Intersectional queer theories are now extremely important.[7] Benjamin Haber (2019) works to join digital and social media theories with queer theories, in which the ephemerality of digital engagements can be explained best through queer theories that have long thought about the transition between the private and public domains—an idea first established by Sedgwick in her writing about the 'closet' as a queer space. Finally, in their development of Oswald *et al.*'s (2005) thesis on queer families, Samuel Allen and Shawn Mendez include the 'five contextual spheres [...] of ability, class, ethnicity, nationality, and race' in their consideration of how hegemony impacts and conditions the establishment and constitution of families, 'although we by no means assert that these are the only contexts that encase the new gender, sexuality, and family binaries' (2018: 76–7). Allen and Mendez also add the variable of time to their theory (78) in order to keep their theory of the queer family flexible and adaptable, concluding that their 'hegemonic heteronormativity model suggests that cis-, homo-, and mononormativity are situated within various contextual spheres, and it accounts for adaptations throughout the life course' (81). Allen and Mendez's queer family theory thus broadens the scope of what constitutes a 'family', adds a more focused intersectional methodology, and also prepares for future change in the composition of the queer family.

As I have indicated, queer theories are multiple not only in their character, but also in their temporality (their use of time): Some focus on the past (Ahmed), some on the future (Edelman, Allen and Mendez), and some on a fractured present, as described by Penney. This present, built on a 'Psychoanalytic temporality is thus a temporality of discontinuity' because 'This temporality features moments of disorienting and unthinkable […] change' in the course of psychoanalysis. The analyst, that is, brings to light features of past events that the patient had repressed. Events are thus 'retroactively' changed and

> future events are likely to change that retroactive assessment in such a way that the meaning or significance of the past […] is constantly subject to change in light of later anticipated retroactive assessments. At any point in time […] something can happen which, from the perspective of a later moment, will have literally changed the past.
>
> (Penney, 2014: 183)

A pat way of categorising these multiple temporalities as a whole is to say that they are queer, and that the wide range of queer theories (beyond their temporalities) testifies to the queerness of queer.

In reviewing the primary texts, next, I use the three tensions I outlined above:

- The tension between the using the past and looking to the future
- The tension around poststructural queer theories that rely on identity
- The tension around 'after' or 'beyond' queer

Using the past; looking to the future

Richard Scott's *Soho* is a collection of queer poetry that details its male persona's[8] experience of being gay in contemporary Britain. Its poems interrogate British gay history—'I am to be [a] homo-historian' (Scott, 2018: 69)—focusing on the well-known gay area of Soho in London. The poems are broadly formal in their construction, with its third section of four, for example, consisting entirely of sonnets. However, these sonnets—as with other forms used in the collection—are not formally strict, but relaxed versions of the poetic forms. In this sense, the collection can be characterised as loosely experimental in form; its true innovation is in the topics it covers.

The opening poem—separated from the sections that follow as if a prologue—demonstrates this innovation by turning to the queer archive in the 'Public Library, 1998' (Scott, 2018: 3). The poem locates an act that is described in the past, but the act is itself enacted on a past beyond even that. Thus, in the public library the persona reads a book of poetry and resents the absence of queer poems. In an act of wilfulness reminiscent of Ahmed's call-to-arms, the persona 'write[s] COCK // in the margins'. In the poem, the graffiti is not presented in line, but is shown typographically in this poem's margins. In doing so, the persona distends the shape of the fourteen-line sonnet, thereby demonstrating his wilfulness to disrupt the orthodox love poem. This is the beginning of the persona's queer practice.

As the poem develops and the persona details all the graffiti he scribbles on the book—'Words stretch to / diagrams, birth beards and thighs, shoulders, fourgies'—he then sees a 'queer subtext' in one of the poems. The fact that this revelation comes in the eighth line that is traditionally the site of the sonnet's *volta*[9] establishes that the poem is playing with, and within, the rules of the traditional sonnet—the poem that is well known for its descriptions of romantic love. A partial revelation of the 'queer subtext' is revealed in the ninth line (and last line of the third three-line stanza)[10] when the persona describes the subtext 'nestled like a / mushroom in moss, *tongue-tree* and *vaunt*'. The simile used to describe the words is itself significant, highlighting a potentially poisonous, parasitic growth (the mushroom) amid the moss that grows in the damp shadows of the forest: This is the queer subtext. The poem referenced is Gerard Manley Hopkins's 'The Bugler's First Communion', first published in his *Poems (1876–89)*, and the lines cited merit fuller quotation:

> Here he knelt then in regimental red.
> Forth Christ from cupboard fetched, how fain I of feet
>   To his youngster take his treat!
> Low-latched in leaf-light housel his too huge godhead.
>
> There! and your sweetest sendings, ah divine,
> By it, heavens, befall him! as a heart Christ's darling, dauntless;
>   Tongue true, vaunt- and tauntless;
> Breathing bloom of a chastity in mansex fine.
>
> Frowning and forefending angel-warder
> Squander the hell-rook ranks sally to molest him[.]
>   (Hopkins, 1986: 147)

The poem tells the story of a priest giving a young soldier his first communion. The lines quoted demonstrate the persona's vigour in giving the wafer to the bugler and following the proper practice of kneeling for communion. The idea of offering a kneeling, vulnerable boy a bodily gift has, at least to the late-twentieth-century mind presented in the poem, more than a whiff of inappropriate homoeroticism. Added to the sexualised language of 'bloom' and 'molest' (again, at least to a contemporary reader), it is clear what Scott's persona was reading in this queer archive.

In response to this revelation, the persona continues the graffiti with renewed zeal, 'and my pen becomes an indigo highlighter inking up what / the editor could not, would not'. This practice concludes with the persona 'illuminating the readers-to-come...', with the pun on the last word left to linger through the ellipsis. Just as the persona found a queer subtext in Hopkins's poem, so the persona leaves his reader with a subtextual pun suggesting a queer reader's playfulness. The last line is strengthened by the nature of the queer reading the persona has undertaken of 'The Bugler's First Communion' that remains a tantalisingly incomplete intertextual reference. The only words taken from Hopkins's poem are '*tongue-true*' and '*vaunt*', leaving the reader to find the Hopkins text for themselves; ideally, the reader will go to find the very text that the persona has graffitied. To this end, 'Public Library, 1998' is both *about* the under-represented queer archive, and it encourages the reader's active engagement *with* the queer archive. That marginalised 'COCK' from the third line now becomes an example, not only of the distending and bending of the sonnet form, but of how the poem is itself subject to a queer graffiti. This collection, too, is now part of the queer archive. In this last idea, we can now extend the archival gesture from dealing exclusively with the archive of the past—that is, the poems in the anthology that the persona was reading—to presenting a queered archive to the reader—that is, the collection *Soho* becomes part of the queer archive. Just as Ahmed's text demonstrated how the 'intimacy of standing against and creativity can take the form of a book' that represents 'our struggle to write ourselves into existence' (2017: 230), so too does 'Public Library, 1998' begin that process in *Soho*.

Soho is not only interested in the queer archive, but also in how the queer subject will experience the future. *Soho* thus engages with the queer tension around the past/future that I sketched above. In '[shame on you faggot for bending Whitman to your will co-]' (the title taken from the poem's first line), the persona ventriloquises homophobic criticisms of 'co- / opting [US poet, Walt Whitman] into your self-help circle- / jerk willing him to yawp across the tattered ages just for you' (Scott, 2018: 64). The criticism levelled at the persona accuses the latter of misrepresenting the archive *as* queer, and therefore also attacks the poem I analysed above, among many others in *Soho*. The accusation goes on to describe how the persona must be feeling:

                    what did you think
leo
    paul
        mark
            jean
                eve
                    michel[11] would be your fore-
faggots signpost your backdoor out of shame shame
    on you faggot and shame on me an italicised quote
    is no talisman

                                        (Scott, 2018: 64)

On the one hand the names signal the persona's accessing the breadth of the queer archive; on the other hand, the lack of punctuation and missing syntactical coherence signal the persona's overwhelmed emotions. These ideas coalesce around the thrice-stated 'shame' that, after Sedgwick's analysis, becomes even more powerful. Sedgwick argues that those who use the word 'shame' 'do not [merely] describe or refer to shame but themselves confer it' (2003: 32) on the victim. To this end, shame is inescapable because it is created as it is pronounced. To say 'shame' to the persona is therefore to defuse the potency of the persona's queer archive wilfulness and to refuse the power of 'an italicised quote' from a queer theorist because it 'is no talisman' (Scott, 2018: 64).

The poem thus puts obstacles in the persona's chosen path, that of making use of the queer archive as an anti-heteronormative resistance. The second page of the poem—significant because the first page of the poem is not full, but the persona moves on to a second to signal that a new page is being written in his mode of queer resistance—is written entirely in parentheses. It begins powerfully:

(… and if I can just push through this decades-long blush this
SHAME SHAME SHAMEFULNESS
will there be something waiting for me[)]

                                        (Scott, 2018: 65)

The persona seeks 'transcendence' from the absolute presentism of feeling shame. After all, shame is 'the place where the question of identity arises most' (Sedgwick, 2003: 37), and therefore anyone feeling shame has their identity shaped by their labelling as shame by another.

But Sedgwick also sees in shame a path to liberation of sorts, because 'Shame, […], transformational shame, is *performance*. I mean theatrical performance. […] Shame is the affect[12] that mantles the threshold between introversion and extroversion, between absorption and theatricality' (2003: 38). In being performed, shame is therefore two further things. First, it is a theatrical front for identity, and not identity itself. Second, it is an opportunity to use shame as a way of 'rais[ing] the question of the status of force and opposition, of stability and variability, *within* performativity', and therefore an opportunity to use performativity to oppose the concept that implicates the victim (Butler, 2011: 169, 184). The developing sense given to shame in Scott's poem is that the future transcendence allows the persona to be 'free from shame but made from shame' (Scott, 2018: 65), thus adopting Ruffolo's future-oriented 'post-queer' version of performativity in which 'performative bodies […] are] *quotes* where the body […] is instead always something given and something created' (2009: 35). We can read the 'body' here as the queer wilful book (in Latin the *corpus*, which comes to mean 'book') that is Scott's *Soho*. At the end of the second-page parentheses, the conclusion to the poem is that 'no shame is your gift from the world to the / world that fucked still fucks you' (Scott, 2018: 65), thus showing how the persona will use their refuted label of shame as way to reflect their renewed and newly-forged identity back to the world. This is the future transcendence of shame that responds to the potential failure of the anti-heteronormative queer archive.

Queer identity

In Michael Donkor's *Hold*, Belinda is a young woman from Kumasi in Ghana, who is invited by wealthy friends of her employers, for whom she works as a maid, to come to London and keep their daughter, Amma, company. Dr and Mrs Otuo ('Nana') worry that Amma is lonely and troubled, and they ask Belinda to keep an eye on her. Amma is British-born and has a vexed relationship with her Ghanaian heritage. On top, or part of that vexed relationship, is Amma's queerness, and during the course of the novel she has to come to terms with her own unrequited love.

In one scene, Amma searches through a trinket box she has filled with items from a summer previously where she met Roisin: 'Ro. Sheen. That name, like Amma's impossible to forget' (Donkor, 2018: 106). As she watches Roisin roll and smoke a cigarette, 'Amma was grateful that her skin hid blushes' (108) because she fancied Roisin from their first meeting. However, she is also embarrassed by 'the unwieldy truth' of queerness, though not just because she is gay, but also because 'no one likes a black girl who likes girls' (108). Amma's queer journey is an intersectional one, touching on what Ahmed says about 'Lesbian feminism of color: [it is] the struggle to put ourselves back together because within lesbian shelters too our being was not always accommodated' (2017: 230). Like Ahmed, Amma is aware that she is multiply marginalised by the intersection of her sexuality and her race.

Roisin, rather than being part of the solution, is tacitly part of the problem. 'Roisin had never been to South London,' we read, 'but Roisin was "curious".' Amma worries 'that Roisin's planned trip was about wanting an ethnographer's look at how the black half lived; Amma was to be her helpful native guide' (Donkor, 2018: 116). In this quasi-colonial narrative framework, it is clear to the reader that Amma is particularly worried about the Black Ghanaian part of her identity, perhaps even more so than her queer identity. Ironically, as Belinda notices at the *Ghanafoɔ*, a gathering of the Twi-speaking Ghanaian community,

> Amma struggled in the *tro tro* tightness, Belinda heard her phrasebook Twi fail. Amma stuttered through limp apologies that amused listeners and [...] Amma was mocked in her mother tongue. An aunty [...] asked if 'this child has the disability? Is the girl your sister afflicted by cruel Down's Syndrome? Is the explanation for the water in her mouth?'
>
> (Donkor, 2018: 84)

It is therefore clear for the reader, if not for Roisin or others at the south London party, that Amma is at least equally uncomfortable—if not more so—in her identity as a young Black woman, as she is as a young queer woman. The aunty's reading of Amma as disabled draws together the queer with the crip theories as described by McRuer.

Back at the south London party Amma is accosted by 'one of the boys [who] decided he had taken a liking to Amma's bottom so he ground it with all his strength. […] She had desperately wanted Roisin to come to her rescue'. With feelings similar to that of shame (discussed above), 'Amma had felt *guilty* at her revulsion' because she knew that she 'was supposed to like this[.] He a big black man, and she a sexy young sista' (Donkor, 2018: 117; my emphasis). The use of the demotic noun 'sista' is significant. The *Oxford English Dictionary* (*OED*) records its meaning as primarily 'An unrelated woman regarded as bound to others by shared experiences or by membership of a particular group, and related senses', and secondarily 'A (fellow) black woman'—a definition that nearly touches upon the cultural and ethnic specificity of the way that Amma uses the word. Indeed, Amma uses the term in an ironic way, both identifying with it and rejecting its underlying premise—that she should identify as a Black woman in a Black community—at the same time. 'The conventional way of distinguishing shame from guilt is that shame attaches to and sharpens the sense of what one is,' writes Sedgwick, 'whereas guilt attaches to what one does' (2003: 37). Here, then, Amma's guilt is twofold. First, she feels 'revulsion' dancing with the man. Second, she would rather be dancing with and/or be saved by Roisin 'cut[ting] the hooded stranger down to size with an exquisite one-liner' (Donkor, 2018: 117). Feelings compel Amma's guilt—feelings that arise from the intersection of her race and ethnicity with her sexuality, an idea cemented when Amma later expresses her 'guilt' (121) at being a member of the privileged Ghanaian diaspora in London.

The sense of queer–Ghanaian guilt is redoubled when Amma comes out to Belinda, who reacts, at first, with hyperbolic incredulity:

> Belinda clutched her knees. 'A homosexual lesbian! On top of all the rest!' She laughed a scratchy laugh. 'You have to

admit, is a bit funny. Funny, funny funny. Someone would
even have joking tears upon their cheeks. Ha. Ha. What?
What? Why you seeing as concern as this? *Won sere* [Won't
you laugh]?'

(Donkor, 2018: 187–8)

This later turns into anger as Belinda tells Amma that she is only
being a '"homosexual lesbian"' '"all for the sake that you want
to say your foolish words about girls. […] If it was my daughter
I might even collapse. [… W]hatever this you have done or want
to do with a girl is no natural thing. Is not. Is wrong. End of the
line"' (Donkor, 2018: 210). It would be easy to dismiss Belinda's
perceived provincial attitude to homosexuality as deriving from
her Ghanaian[13] origins; to do so would ignore the other aspects
of her identity. For example, Belinda is from a working-class
background and is in Britain at the behest and hospitality of the
Otuos. Belinda is also deeply influenced by Christianity, which
affects not only her sense of sexual propriety—'Belinda would
never allow her first kiss to be so public. It would be like a special
ceremony when it finally happened. Quiet and holy and only the
two of them' (136)—but also her sense of family—'"You have a
great power to leave your own mum the most unhappy person
I can imagine"' (210). Furthermore, Belinda's Platonic friendship
with Mary, her colleague in Kumasi, is the kind of homosexual
love of which Belinda can make sense. Mary's funeral bookends
the novel, and Belinda's paralysing guilt at not talking to Mary on
the phone more often (229) combined with her confusion at the
funeral (xi–xii, 292 ff.), where she is one of the chief mourners,
counterposes Amma's anger at being dumped by Roisin (195–
8) and joins the two moments as emotionally complementary.
These identity intersections all condition Belinda's response to
Amma's coming-out, showing how the tension between the
heterosexual-Belinda and homosexual-Amma can be deferred
on to or translated into a tension between heterosexual–working-
class–migrant-Belinda and queer–British-Ghanaian–middle-
class–cosmopolitan-Amma. In this complex position, it is clear
that it would be foolhardy to reduce the queer narrative to a
notionally simple battle over sexuality.

Rather than simplifying or homogenising the nature of being queer in twentieth-century London, *Hold* dramatises not only the intersectional difficulties of being queer but also sets them in the shadow of a more powerful female camaraderie, that between Belinda and Mary. Thus the book complicates queerness by showing off the nature of an intersectional queer identity, and subverts it by showing how Belinda's apparently homophobic position is produced not by mere bigotry or backwardness, but is produced by, and in conversation with, a number of intersecting factors, including the underlying importance for Belinda of her same-sex friendship with Mary.

'After' queer

Louisa Hall's *Trinity* gives us an opportunity to analyse an encounter that benefits from an 'after queer theory' interrogation both in the dominant mode of poststructural queer theories, and then in the mode of Penney's universalism. *Trinity* tells the story of designer of the atom bomb, J. Robert Oppenheimer, through seven (fictionalised) 'testimonials' of those who knew him. Oppenheimer's own testimonial is never given, and he is called different nicknames in each of the testimonials. The testimonials—ranging in date from 1943 to 1966—have interludes told by a narrator of the Trinity atomic bomb test in 1945 in the New Mexico desert. None of the testimonials is told by the same character, and it is as if Oppenheimer exists in these stories as the sun seen from different planets as they orbit him, pulled into his gravitational field and unavoidably blinded by his light.

Whilst the fifth testimonial is overtly queer, telling a story about a lesbian couple in California, I want to pay attention to a testimonial that seems to have little to do with a queer narrative. The third testimonial, set in Paris in 1949, is from a former UC Berkeley colleague of Oppheimer, Andries van den Berg. Andries and his partner, graduate student Jacqueline, welcome Oppenheimer—or 'Opje' as Andries affectionately calls him—and his second wife, Kitty, to their modest Parisian apartment when Opje is in Paris for 'an international conference

on diplomacy in the atomic age' (Hall, 2018: 111). Andries
reminisces about their time together in California, prior to the
atomic bombs at Hiroshima and Nagasaki, when they were active
in the communist-lite movements of union activism. Andries's
world, for reasons that become clear in the course of the testimonial, has shrunk and become dislocated. I argue that it is
possible to read Andries's affection for Oppenheimer as queer. To
do so relies on a theory of the 'closet', which Sedgwick supplied
in her 1990 *Epistemology of the Closet*, because Andries remains
outwardly heterosexual throughout the testimonial, and expresses
no explicit homosexual tendencies. As Sedgwick introduces,
'"Closetedness" itself is a performance initiated as such by the
speech act of a silence' (2008: 3), and it is to Andries's silences
that I will first pay attention as I sketch out what a poststructural,
'orthodox' queer reading would look like.

   The first of these silences is when Andries retreats to his
apartment's balcony before his guests' arrival. Andries worries that
the Opje he knew—'We might not have eaten all week! But even
so, Opje would have had a fine time' (Hall, 2018: 111)—would
not still be the celebrity Opje who was so famous that 'He'd
entered the metonymic realm' (109) and was often represented
solely through his hat. Andries's standing on the balcony already
looks like a significant removal from the domestic space that is
about to welcome the famous Oppenheimer, even before he
admits that when

> at one point Jacqueline came out and asked me to sponge
> off the tables […] I was so caught up in wondering whether
> Opje had changed that I completely forgot what she'd asked
> me. Instead, inspecting those rooftops, I thought that, to a
> certain extent, I would have to 'face facts'.
>
> (111)

Andries's anxiety is clear in the syntax of this last sentence that has
three dependent clauses[14] that all delay his final pronouncement
about '"faci[ng] facts"'. Apparently these facts are Oppenheimer's
necessary change between their shared time in California and
this atomic-age in Europe, but it is interesting that these 'facts'

have already been declared—Andries was already worrying about how Oppenheimer might have changed (111)—and that they do not seem to be so fundamental as to warrant such anxiety.

Perhaps the 'facts' are revealed in a subsequent silence that intervenes in Andries's and Oppenheimer's conversation about the change in Andries's research, which has moved on from 'the monograph I was writing back then, my collection of Native American myths', to the 'new project[…]: an ethnography in photographs, a study of Europe after the war'. As Andries goes on, he admits that he and Oppenheimer 'both knew *without saying it* that it was a new direction for me […] and I found the new subject depressing' (Hall, 2018: 114; my emphasis). There is a clear sense of shame partnered with this silence, with Andries's 'depress[ion]' and unwillingness to speak the subtext—that his new subject was different from his first specialism—signalling Andries's embarrassment. However, we have only Andries's after-the-fact assertion that the silence refers to change in topic, and not to anything else. I also want to question his full knowledge here.

In her reading of Henry James's *The Beast in the Jungle* (1903), Sedgwick points out how the protagonist, John Marcher, is paralysed by a secret that seems to stop him marrying the women he loves—and the woman who loves him—May Bartram. Sedgwick hypothesises that Marcher's secret is a homosexual secret; however, Sedgwick's signature deconstructivist move is to take note of the 'outer secret, the secret of having a secret' (2008: 205). Marcher has told Bartram that he has a secret, but not what the secret contains—because he himself does not know the content of the 'inner secret' that paralyses him. This inner secret—a known unknown, to quote Donald Rumsfeld—is the closetedness to which Sedgwick refers, and I argue that we can transpose this model to Andries's narrative, wherein the 'facts' and the silence about his new research are the outer secret, with the inner secret never revealed. The inner secret's presence is emotionally felt by Andries when he talks with Oppenheimer about the latter's own former research of 'spots of matter' in 'permanent free fall' that

> collapsed into themselves and disappeared, and so did every little thing that passed by them.

Even sound. Even light! Or that's what he told me, sitting
on that back porch in Berkeley. Every little thing that passed
too near those spots bent in and around them and started
to spiral until they'd disappeared, vanished as though they'd
never existed.

Later they called those spots a name. They called them
black holes, I think, but it was Opje who predicted them[.]

(Hall, 2018: 115)

I argue three things here. First that Andries's inner secret is
closeted in a space analogous with a black hole, its contents
utterly unknowable and therefore unspeakable. Second, that
Oppenheimer is a kind of black hole in the text because he, too, is
permanently silenced and never given his own testimonial. Third,
that although we can extrapolate and say that Oppenheimer is the
text's queer centre, he is also the devotee of Andries's unknowable
and unspoken devotion.

For Sedgwick to make the case that Marcher's inner secret is
homosexual in content, she argues that there are spoken signs that
signal his queerness, even if not referencing the inner secret itself
(2008: 202–4). The same is visible in Andries's narrative, such as
his despair that Kitty's hair 'was done in an awful new style, cut
just under her chin, and sort of rounded and sprayed in the shape
of a helmet' (Hall, 2018: 112). He repeats the complaint towards
the end of his narrative about his former partner, Barb, who has
written to him, and mentions that she saw Kitty in the salon:

(So they go to the same salon, I thought, and wondered if
Barb also wore her hair short now, and rounded and sprayed
into the shape of a helmet. Then I imagined a whole bunch
of American women with their hair sprayed in the shape
of a helmet, and I thought, What's happening in California!
Is there some army forming, some battalion of embittered
American women, all wearing their hair like a weapon?)

(Hall, 2018: 125–6)

Andries's denial and lament over the so-called androgynous look
popular in post-war USA seems like a form of 'heterosexual

panic' in which Andries' rejects the becoming-masculine of women, but in a hyperbolic way that supposedly confirms his strict heterosexuality. Despite this panic, Andries nonetheless likes looking at Jacqueline who, on the night of Oppenheimer's visit, 'was looking so sweet, wearing men's trousers' (Hall, 2018: 118).

On top of these signals, there are also the moments of small enjoyment that Andries takes in relation to phallic wine bottles. First, 'Opje grinned, and held out a […] bottle of Château Cheval Blanc', and 'I knew right away that they were the same people' (Hall, 2018: 112–13), which seems to quell his earlier anxiety about Oppenheimer's difference in the intervening years. Second, 'I remembered that I still had three of the good bottles of port I'd salvaged from my marriage to Barb', and that he now gets to share these with Oppenheimer. Indeed, 'as I uncorked the first one, I could smell California. There it was, at the back of my palate' (120). It is the act of reminiscing with Oppenheimer that Andries so enjoys in this chapter, and this bottle, uncorked and ready to drink, fuels the reminiscences, entrenching the drinking–reminiscing cycle. And finally, there is the realisation that he is down to 'the last bottle I had from that case I'd salvaged from the wine cellar at Barb's house. Then I hesitated for a moment, but what better time to finish that bottle than with my good old friend Opje? So then I pulled out the cork' (120–1). This wine is swallowed by both Andries and Oppenheimer as they share in what, in a loose psychoanalytic reading, can be analogised with semen—in other words, a latent homosexual practice. The uncorking of all the bottles could also be analogised with the unstoppering of sexual excess—an excess that, in Andries's narrative, is focused solely on Oppenheimer.

As a final example of the queer subtext that latently voices Andries's desire for Oppenheimer is the recollection of the time that Oppenheimer 'took me riding over a mountain pass near Santa Fe' (Hall, 2018: 110). The sexual frisson of the 'ride' is redoubled by the bottle of wine that Oppenheimer bought: 'Cheval Blanc' translates as 'white horse', thus entrenching the memory as associatively (that is, metonymically) phallic. This becomes an unwitting nodal point for lament later in the chapter. When Oppenheimer and Kitty leave, 'I almost cried, to think of everything that had happened since Opje and I rode over that pass' (121). This again signals the presence of the inner secret, passed off as the 'facts' of the passage of time, but expressed in a latent reference to a sexual frisson between just Andries and Oppenheimer. Thus, the closet is the silent, inner secret of Andries's unspoken 'facts', the contents of which are the homosexual affection, or desire, for Oppenheimer, as confirmed by the spoken, manifest part of the story that suppresses Andries's true feelings.

However, Penney would ask different questions of this chapter. To recall, Penney's 'after queer' argument dismissed the framing of poststructural queer theory as too fixated on a queer identity that, whilst appearing to privilege difference, resulted in concretising the heterosexual/homosexual binary. Penney's response was to use Freudian and Lacanian psychoanalysis allied with Marxist anti-capitalist critique to frame a universal queer theory. Penney's queer Marxism makes a straightforward point in relation to the 'closet' and the idea of 'coming out', that 'not everyone can afford to come out' (2014: 87). This shows how Penney's focus is on the socio-economic factors at play that produce the impossibility of coming out, or the necessity of a silent closet, rather than the individual moments of psycho-sexual struggle. In the case of Andries, there are plenty of socio-economic moments worthy of focus, most of which centre on the nature of post-war internationalist politics that, in the West, grew suspicious of communism and non-Anglo-American identity. Thus, whilst the presence of the closet itself remains the same in the following analysis, the forces that produce the closet, and preclude its opening, are different.

Central to this analysis is the problem of Andries's exclusion from the USA. During their silent discussion about Andries's change of research specialism, Andries tells us that, 'of course, I'd been denied a visa to return to the States' (Hall, 2018: 114). Later, in the letter received from his former partner, Barb, she asks Andries whether

> I ever wondered whether I'd wound up on the blacklist because of my connection to Opje. And she reminded me that all his former students […] had ended up drafted, or blacklisted, or imprisoned for taking the Fifth. Barb said some people in

Berkeley thought he'd given the names of his Communist friends, perhaps to keep his position on the bomb project.

(Hall, 2018: 124–5)

In this revelation, Andries's closeted secret is not necessarily about his desire for Oppenheimer, but at least a desire for re-entry into a liberal political state that permits rides 'over a mountain pass near Santa Fe' (Hall, 2018: 110). To 'face facts' is to accept his exclusion from the USA because of socio-economic and sociopolitical factors, namely Andries's communist sympathies before the war. And the desire is focused on the ability to cross borders through difficult terrain, as that at Santa Fe. Furthermore, the traitor whose actions during the McCarthy hearings led to his political exclusion may be the man (Oppenheimer) who constitutes the object of Andries's sexual desire. In this light, the detestable, imagined collection of US women with new hair styles that look like phallic helmets and, thus, weapons, does not show a 'heterosexual panic' so much as an 'ideological panic'. Thus, by 'inquir[ing] into the ways in which political questions and controversies are shot through with libidinal interest and the vicissitudes of unconscious desire' (Penney, 2014: 90), we are able to supersede the purely individual focus in the Sedgwick-inspired queer reading with the universal, Penney-inspired reading in which the closet is a political one, and only later sexualised.

The ultimate lesson from Penney's disappointment with poststructural queer theory is that it politicises the sexual, when a better approach would be to sexualise the political. Barb's letter is an example of how the political—the communist–capitalist/Soviet–US struggle—is sexualised through the letter of a former lover. As the speaker from the black hole that is Andries's inner secret, Barb symbolises the end of sexual desire, and therefore the end of Andries's political desire to return to the USA from where she writes.

In this chapter, I have summarised the range of queer theories, split between poststructural theories that build on the productive ideas of performativity-as-protest, and post- or after-queer positions that query the usefulness of setting the homosexual/heterosexual binary at the heart of theory. Through these ideas,

I have offered readings of hyper-contemporary writing analysing queer shame and intertextuality, the intersections of race/ethnicity and queer identity, and also the nature of the queer closet. It is now up to you to judge the importance or quality of the debate about the use of the future or past in queer writing, the question of intersectional identity subversion, or the Marxist–psychoanalytic reading of hyper-contemporary writing.

Notes

1 Michael Warner is credited with coining the term 'heteronormative', meaning that the accepted and expected normal social construction is underpinned by heterosexuality: a female–male sexual relationship accompanied by children born of that relationship.

2 'Compulsory heterosexuality' is a phrase coined by Adrienne Rich (1993) that has come to dominate certain strands of queer theory. It describes the way in which society is structured around certain necessary heterosexual relations between citizens.

3 It is worth noting that research into intersectionality has countered Ruffolo's point (defined as 'anticategorical complexity'), with Sylvia Walby arguing that 'such radical deconstruction and destabilization of categories'—for which Ruffolo is arguing—'makes substantive analysis, which requires distinctions between categories, rather hard' (2007: 452). My thanks to Emma Taylor-Collins for alerting me to this argument.

4 Ruffolo would contend this generalisation of his work, arguing:

> The dialogic relation between experience and theory that I am speaking of here refers to the 'politics' in *Post-Queer Politics* where we do not simply need to change the players of the game but how we think about and play the game itself. Post-queer therefore works towards a politics of becoming where experience and theory are dialogically connected without reducing experience to theory and theory to experience.
>
> (2009: 28)

5 Mikhail Bakhtin (1895–1975) was a Russian scholar who established that literature is dialogic in nature and wrote about the interplay between myriad different languages in literature—what he termed 'heteroglossia'. Gilles Deleuze and Félix Guattari wrote two controversial postmodern theoretical texts, *Anti-Oedipus* (1972) and *A Thousand Plateaus* (1980), which together make up *Capitalism and Schizophrenia*.

6 Kristeva's theory itself develops Bakhtin's theory of the dialogic in literature.

7 For a greater explanation of intersectionality, please see above, pp. 27–8, 61–2, 64–6. It is important to recognise that intersectionality has developed independently from queer over roughly the same period of time (the last thirty years or so). However, intersectional arguments hold greater public interest and in some cases have reached similar conclusions to queer in a shorter time frame.

8 Please see above, pp. 86n10, for an explanation for why I prefer to use this term.

9 Italian for 'turn', the *volta* is the moment in the sonnet when the premise established in the opening octave (eight lines) is overturned and surprised in the final sestet (six lines).

10 A three-line stanza is called a 'tercet'.

11 These names refer to: academic and queer theorist Leo Bersani (1931–), French poet Paul Verlaine (1844–96), US poet Paul Doty (1953–), French writer Jean Genet (1910–86), Eve Kosofsky Sedgwick (1950–2009), and Michel Foucault (1926–84).

12 'Affect theory' is concerned with the emotions produced in the reader when they read a text—likewise with the observer of a painting, listener to music, and a theatrical audience member, etc. Affect theorists scrutinise individual emotions and evaluate texts based on the types of emotional responses elicited in the reader/observer/listener/audience member.

13 And of course, to reduce Belinda's ethnic identity to 'Ghanaian' is equally problematic, given the heterogeneous qualities of communities within the nation-state called 'Ghana'.

14 A dependent clause, or sub-clause, cannot exist in isolation, separate from a main clause. In this sentence, the main clause is: 'Instead, I would have to "face facts".' The sub-clauses are: 'inspecting these rooftops', 'I thought that', and 'to a certain extent'. It is also interesting that the main clause is couched in uncertainty and temporal distance through the use of the **conditional** *perfect* ('**would** *have*').

Bibliography

Ahmed, Sara, *Living a Feminist Life* (Durham, NC: Duke University Press, 2017).

Allen, Samuel H., and Shawn N. Mendez, 'Hegemonic heteronormativity: Toward a new era of queer family theory', *Journal of Family Theory & Review*, 10 (2018), 70–86. DOI: 10.1111/jftr.12241.

Butler, Judith, *Gender Trouble*, 2nd edn (New York, NY: Routledge, 2006) [1990].
———, *Bodies That Matter: On the Discursive Limits of 'Sex'* (London: Routledge, 2011) [1993].
Chamberlain, Prudence, *The Feminist Fourth Wave: Affective Temporality* (Basingstoke: Palgrave Macmillan, 2017).
Donkor, Michael, *Hold* (London: 4th Estate, 2018).
Edelman, Lee, *No Future: Queer Theory and the Death Drive* (Durham: Duke University Press, 2004).
Haber, Benjamin, 'The digital ephemeral turn: queer theory, privacy, and the temporality of risk', *Media, Culture & Society*, 41.8 (2019), 1069–87. DOI: 10.1177/0163443719831600.
Hall, Louisa, *Trinity* (New York, NY: Ecco, 2018).
Hopkins, Gerard Manley, *Gerard Manley Hopkins*, ed. by Catherine Phillips (Oxford: Oxford University Press, 1986).
Jeshion, Robin, 'Pride and prejudiced: On the reclamation of slurs', *Grazer Philosophische Studien*, 97.1 (2020), 106–37. DOI: 10.1163/18756735-09701007.
Kristeva, Julia, *The Kristeva Reader*, ed. by Toril Moi (New York, NY: Columbia University Press, 1986).
Luciano, Dana, and Mel Y. Chen, 'Has the queer ever been human?', *GLQ: A Journal of Lesbian and Gay Studies*, 21.2–3 (2015), 183–207. DOI: 10.1215/10642684-2843215.
Miller, Jennifer L., 'Queer theory', *The Year's Work in Critical and Cultural Theory*, 27.1 (2019), 82–99.
Oswald, Ramona Faith, Libby Balter Blume, and Stephen R. Marks, 'Decentering Normativity: A Model for Family Studies', *Sourcebook of Family Theory and Research*, ed. by Vern L. Bengston, Alan C. Acock, Katherine R. Allen, Peggye Dilworth-Anderson, and David M. Klein, (Thousand Oaks, CA: Sage, 2005), pp. 143–65.
Parsons, Alexandra, 'Queer', *The Routledge Companion to Twenty-First-Century Literary Fiction*, ed. by Daniel O'Gorman and Robert Eaglestone (London: Routledge, 2019), pp. 136–46.
Penney, James, *After Queer Theory: The Limits of Sexual Politics* (London: Pluto Press, 2014).
'Queers Read This', Queer Research Directory, 1990, www.qrd.org/qrd/misc/text/queers.read.this [accessed 8 February 2020].
Rich, Adrienne, 'Compulsory heterosexuality and lesbian existence', *The Lesbian and Gay Studies Reader*, ed. by Henry Abelove, Michèle Aina Barale, and David M. Halperin (New York, NY: Routledge, 1993).
Ruffolo, David V., *Post-Queer Politics* (Farnham, Surrey: Ashgate, 2009).
Scott, Richard, *Soho* (London: Faber and Faber, 2018).

Sedgwick, Eve Kosofsky, *Touching Feeling: Affect, Pedagogy, Performativity* (Durham, NC: Duke University Press, 2003).

———, *Epistemology of the Closet*, updated edn (Berkeley, CA: University of California Press, 2008) [1990].

Stockton, Kathryn Bond, 'Queer theory', *The Year's Work in Critical and Cultural Theory*, 24.1 (2016), 85–106. DOI: 10.1093/ywcct/mbw005.

Walby, Sylvia, 'Complexity theory, systems theory, and multiple intersecting social inequalities', *Philosophy of the Social Sciences*, 37.4 (2007), 449–70. DOI: 10.1177/0048393107307663.

4 Class; or, dividing the canon

Theories summary: Class is clearly not a new phenomenon and it remains something that emerges from capitalism: Capitalism produces class differentiation that leads inevitably to class antagonism. Worse still, capital inequality—how much money you have in the bank or buried in bricks in mortar compared with other people—is growing. The problem of the persistence of class is theorised across literature, sociology, history, politics, and economics. For some, class is now about **dispossession by accumulation**: When one person is dispossessed of something, someone else accumulates it. This could be objects or **commodities**, or it could be **family relationships and friendships**. Class is also now felt transnationally across the world, and therefore looking into geographical differences in class is important, whether it's the perceived absence of class narratives in the USA or the emergence of the nouveaux riches in a postcolonial context. **Social mobility** continues to be relevant, especially via education; this is even more so because of the way that universities are increasingly marketised and therefore studying can help you earn more money. There is therefore an uncomfortable causal link between higher education and social standing. Nevertheless, we are warned to be wary of the clichéd stories of social mobility being a natural consequence of being better educated: Who is left out of these social journeys, and how do those who benefit from the bounty education can provide **entrench class divisions** by climbing the social ladder?

Relevant questions

1   Are stories of social mobility depicted in the text, and what emotions attend those stories?
2   Are stories of retail and retail workers depicted in the text?
3   Do any characters experience the breakup of their families or friends' relationships?
4   Are there narratives of how class is felt differently in different geographical locations?

The description of contemporary analyses of class is perhaps the hardest to complete. In part, this is because 'class' is not only a category in cultural discourses, but also exists as an important marker in the social sciences, as well as in historical discourses. These parallel—and sometimes competing—discourses are reflected in the descriptions that follow. I begin with the classical and influential economic historian, Karl Marx, before reaching beyond economics to sociology, anthropology, history, and cultural criticism. These references will sketch out several ways of thinking about class today, with all confirming that class is not a natural fact of society but a description of how societies are constructed.

In *The Communist Manifesto* (1848), Marx and his collaborator Friedrich Engels establish the importance of classes in history: 'The history of all hitherto existing society is the history of class struggles' (2008: 33). This period of 'history' takes Marx and Engels prior to the inception of capitalism in society, and they continue by asserting that

Freeman and slave, patrician and plebeian, lord and serf, guild-master and journeyman, in a word, oppressor and oppressed, stood in constant opposition to one another, carried on an uninterrupted, now hidden, now open fight, a fight that each time ended, either in a revolutionary reconstitution of society at large, or in the common ruin of the contending classes.

(33–4)

The substitution of all of these 'class' divisions with 'oppressor and oppressed' tells us already that Marx and Engels's interest is in how classes are opposed or related to one another in an antag-onistic relationship.

Since capitalism is the dominant underlying force of societies around the world, I will use it as my basis for thinking through contemporary class, rather than those prior forms of class that Marx and Engels catalogued. For Marx in *Capital* (1867), capit-alism describes a set of processes that see material objects given a monetary value, either through making one object out of sev-eral others in the factory (called the 'means of production'), through selling objects (called 'commodities') to other people for money, or by renting out property to other people (often glossed as the 'land'). The conversion of the material into money and back again is the flow of capital. Meanwhile, the working class is itself a product of the capitalist middle class who own the means of production. These capitalist owners require people to work in their industrial buildings and thus become the prole-tariat working class. Moreover, the capitalists need the proletariat to work efficiently each day in order for the capitalist to make money out of their ownership: The longer the labourers work, the more value the capitalists can extract from the commodities they create. For Marx, this is the primary place where class antag-onism is produced because 'the establishment of a norm for the working day presents itself as a struggle over the limits of that day, a struggle between collective capital, i.e. the class of capitalists, and collective labour, i.e. the working class' (1990: 344). Thus an antagonism is established between the bourgeois capitalist and the proletarian working class—and this antagonism is also original in the class structure. That is to say, there is no class without class antagonism. Marx goes further to think about 'not the single capitalist and the single worker, but the capitalist class and the working class', lamenting that

> By converting part of his capital into labour-power, the capitalist [...] kills two birds with one stone. He[1] profits not only by what he receives from the worker [i.e. the commodity that he sells], but also by what he gives him. The capital given in return for labour-power is converted into means of subsistence which have to be consumed to reproduce the muscles, nerves, bones and brains of existing workers, and to bring new workers into existence.
>
> (717)

That is, by paying the worker, the capitalist will not only earn the commodity the worker produces and the capitalist can go on to sell but the capitalist will also earn a profit by paying the worker to be more productive. This, in turn, allows the capitalist to earn yet more money on the next commodity the worker produces, and so on. The capitalist thus profits from the product the labourer makes as well as the money the labourer is paid because it encourages productivity. This profiteering is how the capitalist class as a whole exploits the worker. Capitalism thus produces classes characterised by owners and profiteers, on the one hand, and labourers and the exploited on the other. Moreover, capitalist classes are characterised not only by the level of income and capital gain, but also the manner of that income and gain. The capitalists' continual profit-making means that inequality will only continue to grow because capitalists are only capitalists if they keep making a profit by exploiting the worker, thereby entrenching these class divisions.

Capitalism's inequality is Thomas Piketty's chief focus in *Capitalism in the Twenty-First Century* (2013). He explains that

> When the rate of return on capital exceeds the rate of growth of output and income, as it did in the nineteenth century and

seems quite likely to do again in the twenty-first, capitalism automatically generates arbitrary and unsustainable inequalities that radically undermine the meritocratic values on which democratic societies are based.

(2017: 1)

Again, connecting the economy with politics (just as Marx did, with *Capital* subtitled *A Critique of the Political Economy*), Piketty demonstrates how capitalism produces classes. As with Marx, so for Piketty: these classes are not independent of the economic system but produced by it. Piketty doubles down on these ideas when, while hailing the usefulness of income tax returns in determining levels of inequality, he notes that through the democratising force of income tax, economists can determine the shape and character of the class structure (15).

For Piketty, inequality in the twenty-first century is increasing, and has nearly matched the highs of a century ago in Europe. This is down to two chief factors. First is the continuing importance of capital, defined differently from Marx. In Piketty's terminology, capital combines land and its natural resource value with wealth 'accumulated by human beings (buildings, machinery, infrastructure, etc.' (2017: 59), because capital can be inherited and, especially in its landed form, can accumulate income even while it idles, or while it is passively rented out. Capital contrasts with— and is complemented by—labour income, which accumulates only when the labourer is in the process of labouring. To summarise, Piketty advises that 'it is almost inevitable that inherited wealth will dominate wealth amassed from a lifetime's labor by a wide margin' (34).

The second factor describing the rise in inequality is the rise of a managerial class that has changed the type of capital in the top decile[2] (i.e. the top ten per cent of wealthy individuals) from wealth (as defined above) to income. However, this income is not the same kind of income as the traditional labouring proletariat, but about working in banks, law firms, accountancy firms, management consultants, and the offices of traditional industry, such as in car manufacturers. The managerial class is significant because 'these top managers by and large have the power to set their own remuneration' (Piketty, 2017: 32–3), and therefore

> we have gone from a society of rentiers [e.g. landlords] to a society of managers, that is, from a society in which the top centile is dominated by rentiers (people who own enough capital to live on the annual income from their wealth) to a society in which the top of the income hierarchy […] consists mainly of highly paid individuals who live on income from labor.
>
> (347)

Thus inequality is on the rise in both a traditional capitalist manner—through the capital of wealth—and through the rise of a managerial class who sets their own salaries to the detriment of those whom they manage. Worse still, 'the key issue is the *justification* of inequalities rather than their magnitude' (Piketty: 331; my emphasis) in the twenty-first century, further entrenching class antagonisms based on capital accumulation.

Piketty also considers what he terms forces for divergence and forces of convergence of inequality; in other words, how inequality is deepened ('divergence') or countered ('convergence'). Technology should be a force for convergence because it requires 'greater skills on the part of workers, so that labor's share of income will rise as capital's share falls' (Piketty, 2017: 29). Thereafter, 'Inequalities [should] thus become more meritocratic and less static' (28). However, 'There is little evidence that labor's share in national income has increased significantly in a very long time' (29). Another of these convergent forces is the substitution of 'generational warfare' for 'class warfare', visible in the growing disquiet in the UK between baby boomers who have benefited from the National Health Service and final-salary pensions, and those younger adults who will draw down from average-salary pensions and are treated by a decimated NHS. The prospects of this shift are promising because 'this inescapable biological fact is supposed to imply that the accumulation and distribution of wealth no longer presage an inevitable clash between dynasties of rentiers and dynasties owning nothing but their labour power' and therefore there is less division 'because everyone is first young and then old'. However, likewise with the rise of technological know-how, generational warfare fails to reduce wealth inequalities because 'inequalities of wealth exist primarily within age cohorts, and inherited wealth comes close to being as decisive' (29) as it was in the first mature capitalist societies. Nevertheless, it will be worth considering the presence of generational antagonisms in the primary texts under consideration to see how they manifest, and whether they supplant the classic class antagonisms.

Being either a capitalist or a labourer is not fixed. Lynsey Hanley's *Respectable: The Experience of Class* (2016) charts the author's transition from what she terms the 'respectable' working class to the middle class. Tellingly, this is not solely to do with levels of income or where the author lives, but it also includes a transition in linguistic terms. As such, 'I can't remember the day I started calling dinner "lunch" and tea "dinner", but I know that it happened, because that's what I call them now. That must mean I'm middle class' (ix). By helping us move away from strict socio-economic definitions of class, Hanley alerts us to the nature of class *identity*: It is about how someone feels, rather than how someone is categorised. To this end, Hanley's experience includes both looking 'up' to the middle classes and her feeling of 'anxiety induced by being socially mobile' (ix), as well as looking 'down' on the 'rough' and 'classically working class' (7).[3] Crucially, in Hanley's terminology respectability is a phenomenon of the self because

> Respectability is a property of your specific circumstances: circumstances which permit you, or at least make it easier, to maintain the appearance and feeling of self-respect. The more desperate your circumstances, the less likely you are to be seen as respectable by other people, but it doesn't necessarily affect your own perception of how respectable you are.
> (2016: 11)

To this end, respectability is a tertiary-level feeling in response to class, which is already a secondary-level categorisation arising from capitalism.

Hanley's transition between classes—which involves not only a growing income, a long list of educational accomplishments, but also a shift of home in geographical terms to a more affluent area—alerts us to the psychological impact of what is termed social mobility. She achieves this mobility—if 'achieves' is the right word—by doing well at school and university; in other words, she accumulates not financial capital, but social and cultural capital that she then 'spends' in society. By now 'dwelling'[4] in universities where she works, she has arrived at 'a place where I could make use of who I knew as well as what I knew' (Hanley, 2016: 223). The theory of cultural capital comes from sociologists Pierre Bourdieu and Jean-Claude Passeron. Bourdieu wanted to move beyond 'embodied accumulation' that is found in capital as money, and established

> *cultural capital*, which is convertible, on certain conditions, into economic capital and may be institutionalized in the forms of educational qualifications; and as *social capital*, made up of social obligations ('connections'), which is convertible, in certain conditions, into economic capital and may be institutionalized in the forms of a title of nobility as an additional form of accumulation.
>
> (Bourdieu, 1986: 243)

As Bourdieu describes and Hanley's book testifies, financial capital is not the only source for determining or measuring class position—though in Bourdieu's understanding all capital is useful only if convertible into financial capital.

An important lesson from Hanley's real-world experience of class transition is that class is not only produced by capitalism, nor is it only about 'the ways people are kept apart, and keep themselves apart by the methods we use to sustain class in society' (2016: 226), but also that class becomes an inbuilt, identity-rooted phenomenon. In her powerful terms, being (respectably) working class in a world that encourages aspiration and ascent up the social ladder produces a 'wall in the head', meaning that 'The estate [where I lived] stayed with me long after I moved elsewhere, partly in the form of a strange kind of vertigo when presented with opportunities and experiences I'd grown up assuming were far beyond my reach' (x). In this way, the idea of being socially mobile, both in terms of the metaphorical ladder and the house or flat to which you move, contains a hangover that may manifest in myriad ways, not all of which are positive: 'I resent the idea of feeling guilty about my own socially mobile route through life, even though I feel guilty about it in practice' (189). We have already read about these kinds of feelings in Sarah Perry's *Melmoth*, explored in chapter one, when Helen Franklin passes the 11+ exam to get into a grammar school. In response, her 'mother wept, because she could not reconcile maternal pride with her feeling that she was now marked out among the neighbours—had transgressed, somehow, and would in due course be punished for it' (2018: 58). Hanley's guilt and Mrs Franklin's expected punishment are twin sides of the same social mobility coin. In the discussions below, I will therefore pay attention to social mobility and any attendant emotions.

At one point Hanley comments that 'I am a British person for whom the facts of social class matter' (2016: 6). It does appear to be true that the British have an obsession with class, all the way through society; however, it is also interesting to think through an entirely different consideration of class in terms of the US context. Nancy Isenberg begins her book by noting the

> problem […] that popular American history is most commonly told—dramatized—without much reference to the existence of social classes. It is as though in separating from Great Britain, the United States somehow magically escaped the bonds of class and derived a higher consciousness of enriched possibility.
>
> (2016: 1)

Isenberg proceeds to explain why she thinks class has been overlooked, rooting her reason in the land itself. It was the 'American landscape' that for Benjamin Franklin and Thomas Jefferson, two of the USA's founders, was 'deemed productive of an exceptional society. The founders insisted that the majestic continent would magically solve the demographic dilemma by

reducing overpopulation and flattening out the class structure'
(315). However, Isenberg is also clear that class has and continues
to play a role in US life, 'defin[ing] how real people live' and how
'politicians engage in class issues' (317).

Another complication when discussing class in a US context
is the other major marker of US inequality: race. Isenberg writes
about the nineteenth-century British politician James Oglethorpe
who was able to recognise the economic problems of continuing
with slavery, because 'allowing slavery to thrive would retard economic opportunity and undermine social mobility for average
white men and their families'. Isenberg uses this example to illus-
trate how racial inequalities, in spite of their insidiousness, could
still be measured in economic terms. However, since 'racial dominance was intertwined with class dominance in the southern
states, and the two could never be separated', Isenberg wonders
why 'we continue to ignore the pathological character of class-
centered power relations as part of the American republic's political inheritance' (324). It will be worthwhile to consider this
intersectional issue in the primary texts.

A net result of Isenberg's conception of class being treated
separately to race in US history is that, in the narratives she
excavates, the lower classes in America appear all to be white.
Without restating the entire history, it is interesting that these
disregarded classes have not accumulated wealth but instead
have accumulated a litany of barbaric names. Isenberg catalogues
them: 'Waste people. Offscourings. Lubbers. Bogtrotters. Rascals.
Rubbish. Squatters. Crackers. Clay-eaters. Tackies. Mudsills.
Scalawags. Briar hoppers. Hillbillies. Low-downers. White niggers.
Degenerates. White trash. Rednecks. Trailer trash. Swamp people'
(Isenberg, 2016: 325). These names register the geographical
location of these lower classes and, not unlike Hanley's experience in Britain, these classed locations clearly register long after
they no longer apply. For example, though poor tenant farmers
in the USA at one point ate the clay from the field—earning the
name 'clay-eaters'—that clearly no longer applies, even if it is still
remembered and used to denigrate swathes of the white working
class in the USA. Isenberg's abiding conclusion to all of this is
that 'White trash is a central, if disturbing, thread in our national

narrative' (336), and its 'visibility and invisibility' testify to the hidden obsession in the USA with class.

In what I have discussed thus far, it would be easy to assume that classes are fixed in place, especially in light of the dominance of inherited capital, and that whilst people can move between classes, the classes themselves remain static in their definition and as a result of the forces that produce them. However, as August Carbonella and Sharryn Kasmir make plain, from an anthropological perspective 'a sense of the mutability of class is central to an adequate understanding of its continuing relevance' (2014: 3). Thus, whilst these academics want to dispense with traditional categorisations of the labouring classes—'the affluent worker, aristocracy of labor, labor elite, on the one side; dangerous classes, the great unwashed, lumpen-proletariat, surplus populations, on the other' (4)—they do not want to dispense with class, nor with the idea of a labouring class as a broad category. The way they manage this tightrope act is by zoning in on 'labor accumulation' that offers a 'a sustained focus on the continual making, unmaking, and remaking of labor forces and working classes—politically, culturally, and structurally—through the dual lens of dispossession and disorganization' (5), and finally resting on David Harvey's idea of '"accumulation by dispossession"' (Harvey qtd in Carbonella and Kasmir, 2014: 5). For these anthropologists, therefore, the labouring classes are signalled by their continuous dispossession. For Carbonella and Kasmir, 'dispossession [i]s simultaneously economic, martial, social, and cultural' (16). This entails thinking about the way that 'emergent forms of solidarity often give way to class fragmentation and exclusion, and the multiple ways that people are displaced from their social ties—the bonds of kin and community, however configured—leave many isolated, passive, or in despair' (17). This notion of dispossession will become a useful idea in my textual analyses, below.

By shifting the defining characteristics of the labouring class into dispossession, Carbonella and Kasmir acknowledge that the labouring classes are heterogeneous in their construction, just as Hanley signalled in her division of the working class into respectable and non-respectable. Moreover, Carbonella and Kasmir show that the production and labelling of class 'is inherently political', and that those labels have 'long-term implications for working-class formation and politics. The systemic power of capitalism may well lie in its ability to continually bring myriad forms of waged and unwaged labor into relation with one another across spatial scales' (2014: 13). That is to say, capitalism is so dominant because it is able to create a global system that connects the billionaires of Silicone Valley with the factory workers of Mumbai. These thoughts confirm again that, even from an anthropological perspective, the idea of class is a moveable feast, shifting according to geographical, political, and temporal vectors. They also confirm the possibility of people who are forgotten by capitalism and are therefore not naturally designated into any class at all. In response to this possibility, 'Rather than simply assuming that real people actually constitute capital's outside', Carbonella and Kasmir urge us to 'pay more attention to what relations of production and class fragmentation now look like' (26).

Amid these discussions, it is also important to think through how we can connect class to literature. On a basic level, as Piketty demonstrates, literary writing can document class structures. Piketty's arguments about capital wealth are closely endorsed by his readings of Honoré de Balzac's and Jane Austen's nineteenth-century novels. For example, he observes the importance of wealth and dowries in the decision-making process of Balzac's and Austen's characters, arguing that 'These and other novelists depicted the effects of inequality with a verisimilitude and evocative power that no statistical or theoretical analysis can match' (2017: 2) and that at the beginning of the nineteenth century 'the nature of wealth was relatively clear to all readers' (141). In *Literature and Capital* (2018), Thomas Docherty takes this analysis further by surpassing the presupposition that 'art holds the mirror up to nature', in Hamlet's terms (III.ii.20–1) and by inquiring into 'the conditions in which cultural capital is itself formed, through our institutions' in order to find a response to the 'politicization of letters' (2018: 2). By virtue of the latter, Docherty shows that he is concerned with how literature itself is involved in the politicised process of determining classes.

Docherty's thesis broadly is that written production—and eventually the production of something called 'literature' at the turn of the eighteenth century—is caught up in the historical emergence of capitalism. This process has continued into the marketisation of the university, in which the study of literature has become, by virtue of capital's infection of the university institution, a resource of the state rather than a tool for radical thought. Central to Docherty's ideas is the immaterial turn in capitalism—when central banks printed paper money to represent material wealth such as gold or a mortgaged house—that mimicked the work of writing, as when a poem artistically represents a material object. The immaterial (money; poetry) can confer value on the wealth it represents (the land). This was true as capitalism emerged three hundred years ago, and it is true now in this period of capitalism that represents 'a new phase of capital that is essentially neo-feudal and a rehabilitation of the value of "real estate"' (Docherty, 2018: 130). For Docherty,

> It is this that shapes so much of contemporary fiction, so much of our literature and so much of our cultural activity. Numerous economists identify it as the problem of inequality.
>
> Inequality in the contemporary moment is intimately related to the changing location of value and of wealth. Increasingly, there is an opposition between the two: wealth is material, found in land and property; value has had to occupy the terrain instead of the seemingly immaterial world.
>
> (51)

If, as Docherty argues, literature (with literary criticism) and capitalism are twinned at birth, and if capitalism puts literature and its criticism to ideological use to shore up its existence, then the renewed inequality through capital 'in land and property' as against wage-labour must not only be represented in literature (as Piketty sees it) but also be produced through literature.

Docherty's theories transform the liberating notion of Bourdieu's 'cultural capital' into something more insidious because 'the problem for the student of letters is that the very engagement with institutional forms of literature might itself turn out to be complicit with the contemporary authoritarian turn against culture and its power' (2018: 33). In other words, the perceived left-wing study of literature may in fact bolster right-wing economics and politics. This also means that Hanley's successful strategy of becoming socially mobile through her education consolidates the inequalities that led to class divisions and class antagonisms in the first place. This is especially true when we consider the obverse, that 'to be less well educated [… becomes] itself somehow intrinsically shameful' (Docherty, 2018: 156). Just as Hanley felt anxious and guilty about ascending the social ladder, so there is an emotion associated with failing to become socially mobile. This shame—different in scope from the gay shame I discussed above (see pp. 110–12)—is opposed in Docherty's terms by dignity (155). Since dignity renders humanity valuable, it is therefore part of capitalism that ascribes value to all kinds of objects; similarly, shame renders humanity worthless. Therefore, the shame of the immobile working class is an emotion created by capitalism itself, and the processes that produce and entrench the working classes in the first place. This produces a complex cycle in which the inability to read properly—the failure to go to university, that is—can make the capitally-produced working class feel ashamed. This, in turn, re-entrenches the high value that capitalism places on literature and the study of literature. This, finally, reveals again how literature has become weakened as a radical force against capitalism, where it once might have been used to critique and re-evaluate capitalism's value system and production of classes. Docherty summarises these ideas:

> Shame is a predetermining condition of what we understand as a form of human dignity, or human capital; and such shame relates directly to moral and cultural capital. Intrinsic to this is an argument about our contemporary institutions of value, and above all the institution that prides itself on the advancing of cultural capital, the 'public' university, an institution menaced by the logic of privatization.
>
> (2018: 155)

The continued encroachment of privatisation, not only of the university but of other public bodies (such as public space, the

NHS, or politics, which is now infiltrated by corporate lobbyists) means that the way that literature is now in service to capital will likely continue. Docherty proposes a 'radical geography' to get us out of this predicament—'a literary practice and activity that takes its task to be the discovery of language itself, and an imagining of how we might survive, living on through a mode of inhabiting the earth, an earth that must, now, be re-written' (2018: 233)—but this may seem some way distant.

In *Postcapitalism: A Guide to Our Future* (2015), Paul Mason proposes an alternative way of continuing into the future. Mason is, like many of the other thinkers I have quoted here, worried about the current state of affairs. 'Capitalism is more than just an economic structure or a set of laws', Mason writes (loc. 96–8). 'It is the *whole* system [...] needed to make a developed society function through markets and private ownership.' In this framework, it is clear that Mason is worried about the necessity and persistence of class antagonism, given that capitalism is systemic and not isolable. But Mason also thinks he is witnessing the opportunity to end capitalism's dominance. Whilst two hundred years ago, the proletariat could have brought capitalism to its knees (loc. 157–9), today there is a new kind of class emerging: 'By creating millions of networked people, financially exploited but with the whole of human intelligence one thumb-swipe away, info-capitalism has created a new agent of change in history: the educated and connected human being' (loc. 167–8). Mason's info-networked human coalition could form a supersize class,[5] and they would have the ability to come together in ways hitherto unseen in human history via the Internet. Whilst Piketty doubts the true usefulness of technology to act as a force for convergence of capital inequalities, for Mason, this info-networked class is the promise of postcapitalism.

In my discussions above I have noted that, for the most part, discussions of class are rooted in or emerge from the fact of capitalism. Moreover, the existence of class presupposes class antagonisms. This has manifested in a number of ways. For Piketty, class registers economic inequality. For Hanley class identity mediates sentiments of guilt and anxiety, depending on which way you are looking. Carbonella and Kasmir's labouring classes are characterised by dispossession, while Mason's futuristic info-networked human is a new class that has all it needs to possess in order to undo and undermine capitalism. For Docherty, class is not only driven and produced by capital, but literature has itself been co-opted to be complicit with the machinations of ever-growing capitalist inequality. It is only in Isenberg's consideration of class in the USA that capitalism is not the major force of production of 'white trash', although financial questions in colonial expansion are involved.

Another persistent topic across all these thinkers is the importance of geography in class formation and class antagonism. Whether Hanley's moving to a new house, or Isenberg's American landscape; whether Carbonella and Kasmir's global labouring classes, or Mason's online proto-class; or whether Docherty's neo-feudal capitalism, geography is an important element of contemporary readings of class. It will prove useful in my discussions below.

I will structure my following textual discussions into the following sections:

- Class and dispossession
- Class and social mobility
- Class and geography

Class and dispossession

Nana Kwame Adjei-Brenyah's *Friday Black* is a collection of twelve short stories that poke satirical fun at contemporary life in the USA. For example, the title story offers a mocking portrayal of the post-Thanksgiving US tradition of Black Friday on which retailers across the nation—and nowadays across the world—offer a host of discounts across their products. In representing this phenomenon on the page, Adjei-Brenyah's text reflects the remaking of the working class in the twenty-first century in the retail sector (Silver, 2014: 62). In 'Friday Black' the satirical and dystopic world is almost from the beginning made to seem inhuman and animalistic:

'Get to your sections!' Angela screams.

> Ravenous humans howl. Our gate whines and rattles as
> they shake and pull, their grubby fingers like worms through
> the grating.

(Adjei-Brenyah, 2018: 104)

The implication is that those outside the shutters are animalistic
zombies baying to get into the shop, and the narrator, Ice Man,
is there to placate them. Two pages later Ice Man describes the
scene as the shoppers enter: 'Have you ever seen people run
from a fire or gunshots? It's like that, with less fear and more
hunger' (Adjei-Brenyah, 2018: 106). Violence is only moments
away as 'a woman in her thirties takes off her heel and smashes a
child in the jaw with it just before he can grab the fleece' (107).
Even Ice Man's manager, Angela, is depicted hyperbolically in her
'scream[ing]' before the shutters open in the shop. This is the capitalist USA taken to its extreme; worryingly, it is an extreme not
only in description, as the scenes are immediately recognisable
from images on television screens in recent years.

Crucially, Ice Man is alienated from the objects that he is
selling as much as he is from those to whom he is selling.
Of Marx's descriptions of the four types of alienation,[6] Ice
Man appears to be alienated at least twice over, both from
the 'degraded and dehumanised' customers as much as he is
from 'the product of [his] own labour' (Spencer, 2014: 29–
30). Thus, he is a member of the labouring class whose labour
time produces more capital for the capitalist shop owner. As an
incentive to the workers, the shop owner has created 'a con-
test: whoever has the most sales gets to take home any coat in
the store'. This competition represents a kind of 'institutional
fix' to ward off potential labour-capital conflict—i.e. a strike,
or shop staff resignations as happens with Duo later in the story
(Adjei-Brenyah, 2018: 112–13)—that is designed to 'increase
real wages in step with increases in labour productivity' so as
to share the shop's '*economic gains*' (Silver, 2014: 55) with its
workers. That is not Ice Man's primary concern, however, as
he is instead focused on 'giv[ing] one of the SuperShell parkas
to my mother' (Adjei-Brenyah, 2018: 105). Buying power is

equated with human emotions and Ice Man announces that 'Soon I'll have a five-hundred-dollar jacket as proof to my mother that I'll love her forever' (108). Given the shoppers' own behaviours, and Ice Man's own high emotional valuation of the parka jacket, it is clear that in this world capitalism reigns, and the capitalist classes it produces (capitalist shop owners versus workers) follow suit.

Ice Man's family is suffering because of the vagaries and precarity of working-class life:

> I'm hungry. My family didn't really do the Thanksgiving thing this year—which felt like a relief except I missed my chance for stuffing. I'd offered to help with some of the shopping. My mom had lost her job. I make $8.50 an hour, but I saved. Mom, Dad, sister, me. But then we skipped the whole thing because we don't really like one another any-more. That was one of the side effects of lean living. We used to play games together. Now my parents yell about money, and when they aren't doing that, we are quiet.
>
> (Adjei-Brenyah, 2018: 110)

What Ice Man fails to mention is that 'lean living' is a side-effect of neo-liberal market capitalism that places the burden for equit-able income on individual shoulders. Both Carbonella and Kasmir and Silver—in their shared emphasis on how 'the making and remaking of [capitalist social] divisions is the lifeblood of labor accumulation' (Carbonella and Kasmir, 2014: 11) and 'the recur-rent making and *remaking* of working classes *across time and space*' (Silver, 2014: 47)—draw our attention to the ways in which Ice Man's family divisions are not necessarily a characteristic of Ice Man's family, but of a whole class within the capitalist system. Thus, Ice Man's family fallout is a consequence of the class antagonisms produced by capital's inequalities, demonstrating the way that 'dis-possession by accumulation' (in David Harvey's terms) leads to 'displace[ment] from […] social ties' such as 'bonds of kin and community' (Carbonella and Kasmir, 2014: 17).

The experience of 'dispossession by accumulation' is also vis-ible in other writing. Guy Gunaratne's *In Our Mad and Furious*

City offers us an insight into the formation of a working-class community in this vein. Through five discrete but interwoven first-person perspectives, the novel tells the story of two tumultuous days in London, starting with a lynching of a British soldier, and ending with a mass protest-cum-riot against anti-Islamic sentiment. For instance, Caroline is a middle-aged mother originally from Northern Ireland, now living on a council estate in west London. Her opening narrative follows her as she goes from her flat to a nearby laundrette. On the way, she displays her displeasure at what might be termed the 'non-respectable working class', as she complains to one of her neighbours that 'Every morning I'm made to step past your fucken bin-bags, I should inform the council. You'd do well to stop having so many babies if you can't mind the nappies' (Gunaratne, 2018: 14). This is Caroline's home where she had to move after her partner, John, left her and her son, so that she moved into 'That North Block with its grey and cold' (55). This is one of those estates, similar to where Hanley grew up, that was designed and built in the 1960s as 'a social experiment doomed to fail by dint of its population' (2016: 7). By 'quarantin[ing]' (7) working-class communities in this way, the individuals 'accumulate' a home space, but are dispossessed of a community. This is Caroline's experience of a home she 'had to move into […] with all the rest of the runaways' (Gunaratne, 2018: 54). Far from reworking community or re-planting community elsewhere, the geography of the council estate dispossesses the working-class citizens.

That does not mean that there are not opportunities to form new working-class community ties in response to dispossession. Returning to Adjei-Brenyah's 'Friday Black', it is clear that there are sympathies between the shoppers and the shop staff, illustrated when Ice Man eats lunch opposite a customer whom he had earlier helped. At first the woman is wary of Ice Man, 'hiss[ing] and show[ing] her pointy white teeth', before being assured by Ice Man telling her '"It's okay, […] I helped you"' (Adjei-Brenyah, 2018: 111). He then asks her how her shopping went (she killed two people as she managed to buy a new television), before 'toss[ing] the second [burger] to the woman. She catches it, tears the paper away, and eats gleefully' (112).

Setting aside the grotesque narrative because it is in keeping with the dystopic–satirical genre, I see this moment as particularly poignant. Remembering that Ice Man's experience of dispossession is felt in his hunger (quoted above) as a symptom of his family's degraded tie of kinship, it is therefore altruistic for Ice Man to give away his second burger to the customer sitting opposite him. This gesture is small and drowned by the drama of cannibalistic, zombie-like behaviours on Black Friday—but it is a gesture received gratefully and keenly, nonetheless. This sentiment is reiterated, in a more humane realism, at the end of the story 'In Retail':

> As I tally up the Levi's and think about how to not be Lucy, [a salesperson who committed suicide], this beautiful [customer] who doesn't speak my language will appear behind me and tap me on the shoulder. Out of her bag, she'll pull a red shirt with some flowers outlined with gemstones on it. She will show it to me. It will be so red that it will look like it might be hot to the touch. She'll say, '*Gracias, gracias*,' a few more times and tap my shoulder in parting, and I'll say, '*De nada, de nada*,' which will be a lie, because she is everything.
> (Adjei-Brenyah, 2018: 164)

This community of the dispossessed represents the saving grace in *Friday Black*'s repeated stories of capital dispossession.

It is also worth examining the racial element in working-class USA. In 'Zimmer Land',[7] the narrator Zay wears a mechanised body suit as he walks around a Disney-fied suburb called 'Cassidy Lane', pretending to be a neighbour who could equally be a stranger—this 'module' is designed to 'entertain' (Adjei-Brenyah, 2018: 95). The punters 'Pay-to-Play' (91) the role of suburban citizens when they encounter Zay walking the streets. Invariably, the punters 'kill' Zay in a clear evocation of the Martin–Zimmerman tragedy. The theme park 'Zimmer Land' and the Cassidy Lane module have been designed with easing class antagonisms in mind, as Heland, the park's founder, testifies when claiming that 'Zimmer Land was the "next step in the evolving face of social interconnectivity and welfare promotion"' (99). In other words, it tries to bridge the gap between the white US community that is threatened by the prospect of an errant Black community that is perceived as dispossessing the white community of their sovereign space.

The story offers no easy solutions, and this is the lesson about Black–white inter-class struggle that I take from the story. By the end of the narrative, Heland has introduced the possibility of children taking part in 'Cassidy Lane', much to the consternation of Zay and his colleagues. The story closes with Zay being beaten up by a man who has 'come to shoot me so many times it's almost like we're family' (Adjei-Brenyah, 2018: 102), and this time the punter's son is watching. Whereas before, Zay has activated his mechanised body suit and pretended to 'die', on this occasion Zay 'put[s] the trigger on the ground' as he 'get[s] up slowly'. Zay 'jump[s] up, [and] push[es the man's] arms away'. In spite of Zay's clear refusal to prepare to be shot, nonetheless 'the patron pulls his gun from his waist' (103) and tells his child to stay back. At that point, the story ends, almost as if Zay's inevitable murder takes place at that point, thereby ending the narrative. The story alerts us that, whilst the working classes were able to forge some kind of kinship in 'Friday Black' and 'In Retail', it appears impossible when race is also involved. Moreover, as Isenberg describes, the white punter's class goes completely unspecified throughout the story, redoubling the idea that race has superseded class in US discourses of inter-community discontent. 'Zimmer Land' is thus 'ignoring the pathological character of class-centered power relations as part of the American republic's political inheritance' (Isenberg, 2016: 324) in favour of depicting the Black classed experience.

The abiding and urgent topic of this section, then, is not just about how capitalism produces class differences, but also how capitalism presents moments of both the unworking and the reworking working-class community. The economic exchanges described in 'Friday Black' and 'In Retail' are both alienating to labourer and customer alike, but they do open up to the possibility of inter-human connections. However, 'Zimmer Land'

and Caroline's briefly described experience of the council estate demonstrate the problems of feelings of geographic dispossession and, in the former case, the impossibility of forging new class communities when another barrier—this time race—becomes visible.

Class and social mobility

When considering social mobility, it is important to bear in mind the importance Bourdieu places on education in terms of cultural capital, because

> With the academic qualification, a certificate of cultural competence which confers on its holder a conventional, constant, legally guaranteed value with respect to culture, social alchemy produces a form of cultural capital which has a relative autonomy vis-à-vis, the cultural capital he effectively possesses at a given moment in time. […] It institutes cultural capital by collective magic[.]
>
> (1986: 248)

Educational success can thus be a way of becoming (upwardly) socially mobile. Critically, in Bourdieu's understanding, the educational qualification does not just provide access to temporary social mobility, but to a kind of magically permanent state of social change. Or, in Hanley's terms,

> I don't pay money for my university privileges, paying instead with social and cultural capital. University got me to a place where I could make use of who I knew as well as what I knew. Over the years I've accrued advantages like loyalty points, the bonuses every time I've moved a notch up the social ladder.
>
> (2016: 223)

In her experience of social mobility, though it produced anxiety (xiv), it nonetheless sets doors ajar and has kept them open ever since. Against this utopic vision of education, we must also bear in mind Docherty's idea that, since using education as a path to social mobility is now clichéd, we should be wary of what the cliché continues to hide. This includes the shame of the disenfranchised and under-educated, as well as the retrenchment of middle-class domination by virtue of privileging the educated classes and denigrating the working classes (Docherty, 2018: 156).

Sally Rooney's *Normal People* offers an example of all elements of this educational conundrum: How educational success breeds social mobility, how it produces anxiety on the part of the successful, shame on those who fail or refuse to succeed, and the doubling down of middle-class domination. *Normal People* tells the story of Marianne and Connell, both from a small town in the west of Ireland, who eventually go to Trinity College in Dublin to study where they also have an on–off relationship. Despite their mutual attraction, the differences between Marianne and Connell are stark. Marianne is from a wealthy middle-class family who lives in a nice house with a cleaner. Connell's family includes just him and his working mother who is a cleaner—at Marianne's house.

A discussion over what subjects to study at university takes place just after Marianne and Connell have slept together for the first time. Marianne thinks Connell should study literature but Connell demurs. 'I'm not sure about the job prospects, though', he tells Marianne; in a few pages he flippantly announces that 'I don't care that much about getting a job anyway'. Marianne, regardless, says, 'Oh, who cares? The economy's fucked anyway' (Rooney, 2018: 20, 27). This kind of comment makes sense coming from Marianne for whom money has been readily available, and where the decision about what to study can take place outside a market economy; capital wealth, as Piketty demonstrated, has a habit of being inherited, and therefore represents a stable form of wealth. For Connell, by contrast, the decision is tacitly linked to his 'employability' after college, and therefore the decision about what to study takes on greater significance because of his working-class background. Already in *Normal People* we can witness the tying together of the classed identity, education narrative, and the economy, thereby acknowledging Docherty's point that to study literature nowadays is to enter into a marketplace that has capitalised on literary study:

> [W]here literature is institutionalized, the economy is structured around cultural capital, and not on the primacy of such individual incomes. In this latter case, the value of literature is itself instrumentalized: a literary education becomes the means through which an individual progresses—via the claim of cultural capital—to demand or command a higher salary in the workplace.
>
> (2018: 213)

Whilst Connell has not yet appreciated the way in which the institution and study of literature have already begun to respond to his worry about job prospects, it is nonetheless already hinted at in the text.

The decision to study at Trinity is complicated by Connell's social habits. The complication leads to a non-clinical schizophrenia in which 'he's consumed by a sense that he is in fact two separate people, and soon he will have to choose which person to be on a full-time basis'. This is because 'If he went to college in Galway he could stay with the same social group, really, and live the life he has always planned on'. By contrast, Marianne would be with him in Trinity and 'He would start going to dinner parties and having conversations about the Greek bailout' (Rooney, 2018: 26). Here the shame is not so much about going to university, but about going to a select university in the metropolis (Dublin), which will inevitably be accompanied by a change in social group and therefore behaviour. It is a different shame, but shame nonetheless. In Adjei-Brenyah's story 'The Lion & the Spider', the narrator's shame in a similar situation is expressed as 'anguish' (2018: 121). This is because the narrator has had the opportunity to go to college taken away from him because his father has returned to his native Nigeria to 'see to' 'some business' (115).

However, Adjei-Brenyah's narrator does not have the heart to tell his colleagues that he could no longer go to college: 'So far as they knew, I was deciding between a school upstate, a school in the city, and another one in Connecticut' (2018: 121). Indeed, as it turns out, his colleagues are supportive of the possibility of his becoming a college student and thereby leaving the working classes behind. Underpinning the story is the narrator's absent father. Not only is he absent during the moments of the story, but the story flashes back to a time when his father, due to take the narrator and his friend to the cinema, out of impatience drives off without them. As such, the greatest social and interpersonal struggle in 'The Lion & the Spider' is between the father and son, and not between classes. In this, the generational struggle appears to have replaced the class struggle, as Piketty suggested it might (2017: 29).

The end of the story resolves with the father and son silently mending their relationship, but not before the narrator has internally remarked, '*There's food in the fridge because of me. I went to prom. I imagined you gone forever, and I survived*' (Adjei-Brenyah, 2018: 127). The narrator thus celebrates his successful labour by reconciling with his father who, equally, now respects his son: '"Yes, he's a big man. […] I'll be waiting in the lot. You need a ride, right?"' (127). The generational conflict is resolved, and only now the narrator will be able to go on to college where he will be able to transition to a different social class. Critically, though the story is *about* class mobility and aspiration, the story values endeavour and respectability over and above the ability to be socially mobile. These ideas are endorsed by the fable of the lion and the spider that is also told in pieces during the story itself: The spider outwits the lion when she beats him in a race to the top of the mountain. It is a story that prioritises guile over natural ability, thereby perhaps seeing a way beyond the inherited class system that could be perceived as static.

This is not the way in which Marianne and Connell's story resolves itself. Far from bringing them together in social terms, the experience of Trinity at times drives a wedge between the couple. For example, Connell 'understands now that his classmates are not like him. It's easy for them to have opinions and to express them with confidence. […] They just move through the world in a different way' (Rooney, 2018: 68). Connell has thus begun to witness the lie that institutions tell about the value of a literary education 'because it claims that everyone is always already in equal possession of the truth, their "own" and "owned" truth. This is their capital' (Docherty, 2018: 109): Higher classes nevertheless maintain a greater claim to truth. As if in ratification of this principle, Marianne is one of those who, now away from the school grounds, is popular while Connell is 'lonely' (Rooney, 2018: 73). Their inherited class positions shape their educational experience.

However, Connell has also now begun to benefit from living in the metropolis and studying at Trinity, getting a job by virtue of a college friend. After all, 'Rich people look out for each other, and being Marianne's best friend and suspected sexual partner has elevated Connell to the status of rich-adjacent' (Rooney, 2018: 99). Whilst Connell benefits from the association, he nonetheless feels uncomfortable with his outsider-ness at university. This comes to a head when both he and Marianne have been offered scholarships for their third year. At a hangover-recovery breakfast the morning after the formal dinner announcing their success, the two of them finally talk about how they are 'from very different backgrounds, class-wise'. Marianne subsequently ascribes justifiable feelings to Connell such as 'resent[ment]' at her and 'guilt[]' (173–5) for his success. Importantly, these ideas are only aroused in response to getting the scholarships—that is, by capitalising on their education—and not in response to attending university: 'Everything is possible now because of the scholarship' (159). Connell and Marianne thus most feel their class differences when they begin to fulfil the logic of the capitalised university as described by Docherty.

In the final pages Marianne's own resentment is aroused when Connell is accepted on to a master's degree in New York—a degree for which she did know he had applied. Again, Connell is undecided whether he wants to go, telling Marianne that 'I wouldn't even be here if it wasn't for you' (Rooney, 2018: 265). Her response is telling as she moves from anger to pride:

> It's true, she thinks, he wouldn't be. He would be some-
> where else entirely, living a different kind of life. He would

be different with women even, and his aspirations for love would be different. And Marianne herself, she would be another person completely. [...] All these years they've been like two little plants sharing the same plot of soil, growing around one another, contorting to make room, taking certain unlikely positions. But in the end she has done something for him, she's made a new life possible, and she can always feel good about that.

(265)

Whilst the story of Marianne and Connell is about young people whose lives are entwined for changing reasons—from class antagonism to shared educational aspiration and success—their stories also move beyond a classed dynamic. Beyond the possibilities of education, Marianne recognises that *she* has become the agent of change in Connell's life, helping him to engage with the possibilities that a literary education can offer him. Connell, having once again put the decision in the hands of Marianne ('I don't know what to do, he says. Say you want me to stay and I will' [265]), is given no chance to respond to Marianne's decision that 'You should go' because 'I'll always be here' (26). Ironically, Marianne's final decision—to stay in Ireland while Connell changes, yet again, in New York—actually makes possible a reading of the text that education favours the working classes given Connell's ability to take full, capitalised advantage of his education. Marianne, by contrast, lacks aspiration and therefore lacks the opportunity to change her lot.

In this discussion of education, it has not been easy to isolate a particular bias or prejudice in the texts. In both 'The Lion & the Spider' and *Normal People*, working-class characters have had the opportunity to use education as a springboard to change their classed existence. But it has neither been an easy decision, nor has it had (in Rooney's text) the expected effect. If the texts recommend anything, it is an open mind to the possibilities of social mobility through education and a refusal to treat the clichéd social-ascendancy-through-education motif as fixed in its depiction.

Class and geography

In Novuyo Rosa Tshuma's *House of Stone*, set in Zimbabwe, Zamani is a lodger in a house that his Uncle Fani used to own, and Zamani feels that he should have inherited the house from his uncle. The narrative is told from Zamani's perspective and explores the history of not only Zamani's family but also the Mlambo family—father Abednego, mother Agnes, and son Bukhosi—with whom he lodges, as well as Zimbabwe's recent history as a nation emerging from colonial rule into a difficult independence. Whilst much of what it presents merits scrutiny under the banner of postcolonialism—just as I attempted on pp. 66–9 above—there is also an underlying topic of dispossession that directs our attention towards the classed elements of the text.

Zamani is dispossessed materially by the Mlambo family. When he returns to Bulawayo from London where he has been studying, he is 'shocked [...] to realize how much things had changed, inside me but also outside. [...] It was in that state that I found the Mlambos living in my Uncle Fani's house' (Tshuma, 2018: 321). This deterritorialisation has taken place because of two inheritances, one failed and one successful. First, Uncle Fani's inheritance has failed to pass the house on to Zamani. Zamani thus fails to profit from the nature of capital wealth as it is invested in bricks and mortar. Second, and by contrast, it is Uncle Zacchaeus—Abednego Mlambo's brother—whose will grants the Mlambos sufficient capital to buy the house. '[H]is inheritance, as per his will,' tells Zamani, 'went to my surrogate father [Abednego], mostly in the dismaying form of boxes upon boxes of books, but also, thankfully, in the way of a sizable chunk of money. And thus, the Mlambos were able to [...] buy my Uncle Fani's bigger house[.]' (321). Zamani is thus made homeless and dispossessed by the Mlambos.

It is worth recognising the nature of the inheritance that grants the Mlambos the opportunity to invest in capital wealth. Not only is it the money that Docherty would recognise as 'an immaterialization of capital in which all that is solid land melts into the softness of paper' (2018: 35), but 'boxes upon boxes of books' that, thus willed, represent the capitalisation of literature: the conversion of literary production into some kind of capital. In Docherty's argument, these two objects are thus twinned at an embryonic level. Moreover, this capitalised literature represents an idealised *national* literature, given Zacchaeus's position as a poet who was 'invited to perform at [Zimbabwe's] Independence Celebrations' (Tshuma, 2018: 131) just after Robert Mugabe's Independence Speech. To this end, Zacchaeus's willed boxes of books represent the idealised turn of Zimbabwe's national character towards independent definition as a result of an emerging national literature (Docherty, 2018: 90). Zamani is thus dispossessed by an idealised (yet failed, since Zacchaeus dies unheralded) attempted formation of cultural capital.

Before he even knows that he has been made homeless in Bulawayo, Zamani already begins to recognise the cultural dispossession at work in Zimbabwe. Zamani has made repeated references throughout the novel to 'hi-story', which resembles the idea of 'history' closely enough, but which is finally defined when he narrates his return to Zimbabwe: '[T]hat fiction of many versions'. The definition comes at this point because 'When I returned from my travels […] I found the country living in hi-story. Everywhere, odes to the past were being composed, sung, recited; here, the past lived more vividly than the present' (Tshuma, 2018: 317). Zamani's 'hi-story' might very well be better defined as the battle over what Walter Benjamin famously declared in his eighteen 'Theses on the Philosophy of History': 'There is no document of civilisation which is not at the same time a document of barbarism' (1999: 248). Elsewhere in *House of Stone* this is illustrated in an argument over the 'optics' of 'truth' (Tshuma, 2018: 68). In this vein, we can argue that Zamani is not only materially dispossessed, but he is also dispossessed of a history, made rootless both in geographical–physical and metaphysical terms.

The focus on this aspect of his dispossession is redoubled in two ways. First, by the consideration of his self, and what he might be able to achieve by virtue of the writing of the present narrative. He considers that he is 'cleaving my being from the present to form new bonds with the past' by virtue of 'hi-story', because of which he wonders whether 'I will succeed in saying of the past, "Thus I willed it"' (Tshuma, 2018: 317). The particular use of the verb 'will', in light of the context of his material dispossession, cannot simply be read as a volitional 'will'—'I wanted it to be this way'—but must also be read in terms of inheritance and wealth—'I wanted to create this future narrative legacy'. In other words, Zamani is also interested in gifting his literature to the nation's cultural capital storehouse.

The second way of critiquing Zamani's metaphysical dispossession is the manner in which his Uncle Fani's house was sold. Zamani records that the house was sold, not as part of his Uncle Fani's probate, but 'to one Abednego Mlambo by a Mr Edward Msimangu, registered owner' (Tshuma, 2018: 324). Zamani's dispossession by Old Edward, a former neighbour, is enabled by the fact that Uncle Fani had never had proof of his ownership of the house 'ever since the concentration camp' where Zamani was conceived, and from where Uncle Fani stole him away as a newborn. Zamani writes that 'I suspect the man [Old Edward] knew this, that there was no title deed and no record of an identity document. [...] Such were the new times in the House of Stone[8]' (325). These 'new times' supplant the old times when Zamani could have laid legitimate claim to the Mlambos' house; instead, a cultural and material dispossession now characterises his experience. Geographically, he is deterritorialised in a process not dissimilar from the British colonial practices that dominated the former Rhodesia.

Zamani also makes explicit mention of the way the Mlambos have turned the house into a middle-class home. Though 'The sitting room was never this cramped when Uncle Fani and I lived here', it is because 'We didn't have these plump sofas that lull you to sleep; we didn't have my surrogate father's armchair; and we certainly didn't have the armchair Bukhosi used to occupy' (Tshuma, 2018: 60). Zamani's temptation to complain about these changes is curbed by the confession that 'growing up we were poor [...] and I yearned, whenever his weeping would bounce off the walls and reverberate in our sparsely furnished house, for the comfort of a plush sofa to cushion the sound' (61). Zamani envies these accoutrements of wealth, particularly as they reflect the existence of a happy family, whereas without the furniture, Zamani's experience of living in the home with Uncle Fani is decidedly worse. These home improvements are not, of course, without political ramifications. For instance, Zamani describes the sofa as 'Mama Agnes's struggle for middle-class relevance' (61), and later notes that, 'for the Mlambos, having moved from Entumbane to Luveve, [they] had moved up in the world, and to celebrate this rise in middle-class-hood, had not only acquired the cobalt kitchen table and the kitchen cupboard, but also installed a small boiler' (327–8). These conspicuous consumptions are, according to Russell Belk, to be regarded as the 'ultimate status marker' (2000: 14) for newly-wealthy Zimbabweans. Moreover, the purchase of a house and furnishing it represents behaviour typical of the emerging nouveaux riches in Zimbabwe (5–7), even to the extent of 'striving to materially emulate a global peer group, with special attention to the British and Americans' (14). It would be a stretch to describe the Mlambos as nouveau riche, but their behaviour nonetheless places them within an emerging Zimbabwean middle class who, apparently counter to the national postcolonial drive, want to bridge the geographical divide between the Global South and the Global North. As Carbonella and Kasmir and Silver urged us to recognise, therefore, this working class–middle class transition might appear to be hyper-local, affecting only Zamani, but it is nonetheless connected to a more global capitalism 'in [a] state of continuing collaboration and/or tension with wider class formations, social movements, political networks, and forms of institutional power' (2014: 21). The story of the House of Stone is therefore about much more than either Zamani's homelessness or Zimbabwe.

House of Stone ends with Zamani's confession to the reader that he brought about Bukhosi's disappearance; Zamani is therefore a cuckoo in the Mlambo nest, dispossessing the family of their son. The given reasons for Zamani's betrayal of the Mlambos' trust are interesting:

> Having a perfectly nice family of his own, [Bukhosi] still saw fit to push me out of my filial relationship with Dumo [a

political affiliate]. I, who had already lost everything, losing
not only my past, but also my Uncle Fani, who had tethered
me, at least, to a semblance of a present; losing in the process,
also, all illusion of substantial family roots in which to build
a respectable future.

(Tshuma, 2018: 358)

Aside from turning the tables on Bukhosi and implying that
he, rather than Zamani, is the cuckoo, Zamani's tirade deploys
vocabulary to do with dispossession (e.g. loss) that he immediately associates with the notions of a past, present, and future.
Not just any future, however: a 'respectable' future. This recalls
Hanley's experience of class that, though in a different locale and
slightly different historical period, nonetheless brings her experience of class-transition into dialogue with Zamani's. Yes, Zamani's
story is about grief and benefits from a postcolonial reading, but
it is also rooted in class discourses that bespeak his geographical
dispossession, both on a local level in Luveve, and on a global
level, by virtue of the fallout of anti-colonial revolution.

It is worth asking whether Zamani's narrative—either the one
in which he is a victim, or the one in which he is the murderous
criminal stealing back his place in his Uncle Fani's house—
constitutes what Docherty labelled 'radical geography':

a literary practice and activity that takes its task to be the discovery of language itself, and an imagining of how we might
survive, living on through a mode of inhabiting the earth, an
earth that must, now, be re-written.

(2018: 233)

I suggest that, by prioritising either side of Zamani's fate, *House of
Stone* exemplifies Docherty's radical geography because Zamani's
is a literary practice that seeks *to right* and *to write* Zimbabwe's true
and unwritten histories. In doing so, he tells stories of dispossession and of 'inhabiting the earth', albeit in transgressive ways. To
this end, it is worth recalling the text's final lines when Zamani
turns to Agnes and Abednego, now calling them 'Mother and
Father', and asks them politely, '"When shall I move in?"' His due

inheritance has already had its story rewritten by the Mlambo family, but now he has succeeded in rewriting it once more.

In this chapter, I have described the many ways of approaching class in hyper-contemporary literature. Crucially, whilst theoretical approaches differ—especially through their disciplinary differences, from cultural criticism to anthropology, from history to economics—one thing is clear: Class is a meta-category of capitalism, and capitalist classes are characterised by antagonism. Thus in my engagements with the hyper-contemporary writing, I have explored the antagonisms of purchasing power, of social mobility, and of geographical dispossession. Whether *Friday Black*'s satirical narratives of consumer behaviour are better or worse than *House of Stone*'s radical geography, or whether *Normal People*'s struggle to depict social mobility is more or less important than *In Our Mad and Furious City*'s depiction of a council estate in west London, is now up for debate.

Notes

1 For Marx, the capitalist is essentially masculine.
2 Excluding the top centile, i.e. the wealthiest one per cent.
3 The 'non-respectable' working class to which Hanley refers has also been written about in Owen Jones's 2011 *Chavs: The Demonization of the Working Class.*
4 Hanley's use of this term comes from Martin Heidegger's essay 'Building Dwelling Thinking' (1954) from his *Poetry, Language, Thought* (2013: 141–59).
5 Whilst none of the hyper-contemporary texts I am examining including a postcapitalist class of this type, an example of a text that does explore the info-networked class is Ernest Cline's 2011 *Ready Player One.*
6 Spencer details the four types of alienation:

> First, workers are alienated from the product of their own labour because it is owned by the capitalists who hire them for a specified period of time. They are unable to use the things that they produce to sustain life, since these things are the property of capitalists. [...] Second, it is argued that workers are alienated from the activity of work itself. In

working for capitalists, workers relinquish control over the direction of their own labour within production. What and how work is done is decided upon by capitalists, not workers. […] The third dimension of alienation is the estrangement of workers from their 'species being'. Marx viewed the ability to participate in creative work as an essential part of human nature. The fact that under capitalism workers are unable to exercise any direct control over the product and process of labour means that they are effectively denied the opportunity to work creatively. […] Finally, Marx referred to the alienation of workers from their fellow human beings. Workers confront their own estrangement from their 'species being' in the lives of other workers who are equally degraded and dehumanised by the experience of work.

(2014: 29–30)

7   This title is a direct reference to George Zimmerman, a neighbourhood watchman in Florida who murdered a Black youth, Trayvon Martin, out of a perceived threat. Martin was unarmed.

8   'House of Stone'—the novel's title—is a loose translation of the name 'Zimbabwe' in the native Shona language.

Bibliography

Adjei-Brenyah, Nana-Kwame, *Friday Black* (London: riverrun, 2018).

Belk, Russell, 'Consumption patterns of the new elite in Zimbabwe', no. 288 (William Davidson Institution), 2000, https://deepblue.lib.umich.edu/bitstream/handle/2027.42/39672/wp288.pdf?sequence=3&isAllowed=y [accessed 14 March 2020].

Benjamin, Walter, *Illuminations*, trans. by Harry Zorn, ed. by Hannah Arendt (London: Pimlico, 1999).

Bourdieu, Pierre, 'The forms of capital', *Handbook of Theory and Research for the Sociology of Education*, ed. by John G. Richardson (New York, NY: Greenwood Press, 1986), pp. 241–58.

Carbonella, August, and Sharryn Kasmir, 'Toward a global anthropology of labor', *Blood and Fire: Toward a Global Anthropology of Labor*, ed. by Sharryn Kasmir and August Carbonella (New York, NY: Berghahn, 2014), pp. 1–29.

Cline, Ernest, *Ready Player One* (London: Century, 2011).

Docherty, Thomas, *Literature and Capital* (London: Bloomsbury, 2018).

Gunaratne, Guy, *In Our Mad and Furious City* (London: Tinder Press, 2018).

Hanley, Lynsey, *Respectable: The Experience of Class* (London: Allen Lane, 2016).

Heidegger, Martin, *Poetry, Language, Thought*, trans. by Albert Hofstadter (New York, NY: Harper Perennial, 2013) [1971].

Isenberg, Nancy, *White Trash: The 400-Year Untold History of Class in America* (New York, NY: Viking, 2016).

Marx, Karl, *Capital: A Critique of Political Economy*, trans. by Ben Fowkes, 3 vols, vol. 1 (London: Penguin, 1990) [1867].

Marx, Karl, and Friedrich Engels, *The Manifesto of the Communist Party*, trans. by Samuel Moore (London: Pluto Press, 2008) [1848].

Mason, Paul, *Postcapitalism: A Guide to Our Future* (London: Penguin, 2015).

Perry, Sarah, *Melmoth* (London: Serpent's Tail, 2018).

Piketty, Thomas, *Capital in the Twenty-First Century*, trans. by Arthur Goldhammer (Cambridge, MA: Belknap Press, 2017) [2013].

Rooney, Sally, *Normal People* (London: Faber and Faber, 2018).

Shakespeare, William, *Hamlet*, ed. by Ann Thompson and Neil Taylor, The Arden Shakespeare Third Series (London: Arden Shakespeare, 2006).

Silver, Beverly, 'Theorising the working class in twenty-first-century global capitalism', *Workers and Labour in a Globalised Capitalism: Contemporary Themes and Theoretical Issues*, ed. by Maurizio Atzeni (Basingstoke: Palgrave Macmillan, 2014), pp. 46–69.

Spencer, David A., 'Marx and Marxist views on work and the capitalist labour process', *Workers and Labour in a Globalised Capitalism: Contemporary Themes and Theoretical Issues*, ed. by Maurizio Atzeni (Basingstoke: Palgrave Macmillan, 2014), pp. 25–45.

Tshuma, Novuyo Rosa, *House of Stone* (London: Atlantic Books, 2018).

5   Reviews; or, popularising the canon

Theories summary: It is rare that we come to any text with zero preconceptions. Among the **paratexts** included in a text are its cover, its artwork, choice of fonts and design, as well as the prominence of the author's title, among others. As a subcategory, **peritexts** are parts of the text that are used by the publisher to sell the text. Reviews, by virtue of showing the text off to the public, become such peritexts. Professional reviewers in newspapers and literary magazines think of themselves as mediators between the reader and text; meanwhile, there is huge growth in amateur reviewing online. For example, Amazon uses 'helpfulness' rankings to shape purchasing decisions, while **socially-mediated review sites** like Goodreads showcase millions of reviews. **Ratings** are also important but are used differently. On Amazon, where purchasing is a priority, more extreme ratings are used; however, on Goodreads ratings are more evenly distributed across the 1–5 scale. Ultimately, the kind of review and the topics it mentions can confer a sense of **literariness** on a text, and it is interesting to note how a text is reviewed and what focuses are consistent across different platforms.

The myth has been busted many times over, but I'll say it again: Yes, we do judge books by their covers. 'A beautiful cover caught my eye first,' begins Jane's review on Goodreads of Laura Wood's 2018 *A Sky Painted Gold*.[1] But it is more than the cover that catches our readerly eyes, including the author's name, the title, the title's placement on the cover, the use of endorsements (i.e. snippet review extracts from 'famous' people), the colours, the images, the book's tactility, the visibility of the book's spine on a bookshelf. Book series will often have the same styles applied, such as in J.K. Rowling's *Harry Potter* series: It is possible to date someone's first engagement with the texts based on the editions they have and the cover illustrations that have, over time, begun to model the characters on their film avatars. Publishers and imprints equally have their house style. It is easy to spot the differences between a Penguin and a Ladybird book on a shelf, or a children's book and a book for adults. As semioticians have long argued, all kinds of communication constitute a language, and the composition of a book cover is no exception.

For Gérard Genette, all these elements of a book cover are 'accompanying productions' which 'surround' and 'extend' the text itself and '*present* it, in the usual sense of this verb but also in the strongest sense: to make present, to ensure the text's presence in the world, its "reception" and consumption in the form […] of a book' (1997: 1): what he calls 'paratexts'. He also discusses 'peritexts'—the elements that the publisher in particular has included in the book's production (16 ff.). In *Marketing Literature: The Making of Contemporary Writing in Britain*, Claire Squires extends the idea of peritexts into the process of marketing a book. For Squires, 'marketing is the summation of multiple agencies operating within the marketplace, by which contemporary writing is represented and interpreted, and in which contemporary writing is actively constructed'. To this end, marketing 'is in a very real sense, *the making of contemporary writing*' (2007: 3). Marketing does not just include the work done by the publishers or the marketeers, argues Squires, but also includes the work that serves to market the book, such as book reviews. In this chapter, book reviews are my topic of interest, particularly as they register and convey an idea of quality: They mark out a text as either 'good' or 'bad' literature.

There are two types of book review: the professional and the amateur. Commonly, these reviews both appear online, with professional reviews also appearing offline, as in newsprint or literary periodicals such as the *Times Literary Supplement* and the *New York Times Book Review*. Given the different scope of the reviews for these publications, each necessarily has a different style and etiquette. Moreover, the reviewers see themselves differently. Squires records that 'literary journalists guide the readers of their own newspapers towards certain titles and […] may also assist decisions in a shop or library about which title to purchase or borrow. The reviewer then is a mediator' (2007: 65–6). It is easy to see how the reviewer may unintentionally act on behalf of the publisher's marketing team by acting as a guide and mediator. A marketeer once told me how book review editors at newspapers receive around 200 books on average per week from publishers seeking publicity; there is no feasible way to review all of these books, so the book journalist tends only to write about books they deem as meriting a good review. Professional book reviews, as such, rarely criticise a book, and therefore 'the choices that [the book journalist] makes are highly indicative of the processes of marketing and the concomitant creation of reading communities' (Squires, 2007: 66): The journalist's review becomes part of the book's marketing apparatus, and thus *peri*textual—a part of the text. This also positions the reviewer as 'part of the representational processes of marketing, including sales' (66). In some ways we might see the reviewer as a kind of co-author of the text *as it is received by the reader*.

And so, it is most often in the host of online spaces to review books—be it on Internet-based retailers like Amazon or socially mediated reading communities like Goodreads—that we come across the negative book review. Tom Lin *et al.* note in their article about Internet book reviews that the 'The lack of negative book reviews changed following the emergence of the World Wide Web. Browsing reader reviews on the Internet shows that negative reviews are located throughout the review list' (2005: 463). Judith Chevalier and Dina Mayzlin also note that 'an incremental negative review is more powerful in decreasing book sales than an incremental positive review is in increasing sales' (2006: 346). This alone signifies the different tenor of Internet book reviews, and it is in part or in whole a consequence of two features of the Internet. First, the level of online noise and second, the social nature of online communication. With regard to the former, in order to be 'heard' online, a reviewer has to be able to rise above the huge numbers of book reviews: '[T]he number of Internet book reviews is hundreds and even thousands of times that of the number of reviews published in print versions' (Lin *et al.*, 2005: 461). Moreover, online reviews replicate the way that 'word of mouth' operates in an offline setting. One way of discriminating between reviews is to judge their helpfulness.

Helpful reviews are of interest because the evidence overwhelmingly shows that reviews shape purchasing decisions. Moreover, reviews of books shape purchasing decisions in distinct ways in comparison with other goods. Susan Mudambi and David Schuff have explored how reviews affect purchasing decisions and use the notion of 'search goods' and 'experience goods' as their metric, noting that 'Products can be described as existing along a continuum from pure search goods to pure experience goods' and that 'search goods are those for which consumers have the ability to obtain information on product quality prior to purchase, while experience goods are products that require sampling or purchase in order to evaluate product quality' (2010: 187). Mudambi and Schuff describe how, in general, 'for experience goods, reviews with extreme ratings are less helpful than reviews with moderate ratings, although [by contrast] this effect was not seen for search goods'. However, they notice how when it comes to books, 'moderate book reviews are less helpful than extreme book reviews'. Thus, 'Although books can be considered experience goods, they are a rather unique product category' (195). We must therefore pay particular attention to the ways in which book reviews affect readers in ways different to reviews of other products and purchasers of those products. For a start, the importance of review extremity suggests that emotions have a key role to play in choosing a book.

The book's product categorisation is not the only factor that affects purchasing decisions. Mudambi and Schuff also researched what constitutes a 'helpful' review, given the prominence of these types of reviews on Amazon.com and other online retailers. They 'define a helpful customer review as *a peer-generated product evaluation that facilitates the consumer's purchase decision process*' (2010: 186). Therefore it is not sufficient for there to be a positive or a negative review of a book for it to be helpful; in order for a review to affect the purchasing decision, it must have 'depth'—'the extensiveness of the reviewer comments' (187)—although even a review's depth becomes more or less important depending on the product type (i.e. a search good or an experience good). Pei-Yu Chen *et al.* also researched how review helpfulness impacts on a purchasing decision. They conclude that when purchasers are able to 'rate' a book review for its helpfulness, this can persuade or dissuade other purchasers to buy a book. Moreover, whilst 'higher ratings are associated with higher book sales, higher quality reviews (i.e. reviews with the high proportion of helpful votes) have a stronger impact on consumer purchase decisions than other reviews do' (2008: 23). This is especially true for books that are considered less popular prior to the purchase (21). It is not just the review itself that is important, but also how others have rated it. On Amazon, potential purchasers can organise their reviews according to helpfulness, and some reviewers are even given the title of 'Top 50 Reviewer' or 'Top 500 Reviewer' based on their helpfulness across the site.

The second element worth considering in relation to Internet book reviews is the socially mediated way that reviews are disseminated, and not only through online retailers. In her study of Goodreads, a socially mediated book review website, Lisa Nakamura shows how social media and book discussions can be successfully paired—meaning commercial success for Goodreads, and success for the more than six million readers who use the site. In more detail, Nakamura summarises how Goodreads works:

> It offers all the conventions of social networking—an in-box, notifications, and a status ticker. Classified as a social

cataloguing site, it links promiscuously to other social
networks—*Facebook*, *Twitter*, *Gmail*, *Yahoo!*, and *Hotmail*—
and automatically generates invitations to existing friends on
these networks. *Goodreads* is an exemplary Web 2.0 business: it
is grandly imperial, inviting participants to comment, buy,
blog, rank, and reply through a range of devices, networks,
and services.

(2013: 239)

Nakamura also notes that networks are essential to electronic
books ('ebooks'). The implication is that this is not the case for
print books (2013: 239), but it seems obvious that print books are
also fully engaged with the kind of community that Goodreads
fosters in light of the slowed revenue growth of ebooks,[2] both
in recent years and even more so in forecasts, set against the
continued lively engagements on Goodreads. Goodreads offers
a digital book club where members can recommend books and
discuss them on a 'folksonomic, vernacular platform for literary
criticism and conversation' (242), but is underpinned by an algo-
rithm that tries to perfect the process of 'judging' books. In the
second half of this chapter, I will use both traditional 'print' book
reviews and reviews on Amazon and Goodreads to help triangulate responses to hyper-contemporary literature.

Finally, one particular peritext that interests me is the review
excerpts on book covers, sometimes called endorsements. These
are commonly excerpted from professional reviewers' comments,
or from celebrity reviewers, to validate the book being read.
Squires has noticed how endorsements are not only used to
confer quality on the book but also how they are used to qualify
the text's genre and to place it in comparison with other texts
that readers may have previously enjoyed. The endorsements
also often reflect the content of the book's blurb that likewise 'include[s] generic indicators or comparisons with other
texts' (2007: 78). I suggest that some endorsements are highly
beneficial—think of *The Sunday Times*' endorsement on the first
print run of *Harry Potter and the Philosopher's Stone* (1997) that
compared J.K. Rowling favourably with Roald Dahl—whereas
other endorsements can work against the book. Lynsey Hanley's

pop-academic book *Respectable: The Experience of Class* (2016), discussed earlier in my chapter on class, provides a useful example of this. *Respectable* is, unexpectedly, endorsed by the two-time Booker Prize winner, Hilary Mantel—awarded for her extensive Tudor historical fictions *Wolf Hall* (2009) and *Bring Up the Bodies* (2012). Mantel is quoted as describing *Respectable* as 'Pithy and provoking'. I am confused as to why Mantel is brought in to support Hanley's book. Not because Hanley's book is poor, nor that Mantel's endorsement is worthless. Rather, because the two authors are not, in my mind, complementary; the endorsement jars.

In the following, I explore how professional reviews in newspapers,[3] book cover endorsements (where relevant), amateur reviews, and socially mediated Goodreads, and Amazon reviews and ratings (out of 5 in both cases) characterise the hyper-contemporary texts discussed in this book. In each case for Goodreads, I sorted the reviews with the 'oldest' listed top in order to try to capture the first impressions of a text prior to its general digestion. On Amazon, I used the top-listed reviews according to helpfulness in order to see how purchasing decisions may have been, and may continue, to be affected by these reviews.

Nana Kwame Adjei-Brenyah's *Friday Black*

Friday Black is a collection of twelve short stories contemplating and critiquing the contemporary USA. The tone of voice is predominantly satirical and parodic, dealing with topics such as racism, gun violence, and capitalism. Dystopia is a common thread across many of the stories, while a common thread across the reviews are two key ideas. First, *Friday Black*'s impressionable style and, second, the text's unshakeable contemporaneity.

From 8258 ratings, *Friday Black* has a mean average of 4.1 on Goodreads, and a mode average of 4 (forty-three per cent).[4] Martin Warzala (5★) focuses on the text's important contemporaneity, suggesting that 'The stories will make an excellent TV mini series [*sic*]' and that *Friday Black* offers an 'excellent depiction of the all too real dystopia that is life in a woefully prejudiced dysfunctional American society'. The text's relevance to Martin's own experience of the world is central to his high rating. A third review is particularly interesting since not only does Roxane (4★) commend the author because he 'offers powerful prose as parable', but she also focuses on certain elements that I have also addressed in my chapters above, including 'racism [and] capitalism'. However, Roxane's review is interesting because, on this forum for amateur reviewers, Roxane's review is actually a professional's review: This is Roxane Gay, author of *Ayiti* (2011) and *An Untamed State* (2014). Moreover, Roxane's review is included, in full, on the back cover of the paperback of *Friday Black*. To this extent, Roxane crosses the notional divide that separates socially mediated, amateur reviewers and professional reviews.

On Amazon, *Friday Black* has received a mean average of 4.5 from 102 ratings, with a mode average of 5 (sixty-nine per cent).[5] Daniel Morgan (5★) sees the merit in its ranking, emphatically proclaiming that 'If I could rate it higher than five stars, I would'. Like Martin on Goodreads, Daniel also takes note of the text's contemporaneity, recommending it to 'anyone who's even remotely interested in modern American issues'. Daniel, this time like Roxane, draws attention to the text's exploration of 'institutionalised racism and rampant capitalism'. Lexas (5★) also focuses on the text's relevance to contemporary life because it 'hits hard on reality', while 'The Book Doctor' (5★)—an Amazon 'Top 50 Reviewer', therefore deemed extremely helpful by other Amazon customers—lists *Friday Black*'s 'very prominent real-world issues' such as 'discrimination (between races, cultures etc.), prejudice, capitalism/capitalistic societies, consumerism and materialism', thereby focusing again on the text's contemporaneity.

Tommy Orange's review in the *New York Times* begins by focusing on the year that was 2018, lamenting the endemic racism that goes implicitly uncriticised in contemporary USA. And then, turning to the text, Orange adds that 'Adjei-Brenyah has written a powerful and important and strange and beautiful collection of stories meant to be read right now, at the end of this year' (2018: para. 1), asserting *Friday Black*'s preeminent hyper-contemporaneity. Orange delves deeper into this element of the short-story collection, both noting that the short stories set in a mall, like 'Friday Black' mentioned above, 'explor[e] capitalism and mall culture in a way I've never read before, and also commenting that Adjei-Brenyah 'signal[s] a warning' about the experience of racism in contemporary America. In keeping with the trend set by other reviewers, in the *Guardian* Colin Grant writes that *Friday Black* is 'Composed with brio and rare imaginative power' (2018: para. 4), in part because these 'uncanny tales […] draw on real events […]. They are rooted in soil where reality is already dialled up to 11: this is America, after all' (para. 2). Grant, like others, therefore focuses his review on both the text's style and its relevance to contemporary society.

Given the consistency across the reviews and ratings for *Friday Black*, it is fair to argue that this is the most relevantly contemporary text explored in this book. I will return to why this may be in my conclusion, below. It is also interesting to observe that so many reviewers feel the need to comment on the style of the writing. I see these phenomena as twinned because of the text's tone and genre: Dystopic and parodic satire require a reader's knowledge of and familiarity with 'today' for the satirical elements of the storytelling to be effective. For these reasons, *Friday Black* has become significantly successful *because* of its contemporaneity.

Michael Donkor's *Hold*

Hold tells the story of two young women who both have Ghanaian heritage, but experience it radically differently. Belinda is from Ghana and is invited to the Otuos' house in London to help look after their daughter, Amma. Amma, meanwhile, is gay and coming to terms with her girlfriend breaking up with her, as well as struggling with the Ghanaian strand of her identity. I explored elements of the queer narrative, above, as well as the classed–postcolonial dynamic between the two young women. In the reviews, this classed discourse appears to be of least interest to reviewers, both amateur and professional. Meanwhile, the queer and postcolonial elements of the narrative are routinely mentioned.

Hold has a mean average rating of 3.04 on Goodreads from 928 ratings, with a mode average of 3 (forty-one per cent).[6]

Moray Teale (4★) focuses on the intercultural elements of the story, highlighting how Amma feels alienated from her Ghanaian heritage, and also draws attention to how 'Donkor also tackles the station of Ghanaian women, British racism, [and] homophobia', and alludes to the text's representation of class antagonism when she highlights 'Amma's privilege'. Siobhan (4★) uses her opening sentence to highlight, among other ideas, the text's presentation of 'friendship' and 'shame', two ideas on which I focused, above; Siobhan later adds 'sexuality' into that list of important topics that *Hold* includes, a term that Laura (3★) also discusses in her review. Laura also points to the reverse-Orientalism (to use Edward Said's term) that Belinda experiences in *Hold*: 'The exoticising conventions of Western fiction about Africa, with their detailing of "unusual" practices and customs, are turned on their head as Belinda explores the local area.' Where Laura sees a weakness, however, is in the queer narrative, commenting that 'Amma's struggle with her lesbianism had been short-changed and unresolved'.

On Amazon, *Hold* has a mean average of 3.9 from thirty ratings, with a mode average of 5 (fifty per cent).[7] In spite of this high mode average, K.O. Uzondu (1★) is particularly critical of *Hold*, finding the prose style particularly difficult. Female Reader (3★) enjoyed reading the text, but found some of the plot 'implausible[]'. However, R.D.B Cooper (5★) thoroughly enjoyed the text, particularly because, just having returned 'from a trip to Ghana, this novel gave depth and colour to my understanding of that lovely country'. In other words, R.D.B Cooper uses the book in the way that Said critiqued in *Orientalism*: The textual attitude dominates the reviewer's interest in the text.[8]

The *Scotsman's* review begins with the question of post-colonialism, arguing that in *Hold* 'Africa and Europe bruisingly grate against each other' (1 August 2018: para. 2). However, the *Scotsman's* chief praise is reserved for the text's intersectional elements: 'There is an acute sense that the "immigrant experience" is not one experience but a panoply of difference; and that economic factors as much as origin determine who one is' (para. 8). This accords with my reading, above. Arifa Akbar in the *Guardian* considers the depiction of 'female sexuality' in *Hold*

(2018: para. 4) to be at the fore, though also makes brief mention of 'class differences' (para. 5). This is part of Akbar's general praise for the text's characterisation and authentic voicing of young women in the twenty-first century.

The reviewing patterns for *Hold* are not very significant. Sexuality and postcolonialism are common themes, whilst there is a discrepancy over the authenticity in the voicing of characters. The classed element appears to be least significant to reviewers, which is surprising given the recent rise in popular interest in intersectionality.

Clare Fisher's *How the Light Gets In*

How the Light Gets In is a collection of micro- and flash-fiction short stories, ranging from just five lines long for the shortest story to nearly seven pages for the longest. Structured in four parts, the stories move between a range of disconnected characters, only some of whom feature repeatedly, documenting the experience of living in today's Internet-centred world where interpersonal contact has been reduced to a minimum.[9] As I will show, in the reviews there is a consistent focus on the text's relevance to modern (especially city) life, and an interest shown in the text's structure (most reviewers mention the four-part structure).

On Goodreads, *How the Light Gets In* receives a 3.97 mean average rating, with a mode average of 4 (forty-five per cent).[10] Siobhan (4★) commends the 'sense of accurate detail about everyday life in Britain and characters dealing with tough situations', complemented by the 'enjoyable' level of 'modernity'— that is, the text's importance to contemporary life. Likewise, Fabulous Book Fiend (5★) was 'entertained' because the stories in *How the Light Gets In* 'are born of real life [*sic*] observations'. Fabulous Book Fiend additionally enjoys the text's fragmented structure that, in my reading above, was part of its feminist activism. Jackie Law (5★) also observes that 'the stories deal with the disconnect between people' and concludes that Fisher's is a 'young, modern voice that delves deep into the heart of lived experiences in a contemporary city'. The text's urgent contemporaneity is felt commonly by these amateur reviewers. The review story is similar on Amazon where, from only three ratings, *How the Light*

Gets In's mean and mode averages are both 5.[11] Neverimitate (5★)—an Amazon 'Top 500 Reviewer', and therefore a very helpful reviewer as rated by fellow Amazon customers—describes the collection of short stories as 'shin[ing] a light on individual experiences currently being lived in a UK city'.

No mainstream newspapers reviewed *How the Light Gets In*—a phenomenon to which I return in my conclusion below. However, on Storgy.com, a website for a magazine dedicated to publishing and reviewing short stories, Emily Harrison praises the text's four-part structure as it lends some sense of boundaries to a text that might otherwise appear 'fluid' (2018: para. 2)—in other words, the opposite of how I characterised it in my reading. But, as with others, Harrison is also pleased that some of the *How the Light Gets In* stories are set in northern England because they 'hit close to home (for me)' (para. 8). On Sabotage Reviews, Cath Barton introduces her review by referencing the text's contemporaneity (2019: para. 1), later describing how 'Fisher drills into the alienation of city life' (para. 4). Barton also focuses on the problems created by technology, one of the starting places for my exploration above, noting how 'The inadequacies and delusions of our reliance on technology feature strongly in these stories' (para. 4). Whilst Barton makes mention of 'repeat', one of the stories I paid particular attention to because of its depiction of sexual abuse, she only provides a brief synopsis of the story.

Thus, whilst much of the reviewing of *How the Light Gets In* focuses on the stories' relevance to modern life, thereby proving the text's hyper-contemporaneity, there is no mention made of the narratives of sexual abuse in the text. I find this interesting especially because of the prevalence in recent years on previously unheard stories of abuse and the imperative to listen to those who have suffered from sexual abuse in a tacitly permissive culture. These reviews suggest that, even now, many of these stories may continue unheard.

Zoe Gilbert's *Folk*

Set on the island of Neverness, *Folk* is either a collection of fifteen short stories or a novel—or both. Characters who appear in the first story as children also appear in the last story but grown up with children of their own. It is a mythic fantasy world where realism does not apply, but where real human relationships none-theless maintain. There are stories of human kites, of a musical instrument constructed from the bones of the dead that produces only beautiful music, and a gorse-burning coming-of-age ritual that is not always as innocent as it might be. Whilst I explored the text's presentation of a migrant narrative, the constant threads in the reviews concern the text's genre, the text's structure (novel or short-story collection?), and the text's deployment of the passage time.

From 1048 ratings on Goodreads, *Folk* has a mean average rating of 3.8 and a mode average of 4 (thirty-five per cent).[12] Marchpane (5★) commends *Folk*'s structure that 'works brilliantly to create a sense of the way customs, traditions and superstitions are born out of oral history', while also using the text's 'Melancholy' tone as praiseworthy factor. Emma (4★) praises the text's innov-ation, both in terms of its structure and conception. Furthermore, similar to Marchpane, Emma observes how 'time is the constant thread running through the entire novel, unspooling across the pages—so gradually at times that it's barely noticeable, and so quickly at other times that entire generations transform in the blink of an eye'. Sara (3★), like many of the other reviews, suggests that the text was difficult to 'understand' because of its unusual genre. In spite of this difficulty, Sara nonetheless commented that 'the stories were timeless, and helped support the theory that mythology and folk stories are rooted in truth'. The text's engagement with time and history is a dominant thread running through these reviews.

On Amazon, *Folk* has a mean average rating of 4.5 from forty-nine reviews, with a mode average of 5 (seventy-five per cent).[13] Jane Smith (5★) says that it is one of the 'most wonderful books I've ever read' and particularly praises its innovative structure. A. Kevill (5★) praises the text's originality, adding that 'There is more than a hint of the fantastical about most of them', thereby describing the text's genre. Skycat (4★) focuses on form, pre-ferring to call the text a collection of short stories rather than a novel, but uses that to suggest they could not invest in the characters in the way they wanted to.

Much like the amateur reviewers, genre, structure, and time are Alex Preston's overriding concerns in his review for the *Financial Times*. Preston first tries to pin down *Folk*'s genre by detailing the other texts he was reminded of while reading. Mythic fantasy and magical realism provide the closest generic similarities, but he also thinks of *Folk* as telling stories about locatedness and about 'unexplained, ancient-feeling ceremonies that bind the people to the land and seek to placate the strange forces that may or may not dwell in the caves, hills and rivers' (2018: para. 4). Preston also sees fit to discuss the text's use of time, noting the stories 'never allow[] us the comfort of chronology, but drop[] hints about the passing of time, the growth and change of the characters'. It is the intertwining of these three threads that undergird Preston's review.

In the *Guardian*, Benjamin Myers tries to explain why and how *Folk*'s genre and interest in folk history is important in a contemporary context, writing that the text offers 'a dark historical mirror held up to the harried face of modern Britain' (2018: para. 1); this was one of my main preoccupations of the text when I explored it. In this way, Myers ties up others' ideas about the text into our contemporary moment. For example, 'While *Folk* can superficially be read as fantasy, the concerns of this community of entangled, troubled lives are always grounded in history' (para. 8), thereby characterising the generic mirror as one that reflects contemporary communities in the so-called 'real world' and their struggle to unite amid a fracturing politics.

Thus, whilst all the reviews tend to isolate three of *Folk*'s interesting strands—structure, genre, and use of time—Myers's review shows how these ideas can be thought of as essentially contemporary in the way they enable a critical reflection on our society.

Emma Glass's *Peach*

Peach is a surrealist depiction of a young woman's response to being raped. Following the rape, she envisions the world around her in elemental colours—peach, green, yellow—as also in shapes or objects—fruit, trees, custard. It is a visceral depiction of a post-traumatic response, but the reader is left unsure as to whether or not the depictions are how the protagonist, Peach, sees the world normally, or whether it is a feature of the post-traumatic response. The text's ending, when Peach cooks her sausage-rapist for dinner, is not as macabre as it may seem because of the text's surrealist visuality. In general, the reviews of *Peach* focus on the distinctive style of the writing. Reviewers mostly commend its use of language, though it is not universal. Comparatively, the feminist aspects of the text that interested me are broadly overlooked.

On Goodreads, *Peach* has a mean average rating of 3.13 from 2162 ratings, and a mode average of 3 (thirty-two per cent).[14] Ellis Moore (5★) raves about the book, commending it for its use of language. '*Peach* is saturated in the most beautiful writing I think I have encountered', writes Ellis, also commenting on the text's style since the narrative is 'shown to us through a stream of consciousness, of striking, harrowing imagery and melodic prose'. These ideas are reflective of the paperback's endorsements from the *Independent* ('Poetic') and Alex Preston from the *Observer* ('The language is scintillating'). Siobhan (4★) also notes *Peach*'s 'unforgettable immediate style' and its 'darkly poetic prose'. Meanwhile Izzie Donohoe (3★), who also took note of the text's 'haunting prose', felt that the language was a barrier—'at times […] unclear and difficult to follow'—rather than purely praiseworthy.

On Amazon, *Peach* receives a mean average rating of 3.7 from forty-eight ratings and a mode average of 5 (thirty-eight per cent).[15] The most helpful review from an anonymous reviewer (5★) points to the 'poetic' language as well as the 'grotesquely erotic' and 'absurd' writing. Whilst Rob Peach (5★)—acclaiming the protagonist as his 'vivacious namesake'—also commends the unusual writing style labelling it a 'poetic allegory', another anonymous reviewer (5★) interestingly describes the language as having a 'bubbling pattern' and also characterises the style as 'magical realism'—even if that is not strictly accurate, it still shows a tendency in response to *Peach* to locate and fix the writing style.

Sarah Ditum's professional review in the *Guardian* also commends Glass for her 'poet's ear' that reaches 'for the architecture of sound' and contains 'an imagination full of the bizarre'

(2018: para. 7). For Leaf Arbuthnot in *The Sunday Times* the text's language is either 'distinctive' or 'infuriating' (2017). But, going further, Ditum also tacitly connects *Peach* to fourth-wave feminism, just as I did in chapter one in *Judge for Yourself*, above. Ditum begins her review with reference to slut-shaming: '[T]oday, if a woman says she was assaulted, many will insist that it only happened because she's a slut' (2018: para. 1). For Ditum, this is also a point of critique of *Peach* because, in her view, the text falls into the trap set by the sexual abuse framework (para. 6), and therefore *Peach* is not activist enough within a fourth-wave analysis as I characterised it, in which every text *about* feminism must also be an activist text. Ditum concludes that the text's 'generic formality' (para. 6) at the climax is underwhelming, and laments that 'there must be other kinds of story to tell about being female than ones that end in nothing' (para. 7).

It is interesting that *Peach*'s style is the focus for all the reviewers, with much less coverage over the content of the text. Whilst there are several nods to the text's traumatic narrative, only one of the reviewers I sampled genuinely considered the nature of the trauma and how it relates to the reader's world outside the text.

Guy Gunaratne's *In Our Mad and Furious City*

In Our Mad and Furious City tells the story of two febrile days in contemporary London when, in response to the public lynching of a British soldier in the city at the hands of religious fundamentalists, a series of protests-cum-riots take place in the city's streets. The narrative is told from the first-person perspective of five different characters who all live on or near the Stones Estate—three male teenage friends, and two of their parents—and describes a tapestry of broadly working-class experiences of the city. In my exploration of the text, I was interested in the classed and postcolonial elements, both of which are also referred to by the reviewers. The endorsements and reviews of the text focus on two key aspects: the text's predominating vernacular language and its near-exact representation of contemporary events.

On Goodreads, out of 2250 reviews *In Our Mad* receives a 3.9 median average rating with a mode average of 4 (forty-four per cent).[16] Jamie Garwood (4★) comments that the text depicts the 'multi-cultural diverse mini-universe that is London today', as with Barbara (5★) who tried to explain why the book is 'special' because it represents 'LGBT, BAME and working class [*sic*] voices', and because the characters are 'Believable and empathetic, even the ugly ones'. For these reviewers, the text's contemporenity is cemented by this justifiable reflection of a diverse London— diverse either in its cultural, ethnic, or class makeup.

On Amazon, *In Our Mad* received ninety-seven ratings with a mean average of 4.3, and a mode average of 5 (fifty-six per cent).[17] The UK's top reviews refer to similar aspects of the text to those on Goodreads. Book fiend (4★) also notes the language ('"rap" vernacular') as significant, commenting that it distanced them at first before they could not get used to it, and how the text's characters are all connected. It depicts 'a world away from my experience and that of the majority of readers I suspect' and it is a 'tough, multicultural world of hardships and clashing cultures'. Meanwhile, Kathryn Eastman (5★) also draws attention to the text's contemporaneity by referring to the UK's Windrush scandal[18] and Selvon's immigration to Britain as part of the British Nationality Act (1948) in which commonwealth citizens were invited to Britain to help the country rebuild after the Second World War.

In *The Times*, Siobhan Murphy also points to the text's contemporaneity with her gesture to the 'Lee Rigby-style murder of an off-duty soldier [that] has triggered riots', as also the text's 'London slang' (2018). The *Guardian*'s Shahidha Bari focuses much attention on the council estate and the characterisation of the teenage boys especially, noting that 'What makes this world bearable are friendships, and Gunaratne ensures that they feel precious' (2018: para. 3). Bari also mentions the book's foremost intertext, Sam Selvon's *The Lonely Londoners* (1956). However, Bari also makes the obligatory reference to Gunaratne's distinctive use of demotic language, confirming that 'We are never outside this language as Gunaratne keeps us resolutely in his characters' idiom' (para. 7).

I find it particularly interesting that it is only the amateur reviewer, Barbara on Goodreads, who makes mention explicitly of how the text is referencing working-class life, which was one of my focuses above. More reviewers—both professional and amateur, as well as the endorsements—make mention of the text's contemporaneity, with more or less specificity. This is shown through the references to Grenfell, the murder of Lee Rigby, and the Windrush Scandal. With the latter, several reviewers noted the importance of Selvon's characterisation that, for me, gave an insight into a postcolonial narrative in the text. However, none of the reviews I sampled uses the language of postcolonialism to explain this particular strand of the text's narratives, suggesting that their engagement with the narrative was less critical of what it depicts, instead praising its mere presence. Clearly, the dominant aspect of all the reviews was the explicit mention of the use of vernacular language in the text, implying that this text's particular success includes its aesthetics and stylistics—how it looks and how it makes the reader feels—rather than just in the topics it addresses.

Louisa Hall's *Trinity*

Trinity is a novel about J. Robert Oppenheimer, the historical figure who pioneered research into the atomic bombs that were dropped on the Japanese cities Hiroshima and Nagasaki in 1945. It follows seven characters as they give their testimonials about their own experiences of Oppenheimer over a period of twenty-three years, from 1943 to 1966. Some of these characters are colleagues, others are former friends, or even admiring schoolboys. Importantly, Oppenheimer is never given his own testimony, so we as readers only discern his character in silhouette as the others' testimonials shine light from various angles on this inscrutable and paradoxical character who both brought about the atomic age and campaigned against nuclear proliferation. In my exploration of the text, I focused on the submerged queer narrative, which is obliquely mentioned in the reviews. The trend in reviews of Hall's text is to hold back from narrative detail and maintain the text's mystery, while some reviewers make a concerted effort to pin down the text's genre: It is a novel and not a biography.

On Goodreads, *Trinity* has a mean average rating of 3.43, with a mode average of 3 from 470 ratings.[19] Jessica Woodbury (4★) locates the success of the text in answering questions about Oppenheimer that history has been unable to solve, but also in that it supplants these questions with a more important thread about love. Moreover, among the seven testimonials, Jessica makes an interesting point about the prominence of sexual politics in *Trinity*, noting that 'many of these stories were narrated by women, definitely not what you'd get from a male writer taking on a similar project'. Additionally, Jessica praises the text's inclusion of a queer narrative—this accords with my reading of the text that focused on a queer element of the text. Other reviews are quite generic in their description, often resisting giving details of particular testimonials they liked, though they all mention how the text offers these seven testimonials all detailing their experiences of Oppenheimer. Much like the covers' endorsements, therefore, the amateur reviews are for the most part elliptical in their descriptions.

On Amazon, *Trinity* is now given an interesting sub-title: *Shortlisted for the Dylan Thomas Prize.*[20] Of the twelve texts, this is the only one that has peritextual reference to the IDTP so obviously stated, though others, such as Gunaratne's novel, have it listed on the book's sales page. Clearly, the book prize is part of the way to attract a potential reader's attention to the novel. It also adds a kind of success-rating to a text that, in many ways, remains either under described or indescribable. This indescribability and its general 'elliptical' nature may explain why it has only twenty-six customer ratings, with a median average of 3.9 and a mode average of 5 (forty-two per cent). This suggests that whilst not many people have read the text, many of those who have read it think it is extremely good. In his review, Daniel Morgan (5★) dedicates his opening paragraph to genre: '[T]his ISN'T a biography. I think that's what confuses most people. This is a fictionalised novel set around Oppenheimer's life.' Another reviewer, ericmitford (4★), makes exactly the same point in his opening sentence, while James Brydon (5★) also refers to the fact that *Trinity* 'is not a hagiography', but bolsters his review with narrative detail about the seven testimonials that outline twenty-three years of Oppenheimer's life.

In the *New York Times*, Andrea Barrett calls *Trinity* 'brilliant' (2018: para. 2) and explains that its 'genius is not to explain but to embody the science and politics that shaped Oppenheimer's life' (para. 3). The elements that Barrett praises are the deep characterisation of those giving the testimonials and how they 'mirror the ambiguous tensions of Oppenheimer's personality' (para. 5). Thus, *Trinity*'s success is put down to its nuanced formal structure and the way that Oppenheimer is revealed to the reader not through 'biographical data', but in 'seven thought experiments' (para. 12). Interestingly, therefore, Barrett draws attention not to the text's ellipticism and allusiveness but rather to its excessive detail, even if much of that detail sheds light only secondarily on Oppenheimer himself.

It appears across these reviews that Barrett, the professional reviewer, is the anomaly in acknowledging the level of detail in *Trinity*. By contrast, the amateur reviewers and the endorsements on the book's covers think its ellipticism and secret mysteries most important. Interestingly, my curiosity in the text in the preceding chapter has been on its queer narrative: not its explicitly queer narrative when two homosexual women struggle to make a life for themselves, but the unacknowledged, closeted queer narrative. In other words, my interest has been the mysterious and elliptical in the text, just as many of the reviews have been interested in the secret and elliptical. This suggests that readers' interest in the text's inscrutability is not only an academic feature of *Trinity* but also what makes it of hyper-contemporary interest to readers.

Sarah Perry's *Melmoth*

Melmoth rewrites the myth of the satanic tempter, Melmoth, most famously depicted in the nineteenth-century *Melmoth the Wanderer* (1820) by Charles Maturin. In Perry's version, Melmoth is brought up to date and retranscribed as a woman. The feminist element of the text was what interested me in my exploration above, though it goes unmentioned by reviewers. Instead, their focus is on Gothic genre and its literary antecedents.

On Goodreads, from 8040 ratings, *Melmoth* has a mean average of 3.48 and a mode average of 4 (thirty-five per cent).[21] One of Blair's (4★) arguments about *Melmoth* is precisely its relevance to the contemporary world, complaining that 'it too obviously incorporates modern political perspectives into historical narratives'. Rebecca Speas (5★) enjoys the feelings of 'dread and unease' that *Melmoth* creates and also—like Hannah—points to the text's genre ('neo-Gothic') as an explanation of its mastery.

From 139 ratings on Amazon, *Melmoth* receives a mean average rating of 3.9 with a mode average of 5 (fifty per cent).[22] Despite this high mode average, the top reviews on Amazon are not nearly as positive as those on Goodreads. Lola (3★) 'wanted to love this book' but could not because it fails in its Gothic sensibility: 'I was not scared, there were no goose bumps on my skin, I slept through the night (and the next one). Gothic story? What?' Instead, this is a book that makes you 'think' but leaves Lola 'unmoved' by the 'heroines' struggles'. Catherine G. (1★) disliked the book because its structure failed her. Instead, the text was a 'meandering mess'. However, Anna (5★) is convinced by *Melmoth* and finds it 'horrifying', suggesting that it does land as a Gothic story. This is most keenly felt for Anna in the 'real horror' that is 'humanity': 'the decidedly non-supernatural horrors that humans inflict on each other all the time'. To this extent, it is a Gothic story for today, rather than a mere look back at the Gothic genre's heyday.

In the *Independent,* Lucy Scholes (incidentally, giving *Melmoth* 4★) begins her review by explaining the intertextual background to the text and, crucially, noting that 'In Perry's version of the story, she turns the titular figure into a woman' (2018: para. 2). This, however, is her only comment on the text's feminist representation. Like Anna on Amazon, Scholes asserts that 'the real monsters in Perry's tale are ordinary humans' and therefore that 'human cruelty proves scarier than any spectre' (para. 4). The implication is that *Melmoth* is not so focused on today so much as on the people who inhabit this world today. The review in the *Scotsman* likewise mentions *Melmoth*'s intertextual 'sly subversion' (25 October 2018: para. 1) of Maturin's *Melmoth the Wanderer*, primarily shown through the gender shift of the antagonist (para.

2). The *Scotsman* reviewer praises the text's structure (para. 6) as well as the way it 'places the reader in a remarkably uncomfortable position' (para. 7)—that is, its success as a Gothic novel.

For none of the reviewers is feminism a topic of interest, unlike in my reading. The *Scotsman*'s comment that it 'is an ensemble piece' (25 October 2018: para. 6) approaches the idea of feminism-through-unity the closest. The most common feature of the reviews, instead, is the genre (Gothic) and the feelings this rouses (or fails to rouse) in *Melmoth*'s readers.

Sally Rooney's *Normal People*

Normal People tells a story about two young people, Marianne and Connell, who come from the same small town in the west of Ireland and attend the same school. Marianne comes from a well-to-do family and household, whilst Connell lives alone with his mum and is from a working-class background. Connell's mum is Marianne's family's cleaner. Both Marianne and Connell excel in their studies and end up going to the same university in Dublin, where they have an on–off relationship. Above, my exploration of the text focused on the class antagonism between Marianne and Connell. The reviews home in on the text's characterisation, the contemporaneity of the narrative, as well as the clever use of dialogue; however, the reviewers disagree on most of these topics.

From a gargantuan 194,735 ratings, on Goodreads *Normal People* has a mean average rating of 3.86 with a mode average of 4 (thirty-eight per cent).[23] Possibly from Michigan, London (4★) comments on how quickly they read the book, suggestive of the clear and easy prose style. This accords with one of the book's endorsers, Elif Batuman, who also admits that 'I couldn't put *Normal People* down'. Possibly from Michigan, London also draws attention to the important depictions of 'class difference' in *Normal People*—the latter was also a concern of mine above. Meanwhile, John Purcell (5★) commented that whilst 'The writing is reminiscent of the best of early twentieth century literature, the story is urgently, unflinchingly of our times', thereby both suggesting the text's 'urgent' contemporaneity and its literary heritage.

On Amazon, *Normal People* has received 1785 ratings with a mean average of 5; its mode average is 5 (fifty-four per cent).[24] And yet the three top reviews (as a reminder, based on 'helpfulness') all provide low ratings. Lola (1★) resoundingly rejects any and all of *Normal People*'s alleged qualities. One of Lola's chief criticisms is that she is 'no longer a [member of the] target audience of the book'—that is to say, the text is not sufficiently contemporary, or she sees the book as limited to a certain demographic. Lola also complains that 'important matters like domestic abuse, depression and mental health in general were hugely overlooked', thereby lamenting that it was not a sufficiently activist text. Kate M (5★) complains that the 'characters are two dimensional', in direct opposition to the praise that other amateur reviewers gave *Normal People*. Finally, sue gee (2★) complains that 'It is clearly written by a young person with little life experience and it lacks depth', adding that 'I didn't feel that the characters were "real"'. For a text whose mode average rating is the highest possible, it is interesting both that these low reviews are listed top and that their complaints oppose the very things praised by reviews on another online platforms.

For Orlando Bird in the *Telegraph*, 'The dialogue in *Normal People* is smart and spare' (2018: para. 7), using the same vocabulary as one of the hardback endorsers, Sheila Heti, for whom the text is 'intelligent, spare and mesmerising'. Bird does mention the problematic power dynamics between Marianne and Connell, but does not use the vocabulary of class to explain the relationship. Kate Clanchy in the *Guardian*, however, does refer to Connell's working-class identity (2018: para. 3) and also observes that 'the differences of class and social ease between Connell and Marianne seem to dissolve as the book progresses' (para. 7). Clanchy also makes sure to pinpoint *Normal People*'s depiction of 'thoroughly contemporary' characters (para. 4), even though she also argues that the text is not 'absolutely contemporary' (para. 13) because it seems to call on earlier modernist writing.

Tellingly, across the few reviews I've sampled, the consistent topics of dialogue, characterisation, and contemporaneity are divisive issues. This is surprising because you might expect reviewers to agree that *x* is good, but *y* is bad, and either *x* or *y* outweighs the other. However, it appears that, given these reviews, and the listing as 'top' on Amazon those reviews that criticise *Normal People* so forthrightly, it is legitimate to call the text divisive. This is in spite of its topping the Goodreads ranking for my twelve books based on ratings received (see Table 5.1).

Richard Scott's *Soho*

Soho is a collection of poems, structured in four parts and culminating in the collection's final celebratory paean 'Oh my Soho!' It focuses throughout on a queer life and both the shame and pride the persona feels in living queerly in this day and age. Above, I examined how the queer archive is accessed in *Soho*, and how it *becomes* the queer archive, though this appears unevenly in the reviews I read.

From 315 ratings on Goodreads, *Soho* has a 4.17 mean average and a mode average of 5 (forty-seven per cent).[25] Eric Anderson (5★) praises *Soho* for its 'full frontal engagement with queer experience while vigorously searching for a gay lineage and history to connect to', and also explicitly tethers his ideas to queer criticism by referring to the pernicious effects of 'heteronormative practices'. Martin Newman (4★) intertextually alludes to Stephen Sondheim's lyrics for the musical *West Side Story* when he calls it 'pretty and witty and gay', thereby also reclaiming the word 'gay' as a positive emblem for queer writing—just as queer theorists have reclaimed 'queer' from its pejorative connotations. Neil Fulwood (5★) acclaims *Soho* as a 'pulsating, vital and unflinching' collection, a sentiment that accords with Eric Anderson's idea that *Soho* is 'brazenly sexual'. The text's explicit tone clearly strikes a chord with these reviewers.

On Amazon, *Soho* has received a mean average of 4.15 from fifteen ratings, with a mode average of 5 (sixty-four per cent).[26] For both Daniel Morgan (5★) and Oscar Boyle (5★), the 'visceral' imagery is worthy of particular mention, whilst KGD (5★) says that the collection is 'a must to read for those interested in current poets'. Interestingly, despite the prominence of the collection's queer element, only Oscar Boyle refers to the text's queerness, and even then it is to dismiss its importance: 'Just read it. [G]ay, straight, anything else you may be[.]' Not dissimilar to those on Goodreads, the text's subversive sexual element is not as pressing an issue for the amateur reviewers.

However, in *The Manchester Review*, Nell Osborne begins her review by explaining that '*Soho* is not a celebration of gay freedom or equality or acceptance per se. It leans hard into the shame that corporate, family-friendly or normatively affirmative representations of gay identity and culture often ignore or sanitise' (2018: para. 1). Osborne also thinks about the presence of the queer archive in *Soho* and quotes the idea of the 'homo-historian' (Scott, 2018: 69) from *Soho*, arguing that 'Scott's unyielding poetic eye acts as homo-historian not only of place but of the sensual body' (Osborne, 2018: para. 2). For *The Interpreter's House*, Alison Graham spends much of her review discussing the depiction of the Internet and online worlds in *Soho*. Nevertheless, Graham says that '"museum" is [...] the standout poem of the collection' because it engages with 'a history of queerness' (2018: para. 8): Again, the production and reading of the queer archive are brought to the fore.

I find it interesting that the professional reviewers appeared more willing to engage with an academic discourse that, for the amateur reviewers (and therefore general reading public), appeared to be less important. Instead, for amateur reviewers, *Soho*'s explicit tone and content were more worthy of merit.

Novuyo Rosa Tshuma's *House of Stone*

House of Stone tells the history—and 'hi-story', in the narrator's idiom—of Zimbabwe's explosion out of British colonial control and into independence. It is narrated from the position of Zamani, a lodger in the Mlambo family home. The Mlambos—father Abednego and mother Agnes—are devastated when their son, Bukhosi, goes missing. By way of helping them find Bukhosi, Zamani records the family's experiences of Zimbabwe's transition into an independent nation, alongside his own personal history, born as he was during the independence revolution and its aftermath. The text's approach to history—and its historical fiction genre—is the common thread in the reviews of the text, alongside the importance of the text's postcolonial critique, on which I also partly focused in my reading, above.

On Goodreads, Tshuma's *House of Stone* has a mean average rating of 3.91 from 388 ratings and a mode average of 4 (forty-two per cent).[27] Anne Goodwin (5★) commends it for being so holistically affecting. She notes that it 'is psychologically, historically, culturally and literarily impressive' without going into further detail. Tommi (4★) goes into lots of detail and commends the writing for encouraging further research outside the novel to discover a fuller history of Zimbabwe, concluding that '*House of Stone* is a fascinating blend of history, storytelling, violence, love, patriarchy, and unreliable narration'. Therefore, for both Anne Goodwin and Tommi, *House of Stone* appears to be a novel of many facets, but its genre is fixed as historical fiction (albeit ironised and twisted). Tommi also draws attention to the issue of colonialism in their review, as does Charlott (5★) who points out how the text's depiction of trauma is 'colonial and post-colonial inflicted [*sic*]', thereby drawing attention to one of the text's elements on which I focused, above.

On Amazon, *House of Stone* has a mean average of 4 from twenty-one ratings with a mode average of 5 (fifty-three per cent).[28] An anonymised reviewer (3★) first comments that *House of Stone* is 'a fascinating book historically and quite sad', drawing attention again to the text's historical fiction, just as R.P. Tuckey (4★) calls it a 'story of sickening events'. David Kenvyn (3★) goes further to draw attention to the particular aspects of the text's historicism, in particular the Gukuruhandi massacre, and concludes that 'anyone who wants to understand what is happening in modern Zimbabwe, or even modern Africa, should read this book'. Whilst the term 'postcolonial' is missing from David Kenvyn's review, this final sentiment clearly gestures to this.

Helon Habila's review of *House of Stone* in the *Guardian* also affirms the book's historical focus, even laying some of the blame at the foot of the reader: '[W]e are complicit with the author in this playful, tongue-in-cheek yet serious game of recreating "history"' (2018: para. 5). But Habila also places the fictionalised historical narratives within the discourse of colonialism, writing that

> By the end [Tshuma] has managed to not only sum up
> Zimbabwean history, but also all of African colonial his-
> tory: from devastating colonialism to the bitter wars of
> independence to the euphoria of self-rule and the disillu-
> sionment of the present.
>
> (para. 6)

In the *New York Times*, Dinaw Mengestu yet again draws attention
to the text's revision of Zimbabwe's recent history, but this time
lays some of the colonial-style blame on Zamani's shoulders.
'Zamani's actions and ambitions carry an obviously colonial
overtone', writes Mengestu, adding that Zamani is 'conniving,
earnest and manipulative, brutal and desperate' (2019: paras 7–8).
These ideas accord with my own concluding sentiments about
Zamani's actions. It is interesting that in both these professional
reviews, the newspapers have asked contemporary novelists from
Ethiopia and Nigeria, respectively, to review the book, implying
that *House of Stone* needs to be understood or explained from a
postcolonial perspective.

Thus, though there have been only a few reviews on the amateur review spaces, they have more or less aligned with the professional reviewers' focus, albeit with more or less detail. These
focuses include the text's genre, and its ability to act as a postcolonial critique. Only one of the reviewers (Mengestu) also
makes mention of the text's European intertextualities such as
Nabokov, as I did, suggesting that placing the text within a more
general canon of literature is of less interest to both professional
and amateur reviewers alike.

Jenny Xie's *Eye Level*

Eye Level charts the migrant journeys of its persona through
forty-one poems. The persona journeys from China to the USA
with further stops along the way. In my exploration of the text
I examined the invocations of the idea of migrant hybridity,
concluding that Xie's postcolonial poetry 'disconsoles', in Neil
Lazarus's term, because it defies ready-made expectations of
postcolonial writing. These ideas are more less missing from the

reviews, below, in which the emphasis is on the thematics of loneliness and travel, as well as the magical quality of the writing.

From 803 ratings on Goodreads, *Eye Level* has a mean average rating of 4.16 and a mode average of 4 (forty-two per cent).[29] Caroline (5★) describes how in *Eye Level* 'we find ourselves at once traversing the globe and "tunneling inward."' Furthermore, Caroline explains how '*Eye Level* explores what it means to pass through them, never quite settling', suggestive of the nature of migrancy in general. Jen (5★) likewise refers to the nature of being unsettled, and the use of the clothing imagery, to which I also referred. Richard Weems (5★) is instead wowed by the quality of the poetic voice, noting that 'These poems are chiseled down wonders that cut right to the core of the matter'. Richard makes no mention of context, but specifically refers to certain powerful images in the poetry, not unlike Brenda Shaughnessy, one of the book's endorsers. On Amazon, *Eye Level* has a mean average of 4.2 from eleven ratings and a mode average of 5 (fifty-eight per cent).[30] Both Michael Bever's (5★) and M. Roberts's (5★) reviews are fulsome with praise, but light on detail. For example, M. Roberts writes that *Eye Level* 'shows not only a mastery of language and form, but of voice'. However, Soosiewoo (2★) is 'Unconvinced' because they 'didn't get a feel from it'. Emotions come to the fore, as has been implied by Mudambi and Schuff in their research on reviews.

In *The New Yorker*, Dan Chiasson tacks against the amateur reviewers' interest, instead saying that *Eye Level* 'is a book partly about living and travelling abroad' (2018: para. 2), and claims that the main thrust of the text is its investigation of the philosophical self. At great depth, Chiasson is able to conclude that Xie is 'a magician of perspective and scale' (para. 2). For *The Manchester Review*, Ian Pople also focuses on travel and solitude, agreeing so far with Chiasson in the opening as to quote *The New Yorker* review (2018: para. 1). However, Pople also notes that holiday travel is not the only kind explored in *Eye Level* and closely observes how 'Some of these poems are attached to stories of her own family's migration to the United States' (para. 6), thereby drawing attention to the aspects that interested me. However, the academic vocabulary of postcolonialism is not included, with

Pople instead concluding, much like Chiasson, that *Eye Level* contains both 'realism' and 'mysticism' (para. 7).

The fact that reviewers tend to have skated over the academic vocabulary suggests, I think, not that these aspects of the text are not of interest—travel and the identity of the self are consistently mentioned—but that the majesty and magic of the collection's language overwhelm the opportunity to place the text in a broader discourse.

It is difficult to summarise a textual analysis across twelve texts. There is no distinctive pattern worthy of scrutiny, such as 'amateur reviewers are more interested in contemporary society' or 'professional reviewers are more interested in describing a text's genre'. Instead, the following topics are of interest to reviewers in general:

- What genre the text belongs to; or, how the text defies expected conventions of genre
- How the text made the reviewer feel
- The text's major themes ('The text is about' or 'The text presents us with images/ideas of')
- The depiction of history in the text
- The depiction of the characters in the text
- The text's style and tone

The texts that are most readily connected to contemporary society in the reviews—Adjei-Brenyah's *Friday Black* and Fisher's *How the Light Gets In*—also happen to be parodically and satirically comical, often painting a dystopic portrait of contemporary life. This implies that these genres, which rely on an intimate understanding of society's dynamics and structures, will necessarily elicit reactions commenting on their relevance to modern life.

The Goodreads and Amazon ratings data (Tables 5.1 and 5. 2) tell an interesting story. In both, I have detailed the number of ratings for each text, the mean and mode averages, as well as the standard deviation. As a reminder, I sampled the most helpful reviews on Amazon and the oldest reviews on Goodreads; the

Table 5.1 Goodreads data

Title	No. of ratings	Mean average	Mean average ranking	Mode average	Percentage of mode frequency	Mode average ranking	Standard deviation (σ)	Most consistent ratings rankings
Friday Black	8,267	4.10	3	4	43%	2	0.85	2
Hold	930	3.04	12	3	41%	10	1.00	8
How the Light Gets In	88	3.95	4	4	45%	2	0.95	5
Folk	1,048	3.80	8	4	35%	2	1.00	7
Peach	2,165	3.13	11	3	32%	10	1.17	12
In Our Mad and Furious City	2,216	3.90	6	4	44%	2	0.90	4
Trinity	470	3.43	10	3	34%	10	1.07	11
Melmoth	8,051	3.48	9	4	35%	2	1.03	10
Normal People	195,770	3.86	7	4	38%	2	1.01	9
Soho	316	4.17	1	5	42%	1	0.89	3
House of Stone	391	3.91	5	4	42%	2	0.96	6
Eye Level	805	4.16	2	4	42%	2	0.83	1

Note:
Data captured on 28 March 2020.

Table 5.2 Amazon.com data

Title	No. of ratings	Mean average	Mean average ranking	Mode average	Percentage of mode frequency	Mode average ranking	Standard deviation* (σ)	Most consistent ratings ranking
Friday Black	102	4.50	2	5	69%	1	0.90	2
Hold	30	3.90	9	5	50%	1	1.35	11
How the Light Gets In	3	5.00	1	5	100%	1	0.00	1
Folk	49	4.50	2	5	75%	1	0.97	3
Peach	48	3.70	12	5	38%	1	1.29	8
In Our Mad and Furious City	97	4.30	4	5	56%	1	0.99	4
Trinity	26	3.90	9	5	42%	1	1.14	5
Melmoth	144	3.90	9	5	50%	1	1.35	10
Normal People	1,798	4.00	7	5	54%	1	1.33	9
Soho	15	4.20	5	5	64%	1	1.14	6
House of Stone	24	4.00	7	5	53%	1	1.40	12
Eye Level	11	4.20	5	5	58%	1	1.26	7

Notes:
Data captured on 28 March 2020 from Amazon.com.
* Standard deviation estimate only as Amazon provides percentage data for frequency of ratings figures.

former in order to see how purchasing decisions are most likely to have been—and continue to be—shaped; the latter to take account of the first reactions to any text. The standard deviation (σ) on Tables 5.1 and 5.2 describes how consistently ratings are close to the mean average. A number close to 0, for example, tells us that there is a high consistency in the ratings relative to the mean average, suggesting a more common consensus. A larger number, conversely, tells us that the ratings are quite volatile— that is, lots of people had a range of different responses to the text.

Looking at the data, the first thing that strikes me is that Goodreads has significantly more ratings than Amazon. The second thing, derivative of the first, is how many people who rate books are willing to give them 5 (the mode average) on Amazon. This suggests that those who do rate books on Amazon are likely to be both positive and extreme in their ratings, unlike those on Goodreads who appear more measured in their ratings and reviews. The former phenomenon is in keeping with Mudambi and Schuff's argument that extreme book reviews seem to be more helpful in shaping purchasing decisions (2010: 195). Since Amazon is primarily a shop, as opposed to Goodreads that is more of a digital book club (Nakamura, 2013: 242), we could put this discrepancy down to the service the forum provides. These two ideas converge because, on a platform like Goodreads where more people give reviews and ratings, they are more likely to use the full scale available for rating. Moreover, there is a narrow frequency of the mode average in the Goodreads data, with the most common rating response (i.e. 1, 2, 3, 4, or 5) always being used between thirty-two per cent and forty-five per cent of the time; in other words, the most common rating for any text is *always* given between about a third and a half of the overall time—a span of thirteen per cent.

Amazon's mode frequency in Table 5.2 ranges between 50% and 100%, a much larger span of fifty per cent. This suggests that whilst the Amazon data give us more drastically volatile and much less information than the Goodreads data, Amazon data nonetheless give sufficient information to make a decision that is ultimately binary: to buy or not to buy. By contrast, the more primary concern with rating the quality of the literature on

Goodreads leads to more nuanced ratings, which are nonetheless remarkably consistent across different texts. A cynic could argue that people who give new ratings on Goodreads are easily swayed by the ratings already given; by contrast, and to give readers the benefit of the doubt, the consistency in mode ratings suggests that Goodreads functions well across different forms and genres.

Which books are divisive? We can use the standard deviation measure to help us with this. On Goodreads *Peach*, the surrealist text dealing with a young woman's sexual abuse and subsequent cannibalistic revenge divides opinion the most ($\sigma = 1.17$), whereas on Amazon, *House of Stone*—the Nabokovian-style novel in which visceral scenes of a historically-true genocidal massacre are depicted—is most divisive ($\sigma = 1.40$). This suggests that the main narrative topic is a leading factor in determining the divisiveness in ratings. However, the opposite cannot be claimed based on these data, because *Friday Black* receives the second most consistent ratings on both Goodreads ($\sigma = 0.85$) and Amazon ($\sigma = 0.90$), and yet depicts multiple racist homicides and cannibalism. Therefore, we should look beyond the extreme nature of narrative topics for other variables that may dictate ratings' consistency.

Perhaps the most useful measure of quality—and, at the very least, the most commonly used in day-to-day metrics—is the mean average. By this measure, on Goodreads Scott's queer poetry collection, *Soho*, comes top, while Donkor's *Hold*, a story about the burden of Ghanaian heritage on two young women who are in London for very different reasons, is ranked lowest. On Amazon, Fisher's *How the Light Gets In* is ranked highest with an unsurpassable mean average of 5, but it only received three ratings. By contrast, *Peach* had the lowest mean average with a more than respectable 3.7. *Peach* is therefore the lowest ranked by this metric, and by the metric of volatility—and yet it also received 5 as its most common (mode) ratings response. To use these ratings to qualify a text as either 'good' or 'bad' may become a fool's errand.

It would be easy to use the number of ratings as a judge of quality. Rooney's coming-of-age novel *Normal People* far outstrips any other text on the list in terms of number of ratings, both on Goodreads where the other eleven texts combined have a little over 12.5% of the total responses that *Normal People* received, and on Amazon, where the remaining eleven take a slightly larger chunk of *Normal People*'s share (30.5%)—a nonetheless impressive figure.[31] Should this imply quality? Or does it just correlate with publicity and sales figures? After all, *How the Light Gets In* received not only three ratings on Amazon but also, as I noted above, zero reviews in the mainstream press. Without the sales data we can but assume that rates of response differ widely according to the genre (satirical dystopia is in vogue, so *Friday Black* might expect to receive more ratings than, say, the historical fiction *Trinity*), form (poetry elicits fewer responses than prose in my data, with *Soho* and *Eye Level* tenth and eleventh for ratings ranks on both Tables 5.1 and 5.2), and press exposure. When additionally taking into account the celebrity of the author (both Rooney and Perry have previously been nominated and won awards) versus debut writers whose name has not yet spread among the literati (eight of these texts are the authors' debut full-length publications), I think we can fairly dismiss the usefulness of the metric that describes 'fewer ratings=worse' and 'more ratings=better'.

In fact, I hope that this chapter tells us one thing above all: that reviews and ratings are no doubt influential and have their uses, but they are not the only way of judging a book's quality. Others' opinions on a text must be put into context alongside the other criteria that you use to judge quality. Whether the raw data of ratings, or the more nuanced written reviews, these help us think about the texts and sometimes introduce us to the texts, but they should not be the be-all and the end-all of the judging process.

Notes

1 See www.goodreads.com/review/show/2507863885?book_show_action=true&from_review_page=1 [accessed 20 March 2020].
2 See www.statista.com/outlook/213/100/ebooks/worldwide [accessed 20 March 2020], especially 'Revenue growth by percent' graph.
3 I am using *The Times*, *Guardian*, *Telegraph*, *New York Times*, and *Washington Post*, though not all books are reviewed in all of these publications.

4   See   www.goodreads.com/book/show/37570595-friday-black [accessed 26 March 2020].

5   See www.amazon.co.uk/Friday-Black-Nana-Kwame-Adjei-Brenyah/ dp/1787476006 [accessed 26 March 2020].

6   See www.goodreads.com/en/book/show/37931791 [accessed 27 March 2020]. NB the book is listed under its US title *Housegirl.*

7   See www.amazon.co.uk/dp/B077V2GWW2 [accessed 27 March 2020].

8   For more detail, please see p. 59, above.

9   At the time of writing, we are in the UK and elsewhere under lockdown. Surely the relationships described in Fisher's books are intensifying in this increasingly Internet-connected/decreasingly interpersonal world.

10 See www.goodreads.com/book/show/40095755-how-the-light-gets-in [accessed 26 March 2020].

11 See www.amazon.co.uk/How-Light-Gets-Clare-Fisher/dp/1910312126 [accessed 26 March 2020].

12 See www.goodreads.com/book/show/35892355-folk [accessed 28 March 2020].

13 See www.amazon.co.uk/dp/B075D9CXSK [accessed 28 March 2020].

14 See www.goodreads.com/book/show/34957071-peach [accessed 25 March 2020].

15 See www.amazon.co.uk/gp/product/1408886510 [accessed 26 March 2020].

16 See www.goodreads.com/book/show/35212538-in-our-mad-and-furious-city [accessed 24 March 2020].

17 See www.amazon.co.uk/dp/B073B6S4V4   [accessed   24   March 2020].

18 The Windrush Scandal was a result of the 'hostile environment' policy for illegal immigrants, enacted by then Home Secretary, Theresa May, in 2012. The policy was designed to force immigrants to leave the country who had entered the UK illegally, but an unintended consequence was the forced removal of Windrush-generation immigrants who were in Britain legally, but who had never been given legal papers because there was no prior need. In 2020, an independent review by Wendy Williams concluded that the Home Office showed 'ignorance and thoughtlessness' in their actions, leading to Home Secretary Priti Patel's public apology. See www.bbc.co.uk/news/uk-politics-51961933 [accessed 24 March 2020].

19 See www.goodreads.com/book/show/36461462-trinity [accessed 26 March 2020].
20 See www.amazon.co.uk/dp/B07CXZMB98 [accessed 26 March 2020].
21 See www.goodreads.com/book/show/36628420-melmoth [accessed 27 March 2020].
22 See www.amazon.co.uk/dp/B0788YXDCR [accessed 27 March 2020].
23 See www.goodreads.com/book/show/41057294-normal-people [accessed 26 March 2020].
24 See www.amazon.co.uk/gp/product/0571334644 [accessed 26 March 2020].
25 See www.goodreads.com/book/show/35955748-soho [accessed 27 March 2020].
26 See www.amazon.co.uk/dp/B078HWQ92M [accessed 27 March 2020].
27 See www.goodreads.com/book/show/45894056-house-of-stone [accessed 24 March 2020].
28 See www.amazon.co.uk/dp/B0792M9YCN [accessed 24 March 2020].
29 See www.goodreads.com/en/book/show/36479171 [accessed 27 March 2020].
30 See www.amazon.co.uk/dp/B07B8VFX4J [accessed 27 March 2020].
31 These data were gathered prior to Normal People's popular success as a BBC/RTÉ television show in spring 2020. I would presume the gap has widened since.

Bibliography

Adjei-Brenyah, Nana-Kwame, *Friday Black* (London: riverrun, 2018).
Akbar, Arifa, '*Hold* by Michael Donkor review—a Ghanaian housemaid's tale', *Guardian*, 16 July 2018, www.theguardian.com/books/2018/jul/16/hold-michael-donkor-review-bold-literary-debut [accessed 27 March 2020].
Arbuthnot, Leaf, 'Book reviews: *The Last Ballad* by Wiley Cash; *Peach* by Emma Glass; *Things We Nearly Knew* by Jim Powell', *The Sunday Times*, 31 December 2017, www.thetimes.co.uk/article/book-reviews-the-last-ballad-by-wiley-cash-peach-by-emma-glass-things-we-nearly-knew-by-jim-powell-r9gzdpw3b [accessed 26 March 2020].

Bari, Shahidha, '*In Our Mad and Furious City* by Guy Gunaratne review—grime-infused tinderbox debut', *Guardian*, 13 April 2018, www.theguardian.com/books/2018/apr/13/our-mad-furious-city-guy-gunaratne-review-wiley-skepta [accessed 24 March 2020].

Barrett, Andrea, 'The life of J. Robert Oppenheimer, imagined through his collisions with others', *New York Times*, 19 November 2018, www.nytimes.com/2018/11/19/books/review/trinity-louisa-hall.html [accessed 24 March 2020].

Barton, Cath, '*How the Light Gets In* by Clare Fisher', 2019, http://sabotagereviews.com/2019/08/29/how-the-light-gets-in-by-clare-fisher/ [accessed 26 March 2020].

Bird, Orlando, '*Normal People* by Sally Rooney, review: a smart, cool sketch of mismatched lovers', *The Telegraph*, 8 September 2018, www.telegraph.co.uk/books/what-to-read/normal-people-sally-rooney-review-smart-cool-sketch-mismatched/ [accessed 26 March 2020].

'Book review: *Hold*, by Michael Donkor', *Scotsman*, 1 August 2018, www.scotsman.com/whats-on/arts-and-entertainment/book-review-hold-michael-donkor-270154 [accessed 27 March 2020].

'Book review: *Melmoth* by Sarah Perry', *Scotsman*, 25 October 2018, www.scotsman.com/arts-and-culture/book-review-melmoth-sarah-perry-552953 [accessed 27 March 2020].

Chen, Pei-yu, Samita Dhanasobhon, and Michael D. Smith, 'All reviews are not created equal: The disaggregate impact of reviews and reviewers at Amazon.com', *SSRN* (2008). DOI: 10.2139/ssrn.918083.

Chevalier, Judith A., and Dina Mayzlin, 'The effect of word of mouth on sales: Online book reviews', *Journal of Marketing Research*, 43.3 (2006), 345–54. DOI: 10.1509/jmkr.43.3.345.

Chiasson, Dan, 'Jenny Xie writes a sightseer's guide to the self', *The New Yorker*, 30 April 2018, www.newyorker.com/magazine/2018/05/07/jenny-xie-writes-a-sightseers-guide-to-the-self [accessed 27 March 2020].

Clanchy, Kate, '*Normal People* by Sally Rooney review—a future classic', *Guardian*, 1 September 2018, www.theguardian.com/books/2018/sep/01/normal-people-sally-rooney-review [accessed 26 March 2020].

Ditum, Sarah, '*Peach* by Emma Glass review—turning anguish into art', *Guardian*, 25 January 2018, www.theguardian.com/books/2018/jan/25/peach-emma-glass-review [accessed 26 March 2020].

Donkor, Michael, *Hold* (London: 4th Estate, 2018).

Fisher, Clare, *How the Light Gets In* (Influx Press: London, 2018).

Genette, Gérard, *Paratexts: Thresholds of Interpretation*, trans. by Jane E. Lewin (Cambridge: Cambridge University Press, 1997) [1987].

Gilbert, Zoe, *Folk* (London: Bloomsbury, 2018).

Glass, Emma, *Peach* (London: Bloomsbury, 2018).

Graham, Alison, 'Alison Graham reviews Richard Scott', 2018, https://theinterpretershouse.org/reviews-1/2018/11/18/alison-graham-reviews-richard-scott [accessed 27 March 2020].

Grant, Colin, '*Friday Black* by Nana Kwame Adjei-Brenyah review—both funny and frightening', *Guardian*, 7 December 2018, www.theguardian.com/books/2018/dec/07/friday-black-nana-kwame-adjei-brenyah-review-short-stories [accessed 26 March 2020].

Gunaratne, Guy, *In Our Mad and Furious City* (London: Tinder Press, 2018).

Habila, Helon, '*House of Stone* by Novuyo Rosa Tshuma review—Zimbabwe's story extraordinarily told', *Guardian*, 9 August 2018, www.theguardian.com/books/2018/aug/09/house-of-stone-novuyo-rosa-tshuma-review [accessed 25 March 2020].

Hall, Louisa, *Trinity* (New York, NY: Ecco, 2018).

Harrison, Emily, 'Book review: *How the Light Gets In* by Clare Fisher', 2018, https://storgy.com/2018/09/11/book-review-how-the-light-gets-in-by-clare-fisher/ [accessed 26 March 2020].

Lin, Tom M.Y., Pin Luarn, and Yun Kuei Huang, 'Effect of Internet book reviews on purchase intention: A focus group study', *Journal of Academic Librarianship*, 32.5 (2005), 452–66. DOI: 10.1016/j.acalib.2005.05.008.

Mengestu, Dinaw, 'A first novel explores Zimbabwe's troubled history', *New York Times*, 14 March 2019, www.nytimes.com/2019/03/08/books/review/house-of-stone-novuyo-rosa-tshuma.html [accessed 25 March 2020].

Mudambi, Susan M., and David Schuff, 'Research note: What makes a helpful online review? A study of customer reviews on Amazon.com', *MIS Quarterly*, 34.1 (2010), 185–200. DOI: 10.2307/20721420.

Murphy, Siobhan, 'Review: *Country* by Michael Hughes/ *Early Riser* by Jasper Fforde/ *In Our Mad and Furious City* by Guy Gunaratne', *The Times*, 8 September 2018, www.thetimes.co.uk/article/review-country-by-michael-hughes-early-riser-by-jasper-fforde-in-our-mad-and-furious-city-by-guy-gunaratne-bgvs223sv [accessed 24 March 2020].

Myers, Benjamin, '*Folk* by Zoe Gilbert review—a dreamlike tapestry of island fables', *Guardian*, 8 March 2018, www.theguardian.com/books/2018/mar/08/folk-zoe-gilbert-review-island-fables [accessed 28 March 2020].

Nakamura, Lisa, '"Words with friends": Socially networked reading on "Goodreads"', *PMLA*, 128.1 (2013), 238–43, www.jstor.org/stable/23489284 [accessed 19 March 2020].

Orange, Tommy, '*Friday Black* paints a dark portrait of race in America; fiction', *New York Times*, 23 October 2018, www.nytimes.com/2018/10/23/books/review/-nana-kwame-adjei-brenyah-friday-black.html [accessed 26 March 2020].

Osborne, Nell, 'Richard Scott, *Soho*', 2018, www.themanchesterreview.co.uk/?p=9304 [accessed 27 March 2020].

Perry, Sarah, *Melmoth* (London: Serpent's Tail, 2018).

Pople, Ian, 'Jenny Xie | *Eye Level*', 2018, www.themanchesterreview.co.uk/?p=10457 [accessed 27 March 2020].

Preston, Alex, '*Folk* by Zoe Gilbert—strange beauty', *Financial Times*, 2 March 2018, www.ft.com/content/fa29f9e6-0ccd-11e8-bacb-2958fde95e5e [accessed 28 March 2020].

Rooney, Sally, *Normal People* (London: Faber and Faber, 2018).

Scholes, Lucy, '*Melmoth* by Sarah Perry, review: "A haunting book that speaks to mankind's worst atrocities"', *Independent*, 4 October 2018, www.independent.co.uk/arts-entertainment/books/reviews/melmoth-sarah-perry-book-review-essex-serpent-haunting-a8568846.html [accessed 27 March 2020].

Scott, Richard, *Soho* (London: Faber and Faber, 2018).

Squires, Claire, *Marketing Literature: The Making of Contemporary Writing in Britain* (London: Palgrave Macmillan, 2007).

Tshuma, Novuyo Rosa, *House of Stone* (London: Atlantic Books, 2018).

Xie, Jenny, *Eye Level* (Minneapolis, MA: Graywolf Press, 2018).

Conclusion

The end of the hyper-contemporary

In the preceding pages I have explored how hyper-contemporary literature engages with five major strands of thought. I have used these strands of thought to define the ways that these texts can be judged using these strands, pointing out the various ways that these strands show us the hyper-contemporary elements of these texts.

In my first chapter I explored fourth-wave feminism and focused on the differing ideas of action-through-unity and of fragmentation, the fourth-wave feminist body, and the online world of digital feminism. In my second chapter I detailed how postcolonial and critical race theories help us to read about history and the problem of representation in certain texts, as well as narratives of migration, and also the presence of online narratives in representations of race. My third chapter set out how queer theories, in all their manifestations, help us to read about the use and exploration of the queer archive, how identifying as queer is problematised today, and how theories of 'after queer' or 'post-queer' grant us new insights into the persistence of queer silences. In my fourth chapter I used theories of class to read about how social mobility via education is represented anew, how dispossession is on the rise for those not of the wealthy top ten per cent, and how class and geography continue to be important in hyper-contemporary literature. Finally, in my fifth chapter I explored the helpfulness of public reviews and ratings in determining a book's quality.

Across the chapters I found myself repeatedly heeding the lessons of intersectionality that Kimberlé Crenshaw first espoused during the early rites of third-wave feminism. For example, in my reading of Adjei-Brenyah's *Friday Black*, I benefited from thinking through the consequences of combining critical race theories with theories of class to produce a new, intersecting theory. Likewise, in my exploration of Donkor's *Hold* I turned to theories of queer, class, and postcolonialism, producing a multiply-anchored theory that helped me to read about Amma's and Belinda's experiences in twenty-first-century London. I found this process of intersecting theories not only enjoyable, but also necessary in order to engage properly with these hyper-contemporary texts. If I could venture an argument, it strikes me that the postmodern idea that all identities fracture *ad infinitum* into ever smaller shards of being has been supplanted—or revealed as a proposition emptied of usefulness—by the idea that identities need to be more complex and considered. We do have singular identities, that is, but those singularities are like black holes, densely packed to the point of indiscriminateness. Hence the need for intersectionality to think through the difficulties of twenty-first-century identity where 'identity politics' becomes redundant because no single politics can account for the intersectionally-situated human being.

The process of thinking about intersectional theories is useful beyond the terms I just described. Whilst the chapters were divided into these single theories, it is unlikely that you will ever read a book with one theory in mind, or one theory overshadowing the others to the point of their uselessness. Instead, as you read a text you will see these different discourses emerge with varying frequency and prominence. Equally, there may be other ways of joining discourses across the chapters, as if constructing a rhizomatic set of networks in which there is no starting point. For example, by writing about the 'archive' in different contexts, it implies that there are interconnections between these ideas that mean a fourth-wave feminist theory of the archive will help us to read queer writing, and *vice versa*. Therefore, the experience of reading cannot be limited to single ideas, and you will find that you will have to use more than one chapter to read any one text.

Moreover, as you continue to read you will find that my chapters offer only a starting point. This is because there are other discourses that need to be discussed. For various reasons I did not detail those discourses—either they did not appear at all in these twelve texts or did not appear sufficiently frequently—and they are therefore not included in this book. However, if another random selection of twelve texts were taken, no doubt other discourses would have to be included, from trans★ theories, to disability theories, to ecocritical theories, and also to posthumanist theories.

In addition to these extra theories, there is an argument that this book should also provide greater analysis of particular forms of writing—How does poetry treat a topic differently to a novel to a short story?—as also to particular genres—How does dystopia depict events differently to historical fiction to crime fiction to Gothic? This perhaps should also think about the ways that ebooks and audiobooks are 'read' differently, and how that affects the 'quality' of hyper-contemporary literature. Some more chapters could be offered detailing the different formal and generic demands, and how they help us to judge hyper-contemporary literature.

Moreover, in the examples I have given above, not only are they small instances of using the theories alongside the primary texts, but they also focus on only moments of the primary texts themselves. It is perfectly possible that a reading of queer theory in one part of a text, for example, is countered by another part of a text. In other words, I would be wary of constructing entire arguments based on the examples of close reading I have done. They could be used as part of an argument, but the argument would need to include other elements of the primary texts in order to give a holistic 'reading' of any text—the kind that seminar rooms and book clubs aspire to give.

Hyper-contemporary's end

This is the death knell for hyper-contemporary literature. In my introduction, I defined hyper-contemporary as a period that is quickly passed through, with stress on the temporary nature of the 'contemporary'. Hyper-contemporary literature is unread and unsullied by critical consensus—be that good or bad. It therefore can only ever be hyper-contemporary while these elements continue to be true. As soon as a judgement has been cast, a critical consensus established, the hyper-contemporary is no longer *hyper*-contemporary, receding into the common and garden 'contemporary' only.

Thus the twelve texts that have been my focus in this book are now no longer *hyper*-contemporary. They have entered the far larger world of consensus making and, certainly in my teaching, have entered the university reading lists and syllabuses that confer on them the status of the literary. This is how the hyper-contemporary enters a sort of tenure track, at the end of which is 'literary' or 'canonical' status. Conversely, I will not read some of these books again because I have judged them as 'not good enough' and not worth more of mine or my students' time. 'Had we but world enough and time,' as Andrew Marvell wrote in his 1681 'To His Coy Mistress', then I would be able to read everything ever written more than once over. Sadly, I have neither the space in my house, nor the time in my life, to achieve that. Some hyper-contemporary texts will be taught, and some will not.

However, I am also convinced that 'bad' literature needs to be reckoned with more widely on university syllabuses. For that reason, I am convinced that including texts that I judge as 'bad' on my courses will help develop my students' capacities for literary analysis by showing them the differences between excellent and poor writing. Moreover, there is a chance that my students will convince me that the texts I have judged as poor are in fact better than that. I have long been influenced by my students, and I hope to continue to have my ideas and opinions shaped in dialogue with theirs.

Hyper-contemporaneity may end at different rates with different texts. It may be that, for example, those texts in my 'Reviews' chapter deemed especially relevant to today's world keep producing new readings as ideas and events that their texts reflect keep on happening. For example, Adjei-Brenyah's story of 'The Finkelstein 5' parodically responds to the idea of a white man needlessly murdering innocent Black citizens, only then to escape justice. The US sociologist Whitney Pirtle tweeted on 2 April 2020 that 'In Michigan, my home state, 40% of those who have died from #Covid19 are Black when only 14% of residents are Black. The deathgap [*sic*] is huge and horrific. #BlackLivesMatter'.[1] The continuing focus on the differential experiences of Black US citizens means that *Friday Black* may appear new for a while yet. These thoughts are only tragically redoubled in the wake of George Floyd's murder in May 2020 at the hands of the Minneapolis city police.

On the flipside, perhaps *Friday Black* may become irrelevant sooner because of its intense focus on today's world, much like the third book of Jonathan Swift's *Gulliver's Travels* (1726) is often overlooked because twenty-first-century readers struggle to understand the specificities of the barbed satire directed at Britain's newly-formed Royal Society.[2] *Friday Black*'s hyper-contemporaneity may therefore be more short-lived than, say, *Trinity*'s historical fiction that covers a twenty-three-year period in the middle of the twentieth century—a period of history that will likely never lose interest and the research of which may lead to *Trinity*'s fictions producing new insights not yet accounted for in the critical literature surrounding Hall's text.

What is certain, however, is that the hyper-contemporary will end, one way or another. Or at least, these texts' hyper-contemporaneity will end. But other hyper-contemporary texts will come along in their place.

The end of the hyper-contemporary is the beginning of the hyper-contemporary.

Notes

1 See https://twitter.com/thePhDandme [accessed 3 April 2020].
2 The third book of *Gulliver's Travels* is set on an island in the sky called Laputa, which also controls a landed society called Balnibarbi. In these communities, science is pursued to useless ends; the satire is an implicit attack on some of the members of the Royal Society who conducted unnecessary experiments to great fanfare.

Index